Ebb Tide

PUBLICATIONS

Questions in Arts Administration
Arts Administration
The Privileged Arts
(Ed.) *The State and the Arts*
The West End; Mismanagement and Snobbery
The Theatre Industry
*The Arts In A State; Cultural Management from Greece to
    the Present Day*
Off Gorky Street; Arts Administration in the USSR
Managing the Arts
Weasel Words
The Modern Newspeak
The Power Luncher's Primer
Vile Jelly
The Aesthetic Contract
(With Malcolm Anderton) *Industry and the Arts*
Arts Administration (Second Edition)
Building Jerusalem
(With Mark Jones) *Mr Phipps' Theatre; the Sensational Story
    of Eastbourne's Royal Hippodrome*
(With Robert Protherough) *Managing Britannia*

FOR PERFORMANCE

Hard Times [adpt.]
Swimming With Ibsen
Carrigan Street
Martin Luther King
Garrick's Festival
Story of a Great House [*Son et Lumière*]

EBB TIDE

a Memoir

John Pick

COPYRIGHT © 2016 JOHN PICK

published by ATWP
first published 2016

typeset by The Brynmill Press Ltd
printed and bound by CPI (UK) Ltd
ISBN 978 0 9934431 1 4

Contents

ILLUSTRATIONS

cover illustration *Beachy Head* by Jane Montague

Acknowledgements

I wish to thank Jane Montague for first suggesting that I might write these memoirs, and for her continued friendly support; together with Martyn Pick and Catherine Pick for finding time to explain the mysteries of the laptop and for reading and commenting on parts of the text. I am also indebted to Caroline Gardiner, Tony Crooks, Peter Austin and Brian Freeland for looking at chapters and offering advice. Most particularly I am grateful to Ian Robinson for his typesetting skills, and for heroically refraining from commenting on those passages which (not always flatteringly, or even accurately) refer to him. None of the foregoing is responsible for any undeserved praise, personal slurs or straightforward lies which may be contained in these pages. I alone am to blame, both for my life and the account I have chosen to give of it.

JP

"Is it," Jane asks, "that you don't want your children to read your life story?"

"No, not that."

"Well, what is it then? I think you should try."

"Well, there's another reason."

She smiles across the table: "Frightened you might find out too much about yourself?"

"Frightened that I'd invent somebody who doesn't exist—and never existed."

"All memoirs are part fiction . . ."

Storytelling

WOULD ANYBODY be interested in my story? I've made no great discoveries, championed no worthwhile causes, and have certainly never witnessed at first hand any momentous event. And as soon as I knew anything, I knew that the real world—where significant things happened to the people who mattered, things that got reported in the national newspapers—existed in realms far removed from my surroundings.

I was born in 1936, under the sign of Libra. Retford, Notts, where I entered this world and did much of my growing up in, was ordinariness personified. It could not lay claim to being anything in particular, just a small market town on the Great North Road, through which north-bound travellers passed on their way to Scotland. Its only claim to significance was that it had been there for a very long time. Retford is mentioned in the Doomsday Book, and in its day was a notable Rotten Borough—one that real politicians took some note of. However by the 1930s it had become a dusty relic of its own past. It was (probably still is) for the most part composed of dull rows of semi-detached red brick houses (in one of which I was born and in which I lived for the first eighteen years of my life) spreading outwards from an old market place, with a couple of cinemas, a weekly cattle market and a shallow fast-flowing river which divided East Retford from West—the embarrassingly named River Idle.

The Idle was, truth be told, not much of a river at all, being only about a foot deep and easily crossed by anybody wearing Wellington boots. No boats sailed on it, and no lovers had ever drowned themselves in its murky depths. It features briefly in the local guide books only because they repeat the old canard that Retford got its name because in olden times the red clay of its river bed would be stirred up by cattle being driven across it on their way to the local market (Red Ford, see?). But I have never met anybody who believed this story. There is certainly now no sign of a ford, and the bed of the river is not red, but ordinary grey mud.

War broke out just before my third birthday, though even in wartime nothing extraordinary happened in Retford. True, the street lamps were no longer lit and the windows were blacked out at night time and criss-crossed with tape to prevent us being injured by flying glass when the bombs fell, but they never did fall. In Retford daily life went on much as before. It was still Half Day Closing on Wednesdays, and on Saturdays the stalls still settled into their accustomed places in the old market square. Housewives continued to leave their bicycles in the bike sheds at the back of the Roxy cinema in Carolgate and, their shopping complete, wobble off home with their shopping bags balanced on their handlebars. And although the iron railings around St Swithun's Church had been taken away to be melted down for tanks, on Sundays a small part of Retford's population still shuffled respectfully into its pockmarked old pews.

I started school in 1941 and each morning walked with my mother down Moorgate, crossing Cannon Square to the St Swithun's Infant School, with my Mickey Mouse gas mask slung over my shoulder. At first I could not see the point of education—apparently I told my parents after my first day that I should not return, as I already knew everything they intended to teach me. But I soon came to see school as a necessary, if tedious, rite of passage, though for many years I was an indifferent scholar. I would will the air raid sirens to go so that we could escape lessons and sit in the concrete bomb shelters on Spa Common, where we sang songs and played rudimentary word games with the teachers. If the sirens were disappointingly silent we sat at our desks in the draughty old schoolroom, the gas lamps hissing and flickering, chanting boring tables and listening to Miss Chambers reading stories, telling us again the name of the city that was the capital of France and how much more waste paper than us other classes were collecting for the war effort.

At the end of each day my mother would be waiting among the gaggle of parents just outside the school gates and we would happily walk back up home, with me boasting about the smart answers I had (according to me) given in class and (even less plausibly) how high I had jumped, or thrown the bean bag. This latter was pure bravado, as I was a skinny, rather sickly child, reluctant to engage in acts of physical bravado, and already with a well-developed streak of cowardice. During my recital my mother would remain silent—and, no doubt, deeply sceptical—contenting herself with puffing on her Senior Service. Even then she was a forty-a-day smoker, and she continued steadfastly on this course until after her ninetieth birthday. Knowing nothing then of the health risks involved, I didn't care about that—all adults smoked anyway. What I was much more worried about was the message on the jar of Boots cold cream which I had secretly read on her dressing table. I was worried that my mother, always slapdash, would help herself too liberally to the jar's contents and smooth herself to death.

It was in Miss Chambers' class that I fell in love for the first time. I was sitting cross-legged on the parquet floor in a rehearsal for the coming Christmas nativity, when a girl called Mary Bennett flounced past me and afforded me a brief dizzying glimpse of her white underpants. These aroused no premature erotic fantasies in my weedy breast. Rather it was, as I recall, their dazzling whiteness that so impressed me—not least because they contrasted so sharply with the dingy nether garments favoured by my own family. In that magical moment I determined that when I was grown up I would improve my station in life by marrying her, though I had little idea of what that might actually involve. In the magical moment when I decided to make her mine I conjured up just one image of our future life together. It was the end of the working day, and I would be cycling home from whatever I did for a living to our little semi, where I would see, as I turned into our street, a panoply of brilliant white knickers triumphantly strewn along the washing line outside our home. In my imagination I saw myself dismounting, taking off my cycle clips and standing for a moment beneath the gleaming undies—taking the salute as it were—while homecoming neighbours cycled morosely past, refusing to catch my eye, deeply envious of our Oxydol purity. As with all great love affairs, it had an unhappy ending. By the third year of Infant School we had been torn asunder; Mary's family had moved to Tickhill.

The war brought new members of our household. Having a spare room, my parents had two lodgers billeted on them for the duration. Mr Johnson and Mr Brough were not conventional evacuees, but two research chemists who were working at a secret location nearby to produce materials that were thought to be useful to the troops. They would join us for our early evening meal, and occasionally, to my fascination, show us examples of what they were producing. One such that I remember was a sort of paper which, when you applied a lighted cigarette to it, completely disappeared, leaving neither smoke nor ash. Our lodgers solemnly explained to me that this was the sort of paper they gave to spies, so they would never be found with incriminating evidence on them. They swore me to secrecy so efficiently that even now I feel slightly apprehensive about letting anyone else know about Britain's wartime secrets.

My first small glimpse of the grim realities of war came when I was about four years old and one winter's evening was led out into the back garden to witness a series of lurid orange flashes on the northern horizon. accompanied by distant muffled explosions, and heard my parents agreeing with neighbours that 'Sheffield is certainly getting it tonight.' They might as well have been talking of another country, so far from our rural lives did that city seem. Even so, the bombing of Sheffield did force the war into my conscious mind. I began to suspect that it was just possible, when Hitler had finished with the industrial targets of Nottingham or Sheffield, that he might turn his attention to boskier targets such as Retford. I decided to act. I dragged out one of my father's many spades and laboriously dug a hole at the bottom of our garden—in case Herr Hitler should in the course of his assault come bursting through our privet hedge. The hole was painstakingly fashioned into a deadly man trap by the simple expedient of putting a large stone in the bottom in order to stun the Nazi Fuhrer as he collapsed, cursing horribly, into its depths.

I then covered the aperture with twigs and dead leaves, and forgot about it until the summer when, in the course of a game of Hide and Seek a neighbouring child fell in it, bruising her shoulder and scratching her knee. She swore to her family that I had pushed her in. Neither my denials, nor my explanation that both hole and stone were a vital part of the defence of the realm, were believed. To her indignant parents my mother offered the 'while of unsound mind' defence, explaining, not for the first or the last time, that her only child was afflicted with an overactive imagination and liked to 'tell stories'.

* * *

If my parents were sometimes embarrassed by the way in which the fantasies in my life overtook reality, they made no attempts to draw me back into their more practical universe, and seemed to regard my fanciful mind as a cross they had to bear. They were both sturdy country folk. My mother came from a family of farm labourers in the Trent Valley, and had earned her living as a school teacher until she married and was forced to confine herself to looking after her home (in those pre-war days school teachers had to be spinsters). My paternal grandfather, who knew farming and farm machinery, and could drive a car, had been a general factotum to one of the minor Nottinghamshire gentry, and had in the course of his varied duties fathered six sons, all of whom, like my father, earned their livings in the open air. They never, any of them, ever lost their deep mistrust of built up areas. To his dying day it remained a puzzle to my father that I should enjoy living and working in cities, when I could just as easily have chosen a job where I was surrounded by trees and grass. When I held

an appointment in Cambridge, he was delighted and
spent his days happily walking the banks of the Cam
and inspecting the college gardens, thinking I had come
to my senses at last, but was cast down again when I
inexplicably chose to move back to the bricked-up
barbarities of Nottingham.

My father was a Market Gardener. Working on the
land meant that as far as the War Office was concerned
he was in a reserve occupation, and at the outbreak of
war did not get called up. Indeed a surprisingly large
number of our friends and relatives also avoided taking
part in the real war—though, like my father, they
spent some of their evenings and weekends in uniform
as members of the ARP, or the Retford Home Guard.
But their uniforms, their various drills and manœuvres
seemed even to them to be a sort of play acting—no
more related to the actual war than my Mickey Mouse
gas mask was connected to the realities of trench warfare.

Nor was my family much affected by wartime
rationing and the attendant food shortages As almost
everybody we knew lived one way and another off the
land, in comparison with the less fortunate denizens of
the nearby cities we really ate very well. Some of our food
sources were certainly illegal, though that was of interest
only to the Ministry boffins who occasionally invaded
the local farms, brandishing their Ministry forms. But
they were easily fooled. Meanwhile around Retford
there seemed to be a barter system in operation. My
father would drop off bags of fresh vegetables at the back
doors of various local houses, together with the slabs
of home-churned butter which was one of my mother's
specialities—and in return we would later find half a
dozen eggs, or a freshly shot rabbit, lurking in brown
paper bags in our washhouse. In the shops meanwhile
the housewives duly presented their ration books and
had their coupons snipped out, and all seemingly above
board—but even there mysterious little packages were
slipped into the shopkeeper's hand and exchanged for
something from 'under the counter'.

Not that all rural communities were the same. Even in
wartime there remained a pecking order between the
local conurbations, apparent in the slight enmity still felt

by the citizens of Retford for their nearest neighbour. The town of Worksop was only nine miles away, but it might as well have been on a different continent. Though larger than my home town, it was looked down on by Retfordians, both because it was fairly new (having developed in the nineteenth century) but mainly because it was heavily populated by the miners who worked the local coalfields. Many years previously D. H. Lawrence had noticed what was plain to everyone who grew up in the Nottinghamshire countryside—that there was in those parts a bitter enmity between those who, like their fathers before them, worked on the land, and those dangerous new tribes that had descended from the North to work below it. The incoming miners regarded the farmers as privileged conservative softies, while the farming community in turn saw the miners as dangerous game-poaching radicals. Even after the eighties, when so many mines were closing and many of the younger miners were being re-employed above ground, the old hostilities still simmered. In his retirement my old man played snooker for the Retford Liberal Club in a local league, but would still view with apprehension the prospect of away matches in the Miners' Welfare Clubs. On his return from one he would say how well and hospitably he and his team mates had been received— though still managing to imply that such behaviour was against the natural order of things, as if a tribe of savage cannibals had unexpectedly learned the niceties of folding table napkins properly.

Whatever the reasons, my home town was thought, at least by its own citizenry, to be superior to Worksop— yet in its turn Retford was widely acknowledged to be inferior to another market town on the old Great North Road—Newark on Trent. Newark had both history and style. It had the mighty River Trent (on which proper boats could sail, and in which people could really drown themselves) running through it, and it had a real castle (in which King John had died—poisoned, it was said, by a surfeit of eels fished from the Trent). Equally significant, in those innocent pre-Waitrose days, was that it had a Marks and Spencer, whereas Retford had only a Co-op and a Woolworths. My mother was a Newark girl and when she was bored with housework (which was virtually all the time) would mention these facts in front of my father, a Retfordian, as conclusive evidence that by marrying him she had slipped a notch down the social scale.

And Newark, or at any rate one small bit of it, played quite a part in my young life. Each Saturday my mother would take me the twenty miles or so, by bus, to visit my maternal grandmother, who lived in an old cottage on Newark's outskirts, from whose garden you could actually see the River Trent. Indeed one of the few photographs I have of my very young self shows me, self-consciously posing for the camera, helping my father sail a toy yacht on the Trent a few yards from my grandmother's home.

Yet, unconventional though it may have been, that cottage was undoubtedly a *tabula rasa* for my childish imagination. It was by modern standards quite breath-takingly unhygienic—the sort of dwelling that in later years would have the Social Services buzzing round in droves. On our weekly visits I was left free to explore its disorderly gaggle of old sheds and outhouses without any limit being put on what I could do in there. In them I created flying machines, dens, sniper's nests and a trail of mantraps, all cunningly booby-trapped so that only I could wriggle past them unscathed to what I grandly termed my 'study', fashioned out of fruit pallets wedged in a corner of the rafters, with some old *Picture Posts* as reading matter. None of these constructions was ever touched—I don't think anybody except me ever ventured into the old outhouses—and the remains of my labours, including my 'study', were still there when at the age of twelve I paid my last ever visit to the Trentside cottage, on the day of my grandmother's funeral.

There was of course a reason for her impoverished existence. Her husband, my maternal grandfather, had died when my mother was four. They had lived, like so many rural workers, in tied accommodation on which they paid a tiny rent. After his death my grandmother was allowed to keep the cottage, and she maintained herself and my mother by the only means available to her—taking in paying lodgers. The drawback to this arrangement was that such lodgers as she was able to attract to her primitive home were themselves likely to be near-destitute, and as often as not had to pay for their keep by undertaking odd jobs in the cottage or the garden. When I first visited her she was letting to a cheery labourer called Frank (who had been gassed in the First World War, did labouring jobs on the local farms and whose speech consisted of honks and grunts) and a second lodger (who may or may not have been some sort of companion of Frank's) who seemed to have been what in those days was called 'a bit soft', and whom I was encouraged to call Aunt Nora. The rent the two of them paid must have been minute, but importantly it meant that my grandmother had three people living under her roof and in the days of rationing that meant three ration books. So, taken together with the various meats and vegetables supplied by friendly neighbours, she was able to keep a good, if primitive, table. Already, at that tender age, mindful of the pleasures of eating, I would demand at lunchtime copious portions of her rabbit pie, followed by gooseberry tart and cream.

'Aunt Nora' seemed to do whatever housework was deemed necessary, and was occasionally to be seen wafting a broom around, or shooing perambulating live-stock back out into the yard. Her main duty however was daily to collect scraps and swill from the neighbours to feed the two pigs kept in the sty beyond my grand-mother's woodshed. I have no idea whether the pigs were kept legally or not, but I do know that when one of them was slaughtered each of the neighbours who had helped to feed it would be rewarded with a pork pie or a bit of fry. I would sometimes hear Aunt Nora cheerfully passing on to the pigs, as she fed them, the details of the way their corpses would shortly be dismembered and distributed amongst their patrons.

The cottage had two large downstairs rooms, both lit by gas mantles, and one of them—the parlour—was warmed by a coal-burning range, by which a few scrawny chickens would sometimes settle. On the table in the other main room—the kitchen—there were a few cheap candles, together with a big box of Swan Vestas, in order to light the occupants upstairs to their various beds. Off the kitchen led a larder-cum-scullery, in which jugs of milk, draped in muslin, stood alongside piles of soil-encrusted vegetables and the occasional joint of uncovered meat, around which huge bluebottles droned. This was of course an undeniable health hazard, and a modern Risk Assessor would have closed it with a shudder, but in spite of these medieval arrangements, none of my grandmother's household ever seemed to be taken ill. Nor was there a bathroom as such, just a large kitchen sink with a huge slab of carbolic soap by it. Hanging up on the washhouse wall was a big tin bath which I suspected—though not in any censorious way— was more for show than anything.

Most exciting of all. in the cluster of crumbling out-buildings round the back was a whitewashed privy, which at its rear had a festering trap door, facing out on to the street. Around this was played out one of my most colourful fantasies. I knew that every two to three weeks along the street to the privy trapdoor would come the 'Night Soil Men'—a gang of dangerous-looking beings that even Uncle Frank was in awe of. Once, and once only, their visit chanced to be on a Saturday, so that I saw them in action. In appearance they were excitingly pirate-like, with leather waistcoats and knotted handkerchiefs around their necks but, in lieu of a painted caravan, they clustered themselves around a reeking horse-drawn septic tank which carried at its rear the instruments of their trade. On that one, never-to-be-forgotten occasion I watched their operation with awe verging on adulation. Not until, many years later at the Edinburgh Tattoo, I watched a group of burly soldiers assemble a huge cannon in a matter of seconds and fire it noisily across the Castle arena, did I see anything approach it for military precision.

First, the night soil procession crunched to a stop. Then one of their number stepped forward and wedged the trapdoor open, while another reached in and deftly pulled out the privy can, pouring its dreadful contents into the tank's maw, before swirling it round with a begrimed mop. Then a third man took over, trundling the can back to the open trapdoor and, with a single practised movement, pushed it back into its appointed place. It was all over in a couple of minutes, and they clattered purposefully on down the street to the next trapdoor, making a good deal of noise (it was later explained to me by Aunt Nora) so that anyone who was unfortunately caught in situ could beat a retreat before their privy can was unceremoniously wrenched from beneath them.

I was instantly captivated by the Night Soil Men's glamour. Other children may have harboured dreams of running away to join the circus, but from that day, and for several weeks afterwards, it was the Newark Night Soil men that filled my imagination. I longed to be of their number. I saw myself as a sort of Jim Hawkins figure, willing to trade my childhood so I could become one of their swashbuckling band. At the same time I developed a complementary fantasy that the Night Soil Men, like the pirates of literature, all came from noble families, and that although they might seem to be beyond the social pail (as it were) they were undertaking this necessary work as a patriotic duty. I imagined them going home in the evenings to their posh country seats, bathing in tiled bathrooms, slicking down their hair with Brylcreem and changing into evening dress for dinner. On Saturday nights they would of course mingle at posh restaurants with their kind of people, where a three-piece band would be playing like in the night clubs you saw on the pictures, and where all the women would be wearing fur coats and carrying cigarette holders. And yet none of the bigwigs (except for Mr Churchill, of course, who was in on their secret) ever guessed at the grim but essential weekday work they were undertaking on behalf of the nation.

* * *

People born ten years before me had no doubt looked with dire foreboding on the newspaper headlines of the late thirties—'War Imminent', 'War Looms' etc., but for such as me, born in the mid-thirties, the headlines 'Will there be Peace?' or 'Peace is Near' aroused the same sort of apprehension. Having lived my formative years wholly in wartime, I had come to regard the detritus of war—ration books, hooded bicycle lamps, logs made of folded newspapers, and gas masks in the cloakrooms—as the natural order of things. I did not have any inkling what 'peace' would be like. Genuinely puzzled, I remember asking my father what they found to put in the news in peacetime? 'Oh, murders and things,' he replied vaguely, which did not reassure me—how could there possibly be enough murders to fill all the newspapers every day? The truth was that for several years the war had been a reliable framework for our well-ordered existence. We lived our lives within clearly defined boundaries. Posters told us how to sneeze hygienically, how to repair our clothing and mend our shoes. and on the wireless Gert and Daisy told us how to make shepherd's pie out of snoek, potato and oatmeal. Now all that certainty was disappearing and we were entering uncharted waters.

And peace began inauspiciously. As the end of the European war drew nigh—with the recurrent rumours of bananas in the shops by Christmas—our street, like every other in the land, began making preparations to celebrate its coming. We kids went round the neighbouring houses and smallholdings collecting rubbish for a giant bonfire in a neighbouring field. There was a pooling of flour and eggs to make a big VE cake, and trestle tables were brought out on which spam and lettuce sandwiches, boiled egg salad and ersatz trifles were placed. But the celebrations seemed tentative and strained. One or two of the fathers (not mine) got a bit tiddly, and some of the mothers (not mine) did a bit of dancing to an old wind-up gramophone. But the euphoria did not last. As the day wore on recriminations and arguments grew amongst the grown ups (I began to see why in peacetime murder might become more common) and some of the neighbours' children, apparently unused to the luxuries of peacetime food, were violently sick. It was not a good beginning.

Some months later came Hiroshima, followed by the surrender of the Japanese, and another street party, this time for VJ Day, held in the same field. It was then that I discovered that other people also 'told stories'. At the VJ party I walked around the trestle tables with my new friend Robert, an evacuee from Sheffield who was a year older than me, and whose knowledge of the real world I greatly admired. 'Have you heard about this bomb that's done for Japan?' he said. 'Yes,' I said, 'It was on the news.' 'Did you know it's only the size of a pea?' 'No,' I admitted, 'I didn't know that.' 'One of them could blow up an entire continent,' Robert said, adding for good measure, 'and exploding six of them would mean the end of life on earth.' I did not think for some years to question Robert's inside knowledge. I unthinkingly believed what he had told me, and it confirmed my growing suspicion that this 'peace' would be more dangerous and much less predictable than war had ever been.

So passed the first years of post-war austerity—with queues for everything, and an endless stream of glum news on the radio about fuel shortages, power cuts and the latest tricks of the 'spivs' who were said to flog black market fags and nylons on street corners (though of course there weren't any in Retford). There were still no toys in the shops, sweets were still rationed, and the bananas, when they finally arrived in all their rancid greenery, were a huge disappointment. True, there were a few compensations. I was now able to join the Denman Library (whisked down there by my mother as soon as I was old enough) and grew to love the polished exclusivity of its children's section where I would hope to find in the 'returned books' tray a Swallows and Amazons adventure that I hadn't read. Some of the pre-war comics also reappeared in the newsagents—though they were still full of the old public school stories, with their dormitory feasts, well-stocked tuckshops and playing-field heroics, seemingly oblivious to the fact that their readers lived in a post-war country where the playing fields had been dug up for allotments and tuck was in short supply.

But at least we could now play out of doors without fear of the sirens going. There were not many fields left unploughed, so we generally played in the streets—safe enough in those days, as there were very few cars about. Although I was not by any stretch of imagination an athlete, I was not by nature a loner either, so I joined in the street games of hopscotch and football cheerfully enough. Cricket was perforce my favourite. My father was a good club cricketer, who had played once for his

County (he used to show people a scar on the side of his left hand, caused he said by his failure to catch a ball snicked off the bowling of the great Harold Larwood) and it was an essential rite of passage that as his son I should on occasion accompany him to cricket matches. I was taken to see the first post-war Australian side to tour Britain, and saw Bradman make fifty. Harold Pinter wrote a haiku to mark the event:

> I saw Don Bradman in his prime,
> Another time, another time.

I can, however, remember virtually nothing of the occasion, except the hardness of the Bramall Lane bench on which we sat.

When I was no more than ten years old I joined my father and his brothers in their weekly 'nets' for their local side. Though I was hardly big enough, or strong enough, to wield a full-size bat or throw a proper cricket ball, the team treated me with great politeness, even pretending to be fooled by my feeble leg-breaks, which took so long to reach the other end that nimble batsmen could easily have had two swings at the ball. In this and in other ways, cricket seemed to offer a glimpse of a gentler pre-war world. The radio cricket commentary, with the peerless John Arlott, seems in retrospect to have been the invariable background to a perfect summer's day. Even my mother, whose hatred of cricket was conveyed with the same glowering intensity she brought to her other major dislikes—which included eye shadow, fancy cooking, and (for some reason) Petula Clark—permitted herself an occasional wry smile at his mellow ruminations.

Meanwhile my story-telling was taking new forms. On my bedroom table I was now producing my own comics, with lined paper neatly ruled into little rectangles. In them I drew the tepid adventures of various invented characters—as a rule chirpy little animals dressed in top hats or mortar boards. Even more enterprising—and no doubt of greater interest to any passing child psychologist—were the 'newspapers' that I produced, each complete with banner headlines, cartoons, and even leader comment. Like the regular newspapers, they were designed to shock their readers, but the essential difference was that my 'news' was not partly but *wholly* fictitious—'Queen Mary to Ride St Leger Favourite', kind of thing. It was not that I was exhibiting an early talent for what would later be called 'the satire movement'. It was just that as I hadn't the faintest idea what was really going on in the world, I substituted lurid fantasies from my own moonstruck imagination. However the fact that the content of my 'newspapers' was neither true nor funny did not prevent me from putting a price tag on them—nor prevent my much-put-upon parents from having to fork out good money for their purchase.

I was now also old enough to be taken with my friends to suitable 'pictures' at the local cinemas, and this was a whole new sensory experience. It wasn't so much the films themselves—though Roy Rogers and Abbot and Costello were all right in their way—but the whole sensual experience of cinema-going that I liked. The musty velvet on the tip-up seats, the white smoky beam of the projector, the floury taste of the first post-war ice creams (served in cones of greaseproof paper as wafers were not yet available), the sudden rush of cold air as the doors opened just before the National Anthem started and the local scruffs made a rush for the exits—and finally the delicious salty tang of the three pennyworth of chips (with bits) in Moorgate on the way home.

But the dominant cultural force back then was still the radio, and in my case it was the radio comedians whom I worshipped. I even, like Billy Fisher in Keith Waterhouse's *Billy Liar*, went so far as to write fan letters to the comics of the day. Each week, when it flopped on to the hall floor, I would grab the *Radio Times* to see who was the top of the bill on the Saturday night *Music Hall*, in preparation for what I was certain for a while would be my career. When the show was broadcast I would sit by the radio and write down the catchphrases and jokes, with a view to incorporating them in my act when I became a famous comedian. In that way I relentlessly plagiarised *ITMA, Much Binding in the Marsh, Steady Barker* and of course Charlie Chester's *Stand Easy*, with its snappy topical news items intoned to jungle drums:

Down in the jungle,
Living in a tent,
Better than a pre-fab,
No rent!

I learned all the hoary old routines. As another career ambition at this time was to be a famous radio impressionist—'This is Johnny Pick, the voice of them all!'—I rehearsed impersonations of such as Arthur Askey, Cyril Fletcher and Mrs Mopp from *ITMA*, complete with their stolen routines. Indeed my head was so terrifyingly full of BBC programmes that at school break I would stand in a corner of the playground performing them, with a small crowd of retarded radio junkies around me, poking me in the chest and twisting my nipples when they wanted to change channel.

Then I began to favour the live theatre. In the sitting rooms of my friends' homes, using their curtains as stage tabs, I produced complete shows—inveigling neighbouring children into acting as my 'feeds'. The coloured posters for these extravaganzas, which I pinned to the gateposts along our street, and which invariably featured my name in big red letters, were also produced on my bedroom table. Though occasionally one of the neighbouring children was allowed a brief moment in the limelight while I changed my costume, these shows featured me as top banana more relentlessly than American stars were featured at the Palladium. And I left nothing to chance. I even ordered one neighbouring tot to bang on a drum, boom-boom, Billy Bennett fashion, to show the audience where to laugh.

If my parents ever worried that this precocious, not to say embarrassing, theatricality could possibly harm my schooling, they didn't give voice to their fears, and in due course I strolled through what was in those days called the 'eleven plus' and gained a scholarship to the local Grammar School. On the day this happened, the Headmaster of my Junior School, a nice old boy called Crowder, called me into his study and after congratulating me said rather haltingly that he hoped that now I was going to Big School I would be a bit less giddy, and perhaps work a bit harder?

A few weeks later—with what at the time I thought of as a purely disinterested concern for my welfare—Mr Crowder drove up to our house in his battered old Morris and presented me with a complete set of the *Encyclopaedia Britannica*, twenty-four weighty volumes in all. These, I am ashamed to say, I lugged upstairs and used as the foundations for a new 'stage' arranged in an alcove in the corner of my bedroom. In front of this unconventional platform I strung up a pair of old sheets to act as curtains. Once it was fitted up—and as even I recognised the impracticability of ever luring an audience up the stairs of my parents' house—I contented myself, night after night, with tugging the curtains open and giving long and flowery curtain speeches, graciously thanking my invisible audience for their loyal and unwavering support.

I suppose that at this point my parents might, with some reason, have sent for the men in white coats. After all, the breathless speeches of thanks I was offering nightly to my adoring fans must have been plainly audible to them, and to their visitors. But just as some birds will continue to nurture an alien chick that has by chance fallen into their nest, and whose strange behaviour they cannot account for, so did my parents continue to tolerate the eccentricities of their self-obsessed son.

self-consciously posing by the River Trent

{2}

Pretending

It TRANSPIRED that when Mr Crowder had brought me my copies of the *Encyclopaedia Britannica* he had come to the house with an ulterior motive. St Swithuns School, like many another post-war establishment, was having difficulty in recruiting experienced staff, and so he had taken the opportunity of his visit to ask my mother whether (the pre-war ban on married teachers having been lifted) she would consider returning to classroom teaching and taking up a position at his school? She told me later she had answered him almost before he got the question out. Yes, she would love to have something to occupy her days. She was bored by wifely domesticity and couldn't wait to get back into the classroom.

And with that, everything seemed to suffer a sea change. The Labour Government announced the creation of the National Health Service, with its bold promise of free medical care 'from the cradle to the grave' and, almost simultaneously, the Butler Act, offering free secondary education for all, came into force. 'Gorgeous' Gussie Moran wore lace on her white knickers at Wimbledon and was rebuked by the authorities for 'drawing attention' to 'the sexual area'. O brave new world! With such momentous developments to occupy our minds, we scarcely noticed that North Korea had invaded the South, and that, with an iron curtain being inexorably drawn across Europe, a new Cold War was

about to begin—and that boys of my age were soon
going to be conscripted at eighteen into the armed
forces.

But all that came later. It was in a new and different
world that on a warm September morning in 1948, I
tugged on my new cap and blazer and set off on my
bike for my new school. The Grammar School was much
larger than my old one, and filled exclusively with male
persons who were also rather larger than I had been used
to. However I immediately sensed that I would like it
here—not least because it seemed much more spacious
and less organised than my primary school. With its
dirty windows and funny little staircases, the new school
premises promised to be as much a fantasy playground
as my grandmother's outbuildings had been—old, scruffy
but somehow full of possibilities.

During the war years King Edward's had hosted
another establishment, Yarmouth Grammar School, whose
pupils and staff had been evacuated wholesale to the
safety of Retford. The home team had apparently occupied
the buildings during the mornings while Yarmouth's staff
and students had moved in during the afternoons.
Because of the stringencies of wartime they had shared
practically all the available resources, with the result that
when I arrived there not only were the desks and black-
boards rickety and pockmarked but many of the
textbooks were encrusted with anatomically explicit suggestions as to what the home or visiting masters and
pupils might usefully do with themselves.

The Grammar School was indeed very old. Its origins
—as we were annually informed on Founder's Day—lay
with the charitable instincts of King Edward the Sixth,
who had founded it nearly four hundred years before.
Almost every local grandee, whether Mayor, Alderman
or Councillor, and their fathers and grandfathers before
them, seemed to have been educated there—a fact of
which we were made aware on Speech Days when one
of them would return, pin-striped and pinkly perspiring,
with a Masonic tie pin adorning his ample stomach, to
assure the boys ranged before him that long ago he too
had started life as a humble King Edward's scholar—and
if they would only buckle down and remember the school

motto (*Ex pulvere palma*—'out of the dust a palm') they
too might one day be a successful estate agent, taxi driver
or greengrocer.

We listened docilely, even unto the hundredth explanation of the school motto. True, there were no palms
growing around the school, but there was certainly no
shortage of dust. And the buildings had their own rich
scents. The corridor outside the old chemistry lab, for
instance, smelled of cordite, while the nearby gymnasium
gave off a pungent aroma of stale BO and composition
rubber. As a bonus, the wall bars of the gym also had a
coating of grey slime on them so that by the time you had
climbed up to a secure position, your legs and arms would
be scarred by a series of mud-coloured welts. And although
in theory you could remove these discolorations by washing
yourself in the changing room sinks, such was the
condition of these receptacles, and so primitive were the
adjacent soap and towel arrangements, that those who
tried it found that they emerged covered in streaky grey
stripes, like the Wolf Man in a black-and-white horror film.

Most aromatic of all was the prefabricated school
canteen, in which lunches for a number of the local
schools were daily prepared and from which in the
second half of each morning wafted an awful miasma of
scalded milk, bubbling mince and boiled cabbage. I
cannot remember whether it was because I threw a
wobbly at the prospect of ingesting that food, or whether my
parents had already taken the decision for me, but it was
from the first decided that I should not stay in school, but
should each lunchtime be one of the local boys allowed to
cycle home for lunch. That is what I did—each day I
cycled the mile and a half home, let myself into the house
and devoured the generous cold collation that had been
left out for me by my working parents. Then, after a few
weeks, bored by this lonely ritual, I began inviting other
canteen refusers to join me—and for a while my parents
were surprised by the amount of food I seemed to be
consuming each lunchtime.

However, unlike the way today's parents would react,
mine were pleased that I seemed to be eating my body
weight each day in corned beef sandwiches and short-
bread. For, in contrast to fashionable modern neuroses

about over-consumption, 'eating plenty of everything' was one of my family's maxims for a long and happy life. I can only guess at the roots of this. I imagine that their passion for guzzling had its roots in a fear of tuberculosis, which had laid low several of my ancestors, for the first and crucial symptoms of TB were popularly supposed to be that you would suddenly be 'off your food'. The next stage of TB, or any Retford illness, was that you were 'under the doctor', after which the first signs of recovery would, hopefully, be signalled by the news that you were 'back on solids'. Certainly overeating was felt to be synonymous with the good life, and all their lives my parents would recommend pubs and restaurants less by the quality of what they served than by the quantity; 'I could hardly see over the top of my Yorkshire pudding.' Anybody who worried about the nutritional value of what they ingested, rather than glorying in its bulk weight, was thought to be sickening for something. When a lissom and somewhat fastidious aunt passed peacefully on at the age of eighty-six, at her funeral my decidedly chunky mother gave it as her opinion that she had 'died of dieting'.

Another of the family's maxims was rather more in line with modern tastes. The Picks believed in everybody getting 'plenty of fresh air'. To that end the doors and windows of our house were rarely closed, even in winter, and I do remember visitors huddling closer and closer to the fire in our living room, and even on occasion surreptitiously putting their cycle clips back on, to try to repel the various winds that blew about their persons. On warm still days in summer, when there was a depressing absence of Northerly winds, my parents would fan themselves constantly, and join their friends and neighbours in complaining that all they wanted was 'a bit of air'. Recognising this need, the coastal resorts the locals frequented—Skegness, Mablethorpe and Cleethorpes —all made a great virtue of the sea breezes which whistled off the North Sea and advertised as a major attraction their 'bracing air', as if 'air' were not a commodity available in the inland towns.

Not that anybody had visited the seaside for some time. This was because the UK's beaches had during the war been heavily mined against the feared German invasion—but also because for most people there was no way of getting there. Even after the war few people had cars, petrol was still rationed and the trains were highly unreliable. When we went on our first post-war family holiday, to Mablethorpe in Lincolnshire, even though it was a journey of less than fifty miles it took us nearly a day, with several unscheduled changes of engine, to get there. After we had arrived, and had handed over our carefully hoarded rations for the landlady to cook, we walked down to the beach, but found large sections of it still cordoned off with barbed wire bearing ominous notices saying 'Danger. Do Not Pass'. During the night we were wakened by a series of sharp explosions as luckless dogs, unable to read the warnings, were blown to kingdom come by the lurking mines.

The old promenade was studded still with concrete machine gun nests, on which we played when we were not allowed on to the sands. By way of 'rides' there was an ex-army amphibious vehicle that took children over the beach (3d.) and, with a lot of splashing and screaming, briefly swerved into the sea before returning to its pick-up point. There were kiosks advertising ice cream (Cones 4d.), but they were frequently closed. There were a couple of arcades still open, and in them pre-war penny slot machines depicting 'The Haunted House' or 'The Graveyard after Midnight' that may once have been thought masterpieces of technical ingenuity but which had certainly seen better days. In the back of one of the arcades I found a glass fronted machine with a ragged puppet orchestra of top-hatted minstrels. When a penny was inserted, the puppets jerked spasmodically around to a few wheezy bars of *Twelfth Street Rag*—the timpanist's sticks missing his drum by several centimetres and the fiddler's bow scraping the air well away from his tatty instrument. Years later, returning to the same venue, I found that the minstrels had, in deference to political sensitivities, turned white, and were now playing a snatch of a Marty Wilde number, but they were still conspicuously failing to connect with their instruments.

★ ★ ★

The masters at King Edward VI Grammar School were, I imagine, pretty much standard issue for those days. Quite a few of the older ones, beyond the age for call-up, had remained in post throughout the war, their brief-cases battered, and their torn gowns greening with age. The Headmaster, Pilkington-Rogers, was one who seemed to have been there as long as anyone could remember, living in the dark and forbidden recesses of the Headmaster's House. He walked with a pronounced limp, and distinguished himself from his underlings by wearing a mortar board at all times (we solemnly told each other that he had sworn a dreadful vow never to take it off, and had worn it even on his wedding night). The Head's deputy was a drunken Irish priest called McFerran, who also lived on the premises and who spent every lunchtime in the *Railway Arms* nearby. During the school day 'Mac' alternated alarmingly between violent rages (until opening time) and maudlin affection (every afternoon). In my experience he never actually taught anything, but began each day by bawling at real and imaginary miscreants and spent some of his late afternoons sitting in empty classrooms, head in his hands, sobbing piteously.

Indeed none of the old hands seemed to do much teaching, concentrating instead on being 'characters'. One of them, who allegedly taught religious studies, smiled continuously but said virtually nothing for the two years I was taught by him. Another, 'Tash', a supposed maths teacher, would each morning park his ancient bicycle and, apparently oblivious of any formal time-table, wander dreamily about the school corridors looking for any group of boys that looked as if they might welcome his presence. All these old characters seemed blandly indifferent to the new post-1948 scholarship boys, or indeed to any other manifestation of the post-war world. If they ever referred to a contemporary politician, or a current event, they did so with contempt. More commonly they confined themselves to reminiscences of a lost golden age which, they implied, we and all we represented had been instrumental in destroying.

As the terms passed however they crumbled into retirement and were replaced by a steady trickle of younger, newly qualified masters whom we immediately sensed to be quite different from the caricatures they had replaced. The new intake wore brightly coloured socks and shirts, and earnestly tried to teach their advertised subjects. They mentioned contemporary events. They had up-to-date views. One or two of them were reputed to be so radical in thought that they were suspected by the highly conservative pupils of voting Labour.

With one I became friendly—a young English master called Robert Protherough, a fairly recent Oxford graduate who had not come to teach at the King Edward VI Grammar School out of any deep love of State Education, or indeed of the North, but out of simple expediency. By a strange inversion of fate, the school at which he had held his first appointment did not allow its masters to be married, and Robert wished to marry Margaret, his girl friend from Oxford days. King Edward's offered the only English-teaching post then available and so—fortunately for me, as we have been lifelong friends—he and his new wife fetched up in Retford.

Equally fortuitously, both the Senior English Master and Robert, his new assistant, were great theatre-lovers, and both were heavily involved in the local am-dram society, the Retford Little Theatre. Came the day when this earnest body decided to present the Scottish play, and several of the junior boys, who'd shown a liking for that kind of thing, were asked whether they would like to play small parts in the production. So it came about that the Senior English Master, Howard Bartley, played Macbeth, his assistant Robert played Banquo, and I played the small part of Fleance, son of Banquo, who sees his father murdered. It was a seminal experience for me. More than fifty years later, visiting each other's houses or on holiday with our families, Robert and I will sometimes—to the alarm and con-sternation of those around us—act out with hammy gestures the brief exchange between Banquo and his doomed son:

1990s. The Scene: The Departures Lounge of a Crowded Spanish Airport.

ROBERT (*Suddenly*) How goes the night, boy?

JOHN (*Returning from the Gents, in a lisping falsetto*) The Moon ith down. I have not heard the clock.

ROBERT (*Pointing dramatically upwards*) And she goes down at twelve.

JOHN I take 't, 'tith later Sir.

ROBERT There's husbandry in heaven. Their candles are all out! Is that our flight number? Can you see?

Acting with real people in a real theatre company was of course a step up from treading the encyclopaedias alone in my back bedroom (although perforce the parts were much smaller). I took to it like a fish to water—to the extent that over the remaining school years I played in dozens of shows, at school, at the Little Theatre, with neighbouring am dram societies, with the local rep which briefly flourished in the town, and with my own Company of young performers that I later bullied and bribed into performing in local church halls.

I think it was Edith Sitwell's brother who put in his *Who's Who* entry that he was 'educated during the holidays from Eton'. Something of the sort also occurred with me. I had no particular problems with the school day—though for me the focus was always on the subterranean japes of my schoolfellows rather than on the school curriculum—but a great deal of what I took from those years came from holiday and after-school activities. As Retford was a small rural town, with few other cultural resources, the masters of the local Grammar School, together with the mistresses from the Girls' High School, one way and another ran most of the local societies. It therefore seemed the most natural thing in the world, as we grew older, to meet staff and fellow pupils in the coffee shops or the Denman Library and discuss the books we were reading, or to discuss the exhibited work of local artists with Jack Penrose, the art teacher, or to write up our own programme notes for the local concerts. At such gatherings I still called the staff members 'sir' and they called me 'Pick'. When I later became a Grammar School Master myself, I was sorry that these formalities were giving way to more casual terms.

It was however at play rehearsals that I really came into my own. I chose to believe I was destined to become a famous actor. Indeed for much of the time, and in spite of the occasional distractions from the main school curriculum, I behaved as if I already was one, having myself photographed in profile, with a much-prized cravat (in which I thought I looked irresistible) wrapped around my neck. Even my mother, who had been to school in Newark with the great actor, tried to encourage me by saying that I was the next Donald Wolfit (though even then I knew that wasn't quite right). So when in 1952 the school chose to celebrate its 400th Anniversary by presenting an open-air pageant to the visiting Duke of Gloucester, I took it for granted that I should be chosen to open the proceedings by reciting its prologue.

So it came to pass, at the appointed hour, on a blazing hot June morning, school uniform newly cleaned and pressed, I strode out before the assembled dignitaries and in my best actor's voice began:

> In humble duty to a Royal Duke,
> A lowly scholar of this ancient school,
> I bow my knee—for all assembled here.
> Son of a King, and Uncle to our Queen,
> Who by his presence honours us today,
> As here we celebrate our Royal name,
> By Charter given, four centuries ago.

Then the occasion rather got the better of me. I am told that I stood abruptly, flung back my right arm and pointed sideways (in a gesture which owed more to a cricketing umpire's signal than any self-respecting thespian) and smiled ingratiatingly at the perspiring Duke:

> We beg your Royal Highness now to share
> With us in a brief glimpse of those far-off days,
> When out of piety and Kingly grace,
> Our school first rose to flourish in this place.

Already familiar with the technique of getting a round of applause by exiting on the third beat, I did what I had never done at rehearsal and separated and overstressed the last two words—'this' (one)—'place' (two)—and on the count of three, stuck out my chin and strode majestically off. There was indeed a grudging round of muted applause. But I had meanwhile caught sight of the Senior English Master—himself an accomplished actor and already ashamed of the attention-seeking lickspittle I was rapidly becoming—shaking his head ruefully on the sidelines.

There was perhaps a clearer indication of where my real talents lay in the following year when, as a crafty means of making a bit of money out of Queen Elizabeth's Coronation, I built a portable booth, and made myself a set of Punch and Judy glove puppets. After a bit of rehearsal I inserted a small ad in the local rag and got a gratifying number of bookings, at two guineas a throw, entertaining the various street parties and church celebrations that accompanied the event. The few photographs I retain of that summer suggest that the show was certainly not worth two guineas—though in mitigation, in those pre-television days the bar for popular entertainment was still set pretty low.

*　*　*

Until the outbreak of war, King Edward VI's had been in part a boarding school—in my day two of the classrooms were still called Dormitory One and Dormitory Two—but now the pupils who came from further afield lodged in the town and were counted as day boys. And the 1944 Butler Act had thrown up another anomaly. Boys from Worksop, and the surrounding coalfields, when they passed the eleven plus, were offered places at the school—there being no provision for them in their own towns. As a consequence the first form in which I found myself had only two or three boys in it who came from Retford—the rest were either pupils from further afield who lodged in the town, or (the majority) aliens who came in daily by bus from Worksop, Edwinstowe or Bircotes.

Thus my classmates did not divide themselves up along the usual lines—sporting as against arty types, brawn versus brains—but rather on the basis of the mode of transport they used to get to school. The pupils who came in by bus perforce tended to gang up together, and of course played little or no part in the after-school activities that domiciled Retfordians enjoyed. The day boys who lodged in the town, by contrast, had plenty of free time on their hands and were only too eager to join in with we locals. Indeed, three of the four school friends with whom I remained in regular contact were day boys of that kind.

The fourth was a Retfordian, Ian Robinson, with whom I was destined to have a lifelong friendship. We were interested in the same things (I remember that Ian wrote our second year pantomime) but he differed from me in that he was, from his junior school days, a real academic. I recall (though he claims not to) a cricket match at Babworth when he was thirty or so not out, and on the verge of taking our team to victory when, with murmured apologies, he retired from the crease, got on his bike and pedalled off, anxious he said not to miss a broadcast of *The Tempest* on the Third Programme. Even then we knew that a boundary had been crossed. It was all right to be interested in cricket *and* Shakespeare.

However we do both remember the days when after school we would cycle back to Ian's house and set up a cricket pitch in a nearby field, just for the two of us. It was not a game for sluggards. The luckless bowler had to cover all the fielding positions, even racing round like a dervish to stop the overthrows, while (there being no boundaries) the batsman metronomically galloped to and fro between the wickets, piling up the endless runs. To a passer-by, observing our manic manœuvres, it must have seemed like sports day at the funny farm.

It might be thought remarkable, given the scant attention most of us seemingly gave to studying, that so many of my schoolfellows later achieved a degree of eminence in their fields. One of the day boys, David Norman, became Head of Engineering at the Royal Naval College at Dartmouth, and a Professor at Washington University. Another, Ian Collins, was Chaplain to the late Queen Mother, and led a campaign against the ordination of women. Others became distinguished academics—Brammer a Chemistry Professor and M.N.E.Allsop a Professor of Medicine in Australia. Most distinguished of all the academics was of course Ian Robinson, who followed his illustrious career at Downing by becoming a controversial English Don. Though it must be added that so far as the general public was concerned the best-known of the graduates from the class of 55 was probably Tony Hardisty, who followed Henry Rose as chief football correspondent of the *Sunday Express.*

There ought at this stage to follow a full and frank account of my sexual adventures in adolescence. If King Edward's had been exclusively a working class secondary school, I should no doubt be expected to give a full account of being roughly deflowered by randy mill girls behind the local slag heaps. If it had been a minor public school, the reader would expect to hear of my long walks in the countryside with that particularly attractive flaxen haired youth from the Lower Third, coupled with accounts of the sinister History Beak with his passion for caning young boys' bottoms. But, King Edward's being neither a public school nor a secondary modern, the truth is much more prosaic.

There were certainly no obvious signs of homosexual behaviour, although we occasionally implied that we knew for a fact that so-and-so was a . . . . I choose not to remember the term we then used (in those days 'Gay' was just something which Cicely Courtneidge was). Most of the time, when we talked about sex, we simply boasted to each other about our improbable sexual conquests, and the cunning stratagems we had employed to persuade the opposite sex to come across. But the 'girl friends' in these fantasies were, like the exploits themselves, almost wholly imaginary. For the truth was that we grammar school boys were unnaturally gauche in female company. However, in fairness, we did labour under one cruel handicap. There was a school rule which insisted on us wearing a raucously striped school cap on all our journeys to and from school. Not unreasonably, the local girls did not want to be seen even talking to anyone dressed like Archie Andrews, and so we could not really make any progress until we had pulled on ordinary togs. Nor did the passage of years afford respite, because when you passed into the Sixth Form and were made a 'Prefect', as a badge of office you had to sport a cap with a ludicrous golden tassel on it—something that might have gone down quite well at a Chelsea Arts Ball, but which was inappropriate wooing garb for Retford.

For myself I tried to get round this problem by arranging to escort the more nubile of my fellow am dram actors to evening rehearsals (when I would most likely be wearing my favoured cravat), meeting them at some distance from the rehearsal room, and then taking them on a circuitous route through town in the hope that one of my classmates might see me. Needless to say, these walks were entirely innocent, but in reply to questions the following day—'Oh, did you see me with Joyce? What a raver! We were just off to the Recreation Ground'—I could slyly hint at the depraved couplings that we had enjoyed together. By these sly means I was able to maintain the pretence that I, like some of my classmates, was a ruthless Lothario. But when I did actually lose my virginity, it was I that was seduced. A quietly spoken local Librarian, some years older than me, whom I knew from amdram rehearsals, invited me back to her flat and told me that before we had tea she wanted me to make love to her. She then, with unexpected vigour, demonstrated what she had in mind. What followed was very far from showing me in the role of triumphal male conqueror, and I felt it best not to mention it afterwards, to anyone at all.

❈3❈

Cowardice

THROUGHOUT my school days I always took the easiest option—whether in the choice of subjects at 'A' level (I had passed well in the Sciences at 'O' level, but the Sixth Form courses in Science looked too much like hard work), or in my choice of University. My English masters had suggested that I apply to Bristol—which then offered the only Drama Degree in the UK—but Hugh Hunt's syllabus, aiming to establish Drama as a serious academic subject, looked altogether too demanding, and besides I shrank from being in serious competition with ambitious young actors who would almost certainly be more talented, not to mention more dedicated, than I was. For I had begun to realise that although I may on occasion have reminded my dear mother of the young Donald Wolfit, I lacked that gentleman's exclusive belief in his own talent. I was dedicated to myself, but my primary aim was always self preservation, rather than self enhancement. To steal an old Goon Show joke, I was a devout coward.

Having suggested Bristol, my teachers felt under no obligation to offer further advice, while my parents (neither of whom had been to university) regarded all my professed intentions as further evidence that I was not dealing from a full pack. However, I persevered, looked at a few prospectuses, listened to the stories Old

Retfordians told about their undergraduate days, and was eventually persuaded that the easiest option would be The University of Leeds. It was set in a proper city (a great attraction to a small town lad) and was easily reached by train. One of my school friends, David Norman (who was already there) reported that not only was the university socially vigorous but that Leeds itself had an unbelievably raunchy night life, with throbbing bars and dance halls on every street corner—adding that the city was jam-packed with randy young women. As he told it, young male hunks like us had it made. We would each night have to fight off marauding gangs of lascivious Yorkshire lasses.

When I got there, I have to confess that I never saw much sign of the exciting night life, nor of the predatory young women—but in spite of that, my choice turned out well. Leeds, with its clattering trams, vast shopping arcades and faded civic grandeur, was everything that a Retford lad hoped that a city would be. And the university turned out to be a home from home. The great Higher Education rebuilding programme had not yet started, so the university's premises were still scattered fairly randomly in pre-war terraces and dusty back streets, but all within easy walking distance of the Headrow and the city centre. Bookshops, museums and galleries were thus readily to hand. Europe's leading orchestras played regularly in the City Hall, and there were still—in the mid fifties—four busy theatres. I was later to feel a similar sensation when visiting London, flying in to New York, or coming out of the metro in Paris, but in my student days every time I walked out of Central Station past the Grand Hotel into the sooty bustle of Leeds City Square, I felt my heart beating faster and my footsteps quicken.

The university itself was all I had hoped for—indeed, academically and socially it was very much more exciting than I had expected. Leeds had a surprising number of inspirational teachers and I very soon fell under the academic spell of some of the more colourful among them—including the eccentric Shakespearean scholar, George Wilson Knight, a practising spiritualist who seemed to have no difficulty in conjuring up the great writers of the past at his séances, though it was a little unnerving to be told that S.T. Coleridge or Lord Byron had disagreed with what one had written about them in an undergraduate essay, his more conventional colleague Bonamy Dobrée, the polymath historian Asa Briggs and later, the redoubtable William Walsh, whose *Uses of Imagination* was to lend inspiration to the whole of my teaching life.

And the physical intermingling of town and gown meant that—in contrast to Oxford or Cambridge, where the conventions of College and High Table seemed to set dons apart from students—the Leeds professors perforce mixed with the students on a daily basis. We shared the same streets, trams and eating places—though the war had been over for a decade there was still a British Restaurant under the City Hall, which was remarkably good value. In these circumstances I found I could meet and talk with my personal tutor, Geoffrey Hill, as comfortably as I had once talked with my masters at the Grammar School. Though that easy fraternisation was not to last, it still existed in the 1950s—not least because British universities had not yet begun the expansion programmes that were later to turn them into hi-tech factory farms. And if a university education then felt like a privilege rather than a general constitutional right, it was partly down to the scale of the activity. In those days fewer than 5% of the population read for a degree, and—certainly in the civic universities—students could expect a high degree of individual supervision. Although Leeds was one of the larger provincial establishments, its entire Arts Faculty was then considerably smaller than most modern secondary schools.

And of course another critical difference was that in 1955 the state was still paying—and quite generously—for everything. I don't particularly defend the principle, simply state it as a fact. Once I had been offered and had accepted my place, the local education authority wrote to my parents to say what my personal grant would be. I can still remember my father's incredulous reaction—'All that? For doing nothing but think? I work *and* think.' And in addition the LEA met all lodging costs and fees—so cosseted was my generation that even after four years I had no inkling of how much my university fees were. Out of my personal grant I had enough money to afford to eat out—even, on occasion, to pay for a guest— and those of us who were interested in the performing arts were able to book good seats at the concerts and theatres (dress circle at the Leeds Grand, 3/6d.—about 17 pence in modern money; the gallery at the City Hall some 10p), and even a sought-after box seat at the City Varieties—which specialised in shows with titles like *Ooh La La!* or *Paris by Night* for which theatrical connoisseurs considered proximity to the stage essential—cost only 20p.

In spite of such cultural diversions, I still spent a good deal of time in the opulently stocked Brotherton Library—it was then still the case that students looked for information in books, rather than on the yet-to-be-invented Internet—and was finding, rather to my surprise, that I was beginning to enjoy the discipline of study. I started to bestow upon the more distinguished university staff something of the hero worship I had once lavished on the likes of Frankie Howerd or Norman Evans. For change was stirring within me. Just as my school had encouraged whatever innate creativity I may have had, so was the university now rousing latent academic skills. I began to enjoy learning for its own sake. Some might have called it a stage in the process of growing up.

But the important point is that this maturation began *after* I had gone up to university. In view of this (and as an antidote to those who urge modern youngsters to start planning the right educational paths for their chosen careers almost as soon as they can read and write) it is worth recording that the main reason I went to university at all was most decidedly not to prepare myself for any career. Indeed I had at that stage absolutely no idea how I might earn a full-time living. I just knew I liked the idea of being an undergraduate, and having a period of contemplation before plunging into the real grown up world. I also knew that this was a good way of legitimately deferring, and with any luck avoiding, having to do National Service (which was on the way out anyway, and seemed to me to be a waste of everybody's time). I was of course fully aware that it was all because of my good fortune in being a part of the first generation to benefit from the 1944 Education Act, but I think I am being honest when I say that from the first I had thought of reading for a degree not as a means to any mercenary end but, unfashionable though it may now sound, as an end in itself.

Certainly I had plenty of opportunity to examine my own motives during my undergraduate years, as a number of my fellow students had opted to do their military service before studying for a degree. Not unreasonably, they were resentful of somebody who had so far avoided being called to the colours, and who looked as if he might possibly avoid it altogether. There were long arguments about patriotism, duty to one's fellow men and the nature of cowardice—which became rather more sophisticated as many of us were taking elementary courses in logic—but which were not, at any rate during my first year, anything more than theoretical discussions.

It is hard to convey with any precision the day-to-day quality of my undergraduate years. I lived in digs with an agreeable landlady, Mrs Harman, who looked after four male students in a terraced house just off Woodhouse Moor. The four of us met at breakfast, and again at supper, and gave each other (and Mrs H) guarded accounts of what we had been up to during the day. There was my old friend David Norman, a scientist called Tony Wilson, and Jeff Radley, a geographer. In my conversations with them, I was soon made aware that my time as a liberal arts student was much less structured than theirs. For me there were stretches of each day when it was assumed that I would be reading (which I did) or talking, which I most certainly did as often as I could find anyone to listen. It was really this opportunity for never-ending discussion of everything under the sun which, I gradually realised, might be rendering me less systematic in thought than my scientific colleagues but which, on the other hand, was making me more open to new ideas, and certainly more ready to engage in free-flowing debate. I also saw that in order to be heard, one needed a parade of strong opinions and so for a while I became the worst, and most shallow, kind of student polemicist. In the Spring Term of my first year (the morality of capital punishment being a hot topic of the day) I almost persuaded my housemates to help finance the publication of a pamphlet (which I would write of course) urging the abolition of the death penalty. However, when the others read my rough draft, they decided it was far too strident in tone to convince anybody other than the incorrigibly feeble-minded, and that they had better things to do with their money.

For everyone the undergraduate years offer a chance to reinvent one's personality. I remember experimenting with all the usual costumes and props as I tried to work out what sort of person I was. On occasion I adopted a curved Sherlock Holmes pipe, set off by a wispy beard, and ignited it with cupped hands shielding the bowl from the winds that obligingly howled across Woodhouse Moor ('*The Thinker*'). There was the open-necked black shirt, accompanied by black drainpipe trousers and orange Hush Puppy Shoes, which my friends suggested made me look like Mickey Mouse, but which I thought suggested '*The Poet*'. There was—even less convincingly—'*The Outdoor Man*' (check shirt and Army and Navy boots). About '*The Man About Town*' (sitting at a back street bar with duffel coat suggestively untoggled, nursing a glass of flat Double Diamond) the less said the better.

In order to try to impress my little circle of friends and, on the rare occasions I actually ran across one of the Mill lasses that David had sworn were waiting to pounce on the likes of me, I had developed a number of enigmatic one-liners intended to make me seem mysterious and interesting. I liked to think they were the sort of thing Albert Camus might have murmured to his circle, though in practice they sounded rather more like Albert Modley. 'You wouldn't think it to look at me,' I would say to some girl momentarily prepared to give me her attention, 'but I was actually brought up in Sherwood Forest, and reared by wolves.' But these carefully honed *mots* never worked, and the Yorkshire lasses invariably reacted with something less than uninhibited sexual abandonment: 'Th'art a daft bugger, thee!' The absurdity of all this adolescent posturing was not lost upon my fellow students either, who claimed that I always adopted the character of the hero from the last film or play that

I had seen and lost no opportunity to pass on their judgement: 'We dread it when Pick comes back after he's been to see a Lassie film . . . .'

One remembers the peaks of course—but there were also deep dark valleys. In spite of all the romantic stuff written about university life, I suspect that most undergraduates experience stretches of loneliness or embarrassment or both. Indeed—except for those privileged hooray henrys whose sense of entitlement allows them to think of their own undergraduate boorishness as high jinks—even social successes will often be accompanied by a tinge of self-doubt, as when one's brilliant critical *aperçus* are greeted by imperfectly-stifled laughter. It is part of university student life. I recall only too well both the boredom and the embarrassments. In my first months at university I remember randomly but purposefully striding the city centre streets, wheeling into department stores to stare at goods I had neither the intention nor the means of buying, simply to fill up lonely hours. I remember going to my first university ball, and then spending the entire evening skulking in the shadows because exposing myself to the light would have revealed that the borrowed trousers of my desperately assembled 'dress suit' were in fact a shade of dark green. Another time, with a friend, grandly taking a stage box for four to hear the Carl Rosa Opera Company at the Leeds Grand (£1.15s.) and, in order to impress our girls with our sensitivity to operatic skills, both of us smoking cheroots all evening. Wince and shudder.

However, my undergraduate life was about to be undermined. For there occurred what was to prove a pivotal moment in all of our lives—something which proved an even more pressing moral issue than the abolition of capital punishment. On the 26th July 1956, in the middle of the summer vacation, the Egyptian President, Colonel Nasser, precipitated a major international crisis by announcing the nationalisation of the Suez Canal. This was in retaliation for the sudden withdrawal of promised American and UK aid for the building of the Aswan Dam. War clouds gathered. The UK Prime Minister Anthony Eden compared Nasser's action, somewhat improbably, to Hitler's annexation of Poland. The newspapers were filled with threats and counter threats as the situation threatened to spiral out of control, and we returned to Leeds at the beginning of October with the air crackling with menace. Before Nasser's move 1.5 million barrels of oil had been passing to the West each day through the canal, but now oil supplies had been reduced to a trickle. Petrol rationing was being reintroduced, and at Leeds Central Station that autumn there were no taxis waiting to take us and our luggage up to our digs.

Much worse was to follow. On the 29th October, Israel invaded Egypt and a few hours later (in what was later proved to be a prearranged collusion) France and the UK began to bomb Cairo and to parachute troops into the canal zone, ostensibly to 'stop the Israeli advance'. The USSR threatened to send in their own troops to stop the Western conspirators. The US then starkly warned the USSR to keep out, and for a few days we had to confront the belief that, in the ominous words of a leading US General, 'World War Three is in the Making.'

The impact on city and university was devastating. Both the US and the USSR now had the atomic bomb, so nowhere was safe, and nuclear war suddenly seemed very close indeed. For the first time in my life I engaged with a political cause, and found myself, with hundreds of other callow youths, marching up Briggate and 'demanding' that Anthony Eden withdraw (we waved placards about, so that he should be in no doubt about what he must do). In the university bitter arguments broke out between students of different nationalities, and it was reported that some classes had dissolved into huddled groups doing nothing more than listening to the latest news on the radio. There were rumours that those of us who had deferred our National Service in the expectation that it would soon become an anachronism, were now about to be called up, and used as bomb fodder for the rampaging Soviet forces.

Thus it was that in 1956, at the age of twenty, I lost my dilettante status. Although there were to be other crises of the same apparent magnitude, none would have the same devastating impact. The Suez crisis forced me and my generation to recognise that the 'peace' we had been living through for a decade was even more of an illusion than we had thought. That particular crisis however eventually went off the boil. Israel, France and Britain were forced by the USA into ignominious withdrawal. The USSR took advantage of the crisis to send Russian troops into one of its own satellites. After all that Egypt resumed control of the canal, while the whole terrifying shebang led to the sickness and resignation of Anthony Eden. The remainder of my undergraduate years took on a harder edge. After Suez I took very much more account of the outside world.

★ ★ ★

I continued to act of course, and to direct. I played Iago in *Othello,* and did a toe-curling impersonation of Kenneth More in a short tour of *Doctor In The House.* During two long vacations I was actually paid (expenses anyway) to perform in two al fresco productions (*Teahouse of the August Moon* and *The Little Hut*) staged in the grounds of a local Country Club. I started to write, and co-edited a fortnightly magazine, *Scope* (price 2d.), which reviewed all of the films currently playing in the Leeds area. I followed Herbert Read in having my first critical article, on Rudolph Valentino, published in the University Journal, *Gryphon.* I even wrote some poetic doggerel for publication in little magazines, though its midget tone of would-be sophistication even now brings a blush of shame to my wrinkled cheeks:

IN A COFFEE BAR

He's bearded and he's sueded, that emancipated man,
Smoking by the jukebox as he's leering through the
 plants.
He's a tarzan of the jungle with his coffee in his hand
For he stalks the blonde with falsies and the nylon
 leopard pants.
There are fairy lights and neon, but you still can see
 her eyes;
As they dance across the bottles through the mirror
 round the screen.
I remember naughty Jenny in that coffee bar in spring
When I was young and sensitive and innocent and
 green.

Bearded chap, I bless you for your byrony and
　　impotence
For bringing back the stinging words of that peroxide
　　whore.
The irony of Jenny when I didn't think I ought:
"When you're old enough to know you do, shan't be
　　here any more."
He's put sixpence in the jukebox, that emancipated man
And he's showing her his profile as he stares into the
　　night.
I dream of Jenny anything, and stir my cooling tea
For I'm sozzled and I'm lonely and I fear that she
　　was right. *

I also continued, albeit intermittently, to paint and
draw a little—of which more anon.

The most important thing to say was that at the
end of my second year I teamed up with Ann Clodagh
Johnson, who was to be at my side for the next fifty-
five years, fifty-one of them as my wife. I say 'teamed
up with' rather than met, because the truth was that
we had in a manner of speaking already met twice,
but without either of us feeling the need to take our
acquaintanceship further. For my part I was first aware of
Ann during my fresher year, when a determined-looking
lady suddenly stood up in a packed lecture room and
asked the lecturer—Professor Arthur Brown, whose claim
to immortality was that he had 'invented' the concept of
the inflationary spiral—to please speak up, because she
couldn't hear him. This piece of daring was thereafter
commemorated by the other students—including me—
with cries of 'Speak up, Professor' whenever she entered
a room. So—if I thought about this earnest young lady at
all—I had her marked down as an earnest bluestocking
that no self-respecting young rakehell would touch with a
bargepole.

Her first sight of me was no more alluring. It was the
habit of the Professor of Philosophy, Stephen Toulmin,
to invite all those pursuing any sort of philosophy
course to a garden party in the grounds of his house in

* In *Phoenix*, Vol. 2 No. 1 (p. 42), edited by Harry Chambers. He must
have been short of copy.

Adel woods. Although I am not a natural garden party goer, the promise of free food had led me to accept the Professor's invitation. Ann was later shudderingly to recall this scowling, black-shirted figure alone and palely loitering by a distant bed of roses. One or two of her friends had apparently tried to engage me in conversation, but had been curtly rebuffed. After that Ann certainly felt that a fun-loving girl such as her would want nothing to do with somebody who was not only self-pitying and socially inept, but probably an axe-wielding psychopath into the bargain.

So when we did finally meet, we already sort of knew—and sort of disliked—each other. Indeed, defining, explaining and overcoming that mutual mistrust formed the basis of many of our initial conversations. The setting for our breakthrough meeting was the Leeds Freshers' Conference—a week-long induction to university life at which students from years two and three took on the roles of guide to small groups of new students. Ann had been selected as a 'Team Leader' for the morning session and I was her assistant. We warily chatted over lunch, and discovered that we had a few things in common, particularly that all-important ability to laugh at the same things. I invited her to a film in the afternoon (a weepie, at which we both laughed uproariously) and thence to Leeds' only Turkish restaurant, in which I reduced not only my new companion but also the entire waiting staff to hysterics by my determined efforts to saw through the skewer on the kebab with a table knife (I'd never seen a kebab before). And so are our ends shaped, rough-hew them as we will.

By the third year I was seeing a lot of Ann and although we were not formally engaged, we understood by then that we should probably spend our lives together. So the question now arose of how I would earn my living. What sort of career, if any, should I pursue? Yes, it was still the day of the male hunter/provider—even though Ann, being cleverer than I, would probably have been a much more successful breadwinner. My childhood fantasies of earning my living as a stage performer had receded into the background. Although I had not altogether given up the idea of being a different kind of creative artist, I was I think still more interested in living the life of an artist than in taking the trouble actually to become one. In what was perhaps a last defiant attempt to live the life of a bohemian rakehell, I went for interview at the Leeds College of Art, proposing myself as a postgraduate student, taking with me a few of my sketchbooks and some of my critical assessments of exhibitions which I had seen. The Principal was not unkind about my art work, but soon got down to the nitty-gritty by asking me what thought I had given to financing myself as an artist in training. The answer was only too painfully apparent— none. The scales dropped from my eyes, and I departed with my artistic pretensions in tatters.

As finals approached, my tutor asked me whether I wished to stay on and do research (for which grants were available) but I had by then decided upon another course. I would train as a teacher, and while I was doing so Ann (graduating from her Social Studies course at the same time as me) would take a year's teaching job. Then we would marry and both work as teachers, build up a little capital, keep all our options open and see what life had to offer. Something like that anyway, though I doubt whether either of us could at the time have expressed our vague aspirations so succinctly.

Once more I was blessed by extraordinary luck, for the Leeds Institute of Education—which had for decades been a respectable if boring university department, with a solid reputation for producing sound Secondary teachers—had just that year appointed a new professor. William Walsh, the appointee, was not only considerably younger than most of his colleagues, but also pretty plainly at odds with their rather mechanical view of what education consisted of. Walsh's own belief was that education did not depend upon having the right institutions, nor upon having the right syllabus, nor even upon acquiring a good teaching method—but upon the unique interaction of each teacher and each pupil within the realms of the imagination. It hardly mattered within which system this interaction took place, and it would not necessarily occur within the confines of a formal lesson. For Walsh the primary texts for teachers were not psychiatric or sociological tomes, nor any other kind of textbook, but the imaginative records of those creative artists, such as Coleridge, Henry James or Mark Twain, who had understood and recorded the ways in which a child grows, comprehends and responds to the world.

Then, as now, the prime purpose of school teaching was seen—at any rate by politicians and educational bureaucrats—as being to push as many children as possible through examinations. Walsh was a revelation. I can still remember my interview with him—his fastidious, rather dandyish figure cutting a strange dash in the darkly panelled rooms of the Institute. I felt that what he was saying perfectly encapsulated and made sense of my own introspections—simultaneously giving me a lifelong reason to believe in myself as a teacher, rather than as a classroom mechanic. Though Shaw's glib dismissal of the profession—'those who can't, teach'—was still taken by bar room dickheads as a profound truth, Walsh knew that the obverse was true, that only those that *can* can truly teach.

His influence has stayed with me through half a century of working at every level of education. He must have thought that I was not wholly beyond the pale, for well before the scheduled end of the interview he had offered me a place on his postgraduate course. So began one of the happiest, and most purposeful, years of my life.

⁙4⁙
Compromise

SOME YEARS LATER, when applying for a post which demanded what were rather menacingly called 'out-standing inter-personal skills', I asked my friend John Allen, then Principal of the Central School of Speech and Drama, if he would kindly write a reference for me. Such documents are supposed to be confidential, to be seen only by the interviewers, and I can't now remember why it was that I came to read it. Perhaps John—a man of rare honesty and openness—showed it to me? At all events when I did read it I was startled to see that he had begun his summary of my character with the words; "There are two John Picks...the creative John Pick and his cynical alter ego, highly critical of all artistic pretension". He was otherwise quite flattering, but added that although he personally had no difficulty in dealing with the two warring sides of my character, my colleagues did not always find it so simple. In certain circumstances I was difficult to work with and I did seem to have the unfortunate knack of making enemies easily. In a word, the reference read like an unusually honest, though some-what disquieting, school report.

I was in my early fifties when he wrote it. And I couldn't help being a mite depressed to learn that the long-standing flaws in my character were still so clearly apparent, as I had hoped that by then I had succeeded in hiding them. Heaven knows I had tried for long enough.

With each new job I'd made a conscious attempt to pull
myself together, as it were, and had rather hoped that the
passage of time had covered over the remaining cracks in
my personality. But, no—I was, it appeared, still less than
the sum of my parts, and still conspicuously lacking what
City men rather crudely call bottom. It will therefore
come as a surprise to the reader that my interview was
successful—an illustration of the unfortunate truth that it
is the status of your referees that matters, rather than
what they write.

As far back as 1959, when I entered my year of postgraduate teacher training, I was already making renewed
efforts to train my straggling personality, like ivy, around
some sort of unifying framework. To prepare for my
recently-chosen career I garbed myself in stereotypical
teacher fashion (corduroys and hush puppies, with
leather patches on the elbows of my jacket), bought
and even read bits of the *Times Educational Supplement*,
and bupped away at what I hoped looked like a well-
used briar, as I judiciously weighed up the probable
consequences of at least a few of my actions. And when
that summer I spent a few days at home, I convinced
myself that I saw a look of faint hope in my parents' eyes.
Their weird, self-centred progeny looked as if it might
be going to do something which actually featured on the
RSAA (Retford Scale of Acceptable Activities). At last
they could talk about me to family and friends in terms
that did not involve either lengthy explanation or abject
apology. And I wasn't going to be sectioned, as they had
previously feared, but was going to train to be a teacher.

Before the serious training began we all had to put a
toe into educational waters by doing a couple of practice
weeks in a junior school. I was allocated to Thrumpton
Primary on the outskirts of Retford, a few miles from
my parents' home. As a proactive educational experience
this was unusual in that I did virtually no teaching,
but instead spent my time being taught to write in
italic script by the Headmaster, whose passion it was.
The result of that brief sojourn was that my hitherto
barely legible scrawl was, at any rate for a few years,
utterly transformed. My letters (which even close family
had previously found indecipherable) now looked like

medieval manuscripts, even if the content failed to match their scholarly appearance.

More serious, and lengthier, teaching practices would be undertaken later in the year. The first was at Heckmondwike Grammar School where I learned two valuable lessons in the etiquette of the teaching profession. First, in the final of the HGS staff table tennis tournament, played on the deeply pitted staffroom table, I showily vanquished my opponent (the Senior Mistress)—only to have one of the regular staff take me aside and explain that when senior management choose to fraternise with lowlier mortals and join in their little amusements, they will expect to come out top. The second *faux pas* was worse. I had been flattered to be asked to lead a Sixth Form group studying Goldsmith's *Citizen of the World*. It was not a book of which I had any previous knowledge. In the first class, conscious both of my apprentice ranking and my ignorance of the text, I asked the regular English Mistress—supposedly supervising me from the back of the room—a simple but important question about Goldsmith's main character. It was immediately obvious that she had not read the book either. My question hung in the air. We stared uncomprehendingly at each other. Then a kindly pupil, obviously well used to the gaucheries of student teachers, provided us both with a get-out. 'Miss X won't answer you, sir, because you're not meant to ask her questions. You're supposed to pretend she's invisible.'

My second and final practice was spent in the all-male sanctum of King James' School, Almondbury. Incidentally, although Heckmondwike is still a Grammar School I was interested to see, when I recently looked it up, that King James' School is now an 'Academy'—a curious Victorian term which in my youth characterised comic school establishments such as that presided over by Will Hay. At King James' I remember only two really awkward incidents. First, when trying out my fledgling classroom skills I had cause to write the word 'minimum' on the whiteboard and was embarrassed to receive a round of applause for what the class obviously thought was a well-honed party trick. (Try writing the word in flowing italic script, and you'll see why.) The second occurred when, in the middle of a drama session that was not going particularly well, the door opened and my professor, the revered William Walsh, walked in, looked benignly around him—and then walked out again almost immediately. 'Did you know him, sir?' the class enquired, as soon as he'd gone. 'Bit flash. Looked a bit like somebody taking bets, woodenja say?'

Outside class hours I helped out a little bit with the school production of *Alice in Wonderland*, and remember being particularly impressed by a fleshy youth playing the White Rabbit who demonstrated impeccable comic timing and a remarkable deadpan technique. So I was not surprised when many years later this same Gorden Kaye had a huge success as the improbably attractive René in the BBC sitcom *'Allo 'Allo*.

★ ★ ★

During the working week Ann and I lived apart, for it was still 1959 and nobody knew that the sixties were going to swing like a pendulum do. She had moved into a dingy but spacious ground floor flat in North Leeds with three of her women friends who all, like her, spent their weekends with their boy friends. Above the girls lived a gay bachelor (though I think that in those days we unthinkingly used a different, uglier, epithet to describe such gentlemen) who would occasionally invite them up into his flat for sherry and to show them his most treasured possession—a signed photograph of one of the best-known British leading men of the period, tastefully kitted out in bra, lace-up corsets, nylon stockings and fluffy suspenders. In the interests of good neighbourliness, and because they liked him anyway, Ann and her flatmates hid their surprise and agreed that the gentleman in question looked quite ravishing. It was, as I say, 1959, and notions of consenting adult liaisons, civil partnerships (to say nothing of gay marriage) were a long way into the future.

As for myself I lived with two friends in an even more grotty flat in downtown Leeds, the main feature of which was the bath, which the landlord (who looked like the perpetually mardy character from *On The Buses*) would periodically 'mend' with papier maché and several layers of green gloss paint. Knowing this, and out of common prudence rather than any wish to be unhygienic, we did not trust ourselves to it very often. The cobbled street on to which our little hideaway opened had a pub at one end and a busy brothel at the other, which probably conveys as well as anything the nature of the neighbourhood. It (the flat, not the brothel) was presided over by Mrs Horseful (I think her name was), a screeching bird-like lady who lived downstairs. It was alleged that she had together with her sister been a dancer in a speciality duo on the variety circuit. I never saw any evidence of this—though one of the flat's earlier occupants claimed that he had once been invited down into the lady's private quarters to be shown her scrapbook of clippings.

My two flatmates (who remained friends thereafter) were David Fontana (who had temporarily shelved his intention to be a deeply sensitive novelist in order to follow the same PGCE course) and Ben Roberts, who was not a member of the local university, but an old Harrovian running the family firm which specialised in cinema and theatre advertising. Ben was a bit older than us, and had moved out of the palatial family home in the Yorkshire Dales in order, he said, to enjoy the pleasures of city life. He was not only gregarious but easily the politest man I have ever met. He liked the company of university folk—particularly females—although it has to be said he found most Leeds students a bit dim. However, he was (true to type) invariably polite about David and me and overlooked our comparative lack of sophistication, perhaps hoping that we might one day lead him to our secret store of comely Yorkshire lasses.

No such luck. We didn't know any, and during term-time David and I were totally involved in the course. Although Professor Walsh was always, for us, the highlight of the week, we also enjoyed the training in educational practice which comprised the nuts and bolts of it all. In the evenings the three of us repaired back to the communal flat. We cooked ourselves strange-looking meals, while (it was that sort of time) listening to LPs of Bix Beiderbecke, Satchmo or Humph on Ben's Record Player. On some weekends Ben drove us in his Morris Minor to country pubs out in the Dales where we drank a good deal of beer, listened to little jazz groups and uncomplainingly ingested the pub food of that time—crisps, pickled eggs and—if you were lucky—stale rolls with lumps of orange cheese in them.

This was the late fifties. The Breathalyser had not been heard of, and at the end of the pub evenings we piled into the car and, on the journey home, began to sing. But it was songs of a particular kind. Both David and Ben had undertaken National Service and during their time serving Her Majesty they had learned the scurrilous barrack room ballads with which we made the night air glad. There were several standards—'Eskimo Nell' and 'The Harlot of Jerusalem' for example—but by far the most popular was that string of Bacchanalian limericks which is traditionally punctuated by the chorus:

> That was a jolly good rhyme,
> Sing us another one,
> Just like the other one, do!

It is strange—and perhaps revealing of further flaws in my character—that whereas I have forgotten so much of the fine poetry I learned in school, or had once declaimed on the stage, I can still effortlessly remember so many of these smutty verses. Ben in particular was (still is) capable of reeling off a seemingly endless series of them, each one delicately detailing some closely-observed, if somewhat bizarre, sexual occurence:

> There was a young curate named Pratt,
> Who under an oak tree was sat,
>> Amusing himself,
>> By abusing himself,
> And collecting the drops in his hat.

Following which we would all come in with the chorus:

> That was a jolly good rhyme, etc.

And on and on they would go:

> There was a young sailor from Wales,
> An expert at pissing in gales.
>> He could pee in a jar
>> From the top gallant spar,
> And not even wet on the sails.

Our favourite in those days—even more popular than the young man from Australia who had, for mercenary gain, chosen to paint his botty like a dahlia— was a somewhat surreal account of a West Country schoolteacher:

A schoolmistress who lived in Devizes,
She was up at the local Assizes,
    For she'd taught, on all fours,
    All her girls to be whores
—And awarded french letters as prizes.

I soon learned enough of them to join in, and even (following a little surreptitious research) added a few of my own. Singing them after a night on the ale became a kind of bond between the three of us. I can't offer any excuses for such pathetically adolescent behaviour, except to say that back in 1959 singing them felt like some sort of defiant ritual, a Dionysian protest against the bare-knuckle constrictions of the post-war world. In this regard it was strangely satisfying to discover, much later, that quite a lot of creative chaps of our vintage—Kingsley Amis, Tony Hancock, Robert Conquest and John Osborne among them—seemed to have had the same strange compulsion to sing scurrilous limericks when in their cups. But that was then. I know that significant exemplars of modern culture—Freddie Mercury, Gilbert and George's scatalogical set or Britten's *Peter Grimes*, for example—are of course quite free of any sexual overtones. Such genuinely creative works surely mark the highest and noblest aspirations of our civilisation—in contrast to the base crudities of the banqueting roster of Miss Foster from Gloucester, and the sous chef who roasted and tossed her.

* * *

While all this was going on Ann, by now a full-time Geography Mistress in a Leeds Secondary School, was discovering that teaching a subject she knew absolutely nothing about, even to pupils who had absolutely no interest in it, was still quite a demanding job. In order to prepare her for the coming week we spent many of our Saturday mornings poring over atlases and textbooks trying to work out what Ceylon was now called, or whether (I don't recall why this mattered) corned beef was still canned in Buenos Aires.

Ann was a religious sceptic, who throughout her life found church practices nursery stuff, and those who indulged in them endearing but regressive. So Sundays were given over to our own secular pleasures. On those self-indulgent weekends we consciously tried to immerse ourselves in the high arts—visiting Leeds' excellent museums and art galleries, patronising the Ballet Rambert at the Grand, and sitting through the grainy black and white masterpieces on show at the Art Cinema. We sometimes pulled in a theatre—once going to Bradford to see Harry Hanson's Famous Court Players presenting a much-cut version of *Look Back in Anger* as a broad family comedy. Something of an improvement, we thought. Although it was rather out of our normal price range, when the great Victor Borge announced a one-night stand in Leeds I splashed out four pounds (quite a sum in those days) to book us two comfortable stall seats. Mr Borge gave only one performance and for some reason quite early on a Friday evening, which meant that Ann had to come straight to the show from her working week. The evening was not a success. The theatre was warm and the seats well cushioned, so as soon as she sat down she fell into a deep sleep, and didn't catch a word of it. Years later, fed up with me telling the story at dinner parties, she publicly gave me back the price of her ticket.

As Easter approached, we began to give some thought to more mundane matters such as what post I might occupy, and where we might live. Then one memorable day the English tutor called me into her office and told me that I was going to get a course distinction and some sort of prize (that apparently was the reason the professor had looked in on my class at King James), but—much more to the point—that she had a teaching post in her gift which could be mine for the taking. This was at the Leeds Grammar School, then still in its old buildings by Woodhouse Moor. So a settled future beckoned! I could join a prestigious public school as an assistant teacher, Ann could continue to draw a salary teaching geography at Intake School, until eventually we could settle down

and breed, no doubt occupying a tastefully modernised
cottage in one of the more sought-after villages on the
outskirts of Leeds, before taking our places in the lower
rungs of respectable Yorkshire society.

We did not hesitate for very long. Faced with that kind
of career path the answer had to be 'no'. Though we had
enjoyed our time as students in Leeds the prospect of
settling down there and becoming pillars of respectability
in a place where we had once kicked over the traces,
seemed suddenly too much like being sentenced to a
decade of compulsory community service. I thanked the
tutor for her kindness in thinking of me but said that I
should not be applying.

Then, as sometimes happens, serendipity took over.
Robert Protherough—my English Master friend from my
schooldays—had just been appointed Head of English
at Bilborough, a newly built Grammar School ('Very
South Bank' he said in his Christmas circular) on the
edge of Nottingham. Bilborough was now advertising
for someone to teach English and Drama in Robert's
Department. I applied and, armed with my first class
teaching qualification, and equipped with quite a lot of
inside knowledge about my future department head's
likes and dislikes, I got the job. Ann (it was so easy, then!)
followed this up with her own application to the local
Education Authority, and was in turn appointed without
interview to teach Civics and English at the William
Sharp School, set on the same site as Bilborough. This
happy combination of circumstances did not seem in any
way unusual. In those far off times graduates could more
or less choose not only what they would do, but also where
and with whom they would do it.

There remained only the necessity of getting formally
married (in those days teachers and the like simply did
not 'live in sin'—as a lot of older folk still called it).
Marriage itself did not seem to present a problem, but
the formalities did. We had never been officially engaged,
so neither of us had ever had reason to communicate
with, or to visit, the other's parents. We were suddenly
aware that this would have to be put right. Ann's parents
certainly wanted to have a look at me before we plighted
our troth, and so did my parents want to meet Ann. In

their case—mindful of my long-standing preference for fiction over fact—they probably harboured doubts about whether the 'Ann' I spoke of actually existed.

One of the few things that life has taught me is that there is no way in which you can ever understand the dynamics which hold other people's families together. Ann was obviously very fond of her family, though she had left home to go to university as soon as she possibly could. In her description of her parents she had painted them as being highly conventional, and rather patrician in outlook. Her mother, she told me, was very kind but a bit of a Liverpool snob. She had been perfectly happy to let her young daughters wander the streets of Liverpool, rubbing shoulders with drunken sailors, the Maggie Mays of Scotland Road and the dockside knife gangs, but drew the line at them ever going to Blackpool, because it was 'common'. Ann was certainly worried that we would not get on. I should judge her parents, who voted Tory and were supporters of the local Tennis Club, to be too conventionally middle class. They in turn would come to the conclusion that I—who neither played tennis nor habitually voted Tory—was clearly a dangerous leftie of dubious character.

Neither expectation was realised. Ann's mother turned out to be an eloquent softly-spoken Irish Protestant, perfectly happy to tolerate young men with unsound opinions provided they would debate with her. She soon told me her story. As a young girl she had come over to Britain to work in the Civil Service, and had met and married Ann's Liverpool-born father in her late twenties. They had made their home in Liverpool but retained strong links to the Emerald Isle and even after their two daughters had been born and war was raging still made a pilgrimage each summer to see the family in Southern Ireland. Ann's father was not a natural lover of the Irish, having no taste for disorder, but tolerated these yearly sojourns out of love for his wife. Above everything Ann's mother loved talking, and once she had got over her slight disappointment that I knew nothing whatsoever about Irish politics, engaged me in long and wordy disputations over matters such as the superiority of the public schools (they had sent both their daughters to

Merchant Taylors'), the looming menace of the unions, and what Harold Wilson's Government might mean for the future of British civilisation. Meanwhile Ann's father, who had long ago made up his mind on these and all other topics, held his peace behind the *Daily Mail*.

But if Ann's parents were a surprise to me it was nothing compared to the shock that my parents were to Ann. In their centrally-heated Liverpool home Ann's parents played music during meals. Her mother went regularly to the theatre and they watched the *Brains Trust* on television. In their home meals were refined affairs, both in their preparation and consumption. Back at the Pick ranch, things would be very different. I had tried to prepare Ann, both for the extreme ordinariness of Retford (very different from the tumultuous streets of Liverpool) and had hinted that in every way my parents lived much closer to nature red in tooth and claw than did hers. Even so she still found it a bit of a shock to enter a house in which all the doors were constantly thrown open, in which my mother wandered from room to room plucking newly-slain pheasants for supper, and where my father's idea of entertaining his son's Intended was to take her out to admire his composting arrangements. However, she played up to it all very well, even conjuring up some enthusiasm for the various specimens of flora and fauna that were presented for her inspection and approval. With the result that my parents (who had no doubt been expecting me either to turn up with an invisible friend, or some city sophisticate combining the worst attributes of Catwoman and a Bride of Dracula) were delighted by Ann. When at supper she bravely asked for more shot-filled pheasant the deal was done.

And so it came to pass, in a slightly bizarre ceremony at Ann's parents' local church. Her father had asked us whether we wanted a big wedding and reception like her sister had enjoyed, or whether we would just like the money? No contest there. At the Wedding my parents duly met Ann's parents (a no-score draw, we decided) so the family sextangle was complete. Ann's only guest was her sister Pat, always known as Tish, who was her Maid of Honour, while my sole invitee was my old school friend David Norman—who, by his strong advocacy of

Leeds as a good place for crumpet had, in a roundabout way, been responsible for our meeting. The congregation was completed by Ann's father's brother Uncle Percy and Aunt Vera, his wife.

David assumed the duties of Best Man and it was no fault of his that a particularly virulent muscular problem in his shoulders and neck had on the day rendered him alarmingly lopsided in his appearance and gait. This meant that as he lurched unsteadily down the aisle to take up his appointed place, accompanied as he was by a sudden peal of organ music, we were all irresistibly reminded of Charles Laughton's memorable performance in *The Hunchback of Notre Dame* and, much to the disapproval of the presiding vicar, collapsed into fits of unstoppable giggles. Nevertheless we were legally married. Toasts were drunk in a nearby hotel, and Uncle Percy, always the most generous of men, gave my father half his timber importing business—a contract which had no legal standing since by then both parties were palpably drunk. Then it was off to London for a few days before we returned to our Nottingham flat, furnished it quickly and cheaply, and settled down to live happily ever after. Although it was not of course quite as simple as that.

JP with Ben Roberts

❊5❊

Dissimulation

MY TWO YEARS as a provincial Grammar School teacher are in many ways the hardest of all to write about. Words have to be written consecutively, but the events which they describe are sometimes unrelated to deeper shifts of personality and attitude, which beat to a quite different rhythm. So it was then.

I was now living in Nottingham, married to the delightful Ann, and with a pleasant and easy job. The days were filled with love, friendship and laughter, yet beneath the surface something was beginning to stir. The dreams of childhood and adolescence—which should perhaps have been discarded long ago—were at last being stored away for good, while other, as yet ill-formed, ambitions were trying to gain admittance. Finally I forced myself to acknowledge that I had neither the single-mindedness nor the driving ambition to succeed as a professional artist. Yet on the other hand I was becoming increasingly aware that I did not want to spend the rest of my life as a schoolmaster either. As a result other, if so far misty, horizons began to beckon.

Meanwhile, daily life occupied me happily enough. As a result of our having two reasonable full-time salaries, Ann and I were able, for the first time in our lives, to fashion for ourselves what people were later to call a 'lifestyle'. Though we sometimes 'hopped over' to France in our vacations, and occasionally 'dropped down' to London for shows, there was sufficient artistic life in provincial Nottingham for us to convince ourselves, perhaps naïvely, that we were living in the vanguard of a vaguely perceived cultural revolution. Upon arrival in the Midlands we had found ourselves caught up with a group of determinedly 'with it' colleagues and friends who listened to jazz, earnestly read and discussed the latest kitchen sink novels (including, this being Nottingham, the works of Alan Sillitoe and Stanley Middleton), saw everything at the (old) Nottingham Playhouse, and studiously attended the private views at the tiny Midland Art Gallery—then set in one large room above Boots off Slab Square. As outward signs of our new cultural status, we all proudly displayed our virtually identical racks of paperback books—*Billy Liar, Lucky Jim, Saturday Night and Sunday Morning*—and LP records—*Chris Barber, Acker Bilk, Noël Coward in Las Vegas*. From the Midland Group we bought a couple of abstract paintings and hung them in our little flat, to the polite bafflement of Ann's parents, and the barely-hidden scorn of mine. We even gave little *dinner parties* for our group, with the sort of menu that *Guardian* readers like ourselves would be sure to enjoy—sticky sherry, followed by a 'continental' entrée (served with rice, still in those days a slightly exotic accompaniment) and cheese board, all washed down with *Mateus Rosé*.

Meanwhile my work at the grammar school was (in contrast to many people's first experience of teaching) virtually problem free. The pupils, boys and girls, were quite extraordinarily polite and seemingly grateful for the opportunities Bilborough offered them. I've already said that personally I was extremely fortunate in having my old teacher, and friend, Robert Protherough, as Head of English—but there were many other interesting staff members, including the painter Ken Rowat as Head of Art, and in charge of music the scholarly Ian Bartlett (whose work on Purcell was later to be much admired). Almost everybody on the arts side had strong interests outside the school. In my short time there Ken Rowat had a London exhibition, and Robert wrote an excellent adaptation of *Great Expectations* for Val May at the Playhouse. I did some more stage work, including a short run as Vladimir in Samuel Becket's *Waiting for Godot*—

which masterly work captivated me completely. I learned Vladimir's part in less than a day—for although it appears to be made up of *non sequiturs,* Becket's dialogue is in fact imbued with a deep poetic rhythm, and simple to memorise. Thereafter I always went out of my way to see productions of Becket's plays and, for many years, when I was asked if I had a religion, I would murmur 'Samuel Becket'. By way of explanation I would intone one of Vladimir's bleaker lines:

> We give birth astride of a grave. The light gleams for an instant, and then it's gone.

I never met the great man, but I always pestered those fortunate people who had, to tell me what he was really like. The oddest reply came from the actor Richard Goolden (who played Mole in the London production of *Toad of Toad Hall* each Christmas). It appeared that Richard used to go on holiday each summer with Sam Becket and one or two of his fellow actors to a small seaside resort in Normandy, where they would spend their time, not in philosophic discourse, but in playing scratch games of cricket on the beach. So, in reply to my question as to what the dramatist was 'really like', Richard cackled darkly and said, 'Couldn't play leg breaks.'

Bilborough Grammar School was set on the Western edge of Nottingham, amongst woodland and extensive playing fields. It was a shiny new building, with glass everywhere, and bright metallic handles on the doors and windows that tore at the sleeves of the staff's gowns. Its pupils, largely drawn from neighbouring post-war estates, were generally encouraged by their working class parents to make the most of the educational opportunities which they had never had. And BGS offered a remarkably broad education. As after-school sporting activities it offered rugby, cricket and athletics for the boys, tennis, hockey and lacrosse for the girls, netball, gymnastics and yoga for both. There were choirs, an orchestra, a thriving art club, a ballroom dancing group, a debating society (which successfully debated against Nottingham University) and a very active drama society. With two other staff members I also ran a weekly film society. The school magazine was not the usual tedious roll call of house reports and first eleven matches but instead Robert edited a lively compendium of creative writing, original art work and satirical observations which, rightly, won a national prize.

The arts, sciences and sport were nicely balanced. Most of the staff, myself included, took their share of sports coaching duties. My particular charges were the school Under 14 Cricket team. Realising they weren't much good at actually playing the game I set out instead to teach them some of Stephen Potter's principles of Gamesmanship. After a few matches my training began to bear fruit. Our opening batsman, having miraculously survived for a couple of overs would, after missing some harmlessly wide ball, start to walk off. When asked why, he would say 'I touched it. You may not have heard it but I know that I was out.' Only after it was pointed out to him that the wicket keeper had in any case dropped the ball, was he persuaded to stay. But then, of course, for the rest of the game, the opposition didn't feel they could appeal at all—even when he was blatantly lbw to a perfectly straight ball.

Another ploy was the 'liquorice stick' routine. If the opposition batsmen were doing well they would soon hear the fielders discussing whether it would be fair to let our fast bowler 'have his liquorice'. Eventually they would decide it was time. The captain would solemnly unwrap a small nuggest of the stuff and the bowler would slowly eat it, breathing deeply. The wicket-keeper, slips and in-fielders would move back five or six feet, looking apprehensive. The bowler, lips blackened and muttering apishly to himself, would retreat several paces. By the time he began his run in, the batsman, convinced the ball was going to come down at least twenty miles per hour faster, would begin his own retreat to square leg— so that the ball—which of course came down at exactly the same easy pace as the previous ones—would trickle unhindered on to the wicket. By these means, and by covering the visible parts of the boys' anatomies with a selection of bloodstained bandages and elastoplasts, the Under 14s often managed to hold their own against teams that could actually play the game.

* * *

Even after a few weeks I was beginning to wonder whether this schoolmaster lark was not, for me at least, all too comfortable and easy. As happens with all sorts and conditions of men, I craved an enemy. I had had it all too easy. For almost twenty-five years of my life I had faced no great privations nor hardships, had always been able to take the easiest course and had always, it seemed, been rewarded for it. Somewhere deep inside me I began to feel not only guilty about my continuous good fortune but also slightly resentful of the way in which Britain's new Welfare State was still cosseting me. Could I not stand upon my own two feet? I needed to shake myself out of what was already beginning to look like an over-comfortable life, get out of my comfort zone, and set myself new challenges.

Recently I have enjoyed reading Roy Strong's frank account of his early life, *Self-Portrait as a Young Man*, not least because we were both born around the same time into relatively unprivileged homes, and both made comfortable livings not as artists, but as administrators and critics. But there, of course, any similarity ends. In his memoir Sir Roy describes his bleak and poverty-stricken childhood, coping with an inadequate father and bullying elder brother pouring scorn on his artistic pretension. Nor did his difficulties end with his school days:

> One of my earliest encounters on reaching the university was with a girl who cross-examined me as to which public school I had attended and to which London club my father belonged. My negative replies meant that I was immediately cut.
>
> The years of my degree and post-graduate studies were years of unremitting slog. I knew that any failure would bring to an abrupt end what I aimed to achieve.

The contrast with my own comfortable passage through school and university could hardly be more stark. Sir Roy had faced hardship, bullying and social rejection. For him, university was unremitting toil, whereas for me, it was a continuation of a comfortable, if unremarkable, existence, quite free of privation, violence or the poisonous fangs of snobbery. Yet by his twenties

Strong was making a name for himself as a talented
exhibition organiser, and at the age of 31 was appointed
the new Director of the National Portrait Gallery. He
adds: "Without the 1944 Education Act, which put in
place what was in effect a social revolution, none of this
would have happened."*

I too had been a beneficiary of Butler's remarkable
Act, but whereas Sir Roy, with all his difficulties, had
driven his ship of fate relentlessly forward, I in my
twenties was still allowing mine to drift. Here I was,
three years after graduation, still engaged in explaining
Lady Macbeth's motives to Lower Five B, and parsing
some of Conrad's more convoluted sentences to a
politely indifferent 4A. It wasn't that the work was not
worthwhile, it was a dawning realisation that with all the
privileges that my generation had enjoyed, I should do
more with life than this. So I began to be possessed, not
with a newly roused ambition, but with a new sense of
obligation towards all those people—my parents, family,
schoolteachers, university tutors, Mr Butler even—
who had provided me with the means to do something
distinctive with my life.

And although I am sure that it was as much as anything from a simple desire to supplement my income, I
regard the time that I offered my services to Nottingham
University's Adult Education Institute as being something of a turning point. One day, at the end of the day's
teaching I went to see the Institute's Director, Walter
James, to offer myself as a tutor. As usual, I oversold
myself. I declared myself not just interested, but a
passionate and totally committed believer in Adult
Education—suggesting none too subtly that I was the
kind of once-in-a-lifetime tutor able to combine the
soaring oratorical skills of a Michael Foot with the
sympathetic understanding of a Patience Strong. After
listening to all this nonsense, and taking a longish look at
the callow young man posturing before him, James
brought me down to earth by asking what actual experience I had of teaching adults. The truthful answer would
have been none at all—but I temporised by saying

* Roy Strong, *Self-Portrait as a Young Man*, Bodleian Library Press, 2012

(truthfully) that I had followed a short elective on adult education when studying at Leeds with Professor William Walsh which had inspired me. At the mention of Walsh's name James began to take me a little more seriously. He murmured that he did have one class that was looking for a new tutor for a short series. Did I know anything about D. H. Lawrence?

I immediately expressed my unstinting admiration for David Herbert and all his works (I did, to be fair, know two or three of his novels, some of his poetry and one of his plays). Well, James said, I have to tell you that we have a group that meets in Eastwood (the Nottingham suburb into which Lawrence was born, and which forms the background for several of his early novels), and they're all Eastwood folk (I said that was marvellous news). They've had a very good tutor until this year, James added, but now he's 'left us'. (I later learned it was Malcolm Bradbury—whose first novel, *Eating People is Wrong,* was about the frenzied sexual couplings of the staff of an Adult Education Department of a Midlands University— who had just 'left them'.) The Eastwood group started out a year or two back by studying Lawrence but in recent years they had branched out a bit, but now, James gathered, they wanted to have another look at their own literary prodigy. 'Do you think you could give that idea some thought?'

'Certainly,' I said, still unaware of the minefield ahead. 'It sounds just up my street.'

'And, I don't doubt, up theirs. I'm sure they'll enjoy your company,' said James enigmatically. I did not, even then, heed the warning, momentarily forgetting that when an academic says 'I'm sure' in that emollient way, it means that he strongly suspects the opposite is the case.

And so it came to pass that, a few weeks later, early on a Monday evening, an earnest-looking young man in a well-worn duffel coat could be seen boarding the Eastwood bus in the foggy town centre. He was clutching to himself a briefcase containing a couple of Penguin editions of D. H. Lawrence's novels, a brand new copy of F. R. Leavis' recently published book extolling the virtues of the great man, and a wad of scholarly-looking notes (none of which, as it happens, would ever be used). A

keen-eyed observer might also have noted that the young
man's lips were moving as he wiped the steam from the
inside of the bus window, and asked himself why? There
is a simple, if slightly embarrassing, answer. The young
man was practising critical epigrams intended to stir his
adult pupils to animated debate (though, in the event,
they too remained unused).

Slowly the bus jolts its way through Nottingham's
dimly-lit suburbs, briefly transverses what might have
been recognisable as a strip of real countryside and
then plunges down into the Stygian gloom of Eastwood.
This is of course a township familiar to every Lawrence
reader. An old mining community comprising rows of
back-to-back houses and guttering gas lamps. 'Ugly,'
Lawrence called it in 'Nottingham and the Mining
Countryside'.

Our young tutor alights at the designated stop and
looks about him for the school in which, he has been
told, the class will be held. Ah, there it is! A Victorian
workhouse with a few prefabricated sheds bolted incongruously to its side. There is very little light. He stumbles
awkwardly up the darkened drive and passes inside. To
be greeted by a smell of old plimsolls and soured milk
bottles—so different from Bilborough, which smells of
soap and polish. He walks warily up the stone-tiled
corridor and gingerly opens the door of the one room
which has its lights on. There, huddled around an
exhausted looking stove, his students are assembled.
One man and nine women. All of them very much older
than him.

They do not rise but in reply to his bright 'good
evening' smile thinly, then glance surreptitiously at each
other as if his appearance had confirmed all their darkest
suspicions. The man arranges a rug over his knees. Some
of the women already hold a paperback copy of the first
novel to be studied on the six-week course, Lawrence's
The Lost Girl. He notices with a little tug of alarm that
some of these copies are already dog-eared and one or
two have slips of paper already inserted between the
pages. But he puts this down to their literary interest—
he does not yet know the full extent of his coming
humiliation.

"Hello, my name's John." (Too ingratiating! Lower the voice a bit!) Well, it's very nice to meet you all. I'm sure we're going to have a rewarding time reading, or re-reading, D.H.Lawrence. I see that some of you have already got copies of *The Lost Girl* and I expect some of you have already read it. But for those who haven't I'll just tell you what sort of a book it is. It's about a community much like Eastwood, in fact. It all starts when, one Tuesday, the travelling picture show comes to the town . . . .

"Wednesday." A male voice, accompanied by a defiant tug on the rug.

Smiling still—thinking the old man must be deaf—and raising his voice slightly, "No—Tuesday."

"Wednesday. T'Kinema coom 'ere on Wednesdays. Allus Wednesday" Some of the others nodded.

I will not go on. Even at a distance of half a century the memory is too painful. The group, all of them, had not only known David Herbert Lawrence as a young man—known in every sense of the term, as old Mrs Moore proved when she took me back to her house one night after class and proudly showed me a sheaf of letters the ardent young Bert had written her—but they had also known his family, *and* the people and events on which he had based his novel. So their major interest, indeed their only interest, then and in successive classes, was to 'correct' Lawrence's account of events. What she was really called. Where it really happened. What the village gossips really thought about it all. In the process of course they thoroughly enjoyed themselves (though as my teachers rather than my students) and it gave me an extraordinary insight into the way in which a great novelist can take commonplace events and spin them into something so illuminating.

My final Eastwood lesson was delivered by the non-speaking school caretaker (I don't know whether he was actually dumb or found himself unwilling to commit himself to a discussion in case it led to him being asked to do some work). At all events I had been told he always came in to the last twenty minutes of class each week to listen to the discussion. We had that evening been talking about the 'Throttle 'a'penny mine', a small open-cast set-up that features in *The Lost Girl*. As I was pulling on my coat and scarf after the class he beckoned me to follow him, got out his torch and led me silently to a distant corner of the school playing field. There he pulled aside a sheet of corrugated iron and gesticulated for me to look at what was behind it. And there, undeniably—its rotting prop timbers still plainly visible—was the very mine!

But what could have been a total humiliation was in fact a seminal experience. I shall forever be grateful to my Eastwood group. I realised how much more rewarding it was to work with people who had lived their lives, and who had it in them to instruct you, rather than spend your time filling empty young vessels with the 'right' responses. And I was chagrined to be made to realise, after all those years of education, how very ignorant I was. I had the undergraduate's response to Lawrence off pat—I could fill pages with analysis of his novels, and with what Murry and Connelly and Trilling and Leavis had said about him—but about the essential Lawrence, the life force that captivated our group each week in the Eastwood Secondary School, and about whom his neighbours and friends still reminisced and fretted, I knew nothing at all. So even as my book learning was being exposed for the tawdry and shallow thing it was, I began to sense that I must, somehow, turn again to scholarship—only this time looking at things from a broader perspective, what was *lived* as well as what was painted, performed and written.

★ ★ ★

Meanwhile, there were children to be taught, and plays to be produced. I decided, at the beginning of my second and (as it turned out) final Bilborough year, to produce a full-scale modern dress version of *Romeo and Juliet*. If the Head had any worries about introducing into his orderly school a play obsessed with the pleasures and pains of teenage sexual desire, he held them in check and gave his full blessing. I had then to convince two other people that the project was worthwhile. The first was the school caretaker, Mr Beadmore, who regarded the highly polished stage of the school hall with the same devotion that papal novitiates lavish on the High Altar of the Vatican. I had to tell him that not only would we have to perform the play on a non-reflective surface, but that a complex multi-level set would mean that some screws might have to be inserted in the beautifully polished woodwork. It is greatly to his credit that he swallowed his every caretaking instinct, and agreed.

The second person I had to convince was Gill. Now Gill was actually a fourth form pupil at the school. He was obsessed with art and design, who before my advent had made himself responsible for all the sets and set ups that appeared on the school hall stage. To this end, he had taken over the scene dock, with its large sliding doors, set in the wings—as a workshop and store, and as his own personal office. By the time I arrived even Mr Beadmore was not able to gain entrance to the scene dock because Gill had the only key to the large padlock which secured the door. At break and lunchtimes Gill and his two or three trusted acolytes would disappear into their sanctum, brew their own coffee and discuss upcoming designs. The staff—including the Headmaster—had to knock on the door if they wanted to discuss anything. I was probably more nervous about getting Gill's support than about anything else, but fortunately, after making one or two little amendments to my plan for the set, he gave the idea his blessing.

And, to cut to the chase, the production was a success —a success in ordinary stage terms, but much more importantly as a social force. For a while *Romeo and Juliet* held the school in its imaginative grasp. It affected everything we did and changed all our relationships. Classes in history, religious studies, geography, civics and even the sciences, drew their examples from the one thing which for a brief time we had in common—the inter-family rivalries of the Montagues and Capulets in fair Verona. In its way it was as seminal to me as the Eastwood class had been. I sensed that the drama could be much more than an after dinner parlour game. It could shape the way we live, giving meaning to the confused myth and symbol in which we live our ordinary lives.

I knew as soon as I saw the advertisement that this was the job for me. The Cambridgeshire College of Arts and Technology (later to become Ruskin University) was advertising for a Drama Lecturer. The terms of appointment were open and generous—but it offered a chance to re-search, to teach older people and to work seriously in drama in an ancient University city where, by good fortune, I already had friends. It was a gift from the Gods.

When I was called for interview I was, by some sortof fateful coincidence, performing at the Nottingham Theatre Club, once more playing the Scottish Play—this time as Banquo. I had to miss a couple of performances and Robert—who had been Banquo to my Fleance ten years before—deputised. I had never in my life been so determined in inter-view and, although in competition with a strong field of experi-enced teachers and budding theatre di-rectors, the appearance of this orange-tanned aesthete (I was never very good at removing stage make-up) who spoke with such passionate intensity, leavening his discourse with modish educa-tional jargon, duly prevailed. I was given the job. And so to the next chapter of my adult life — neither schoolteacher nor actor, but either spoiled.

moving into older parts

❦6❧

Cambridge

MOVING TO CAMBRIDGE presented few problems. As soon as my appointment was confirmed Ann wrote to the Cambridgeshire Education Authority and almost by return of post came the offer of a job for her, teaching English at one of their dinky Village Colleges. It was like that in those days. So after a couple of weeks' holiday we gathered together our personal effects, put our few sticks of furniture into store, said au revoir to our Nottingham friends and took the train to Cambridge, eventually decanting on to that bleak ribbon of a railway platform (Kafkaesque, as Kingsley Amis called it), which is in turn set inconveniently far from the city centre.

As we had arrived during the university vacation, we were able to take cheap lodgings, before searching for a more permanent home. Again, our luck was in. We found a rented ground floor flat on Parker's Piece, conveniently just around the corner from my new berth in the Cambridgeshire College of Arts and Technology (I later discovered that if you stood in the corner of one of the College's Common Rooms, you could actually see into our bedroom, though I veiled this information from my more prurient colleagues). The stop for the bus out to Ann's village college was nearby, and as a bonus we had a dazzling view from our front windows, across the park, past rows of immemorial elms, almost to the gates of Downing College, no less.

As soon as we had taken delivery of our stored furniture (which mysteriously arrived soaking wet, leading to many weeks of haggling over the bill) we set about making contact with those people we already knew in the town. I met an old drama chum from Nottingham days, Stephen Frears (later to be well-known as the director of *My Beautiful Launderette* and *The Queen*), who offered me an insight into the precious world of Cambridge theatricals. He was at the time directing the musical *Expresso Bongo*. Though he had betrayed his Leavisite teaching by becoming popular, its librettist Wolf Mankowitz had studied in Downing, and his musical was a regular feature on the university's drama scene. Stephen told me he was puffing his show as 'a landmark in Cambridge productions of *Expresso Bongo*'.

Then there was my former school friend Ian Robinson, who had taken a first at Downing and currently occupied a Fellowship at the very new Churchill College, where he was writing his doctorate. Ian kindly took it upon himself to take us on tours around some of the lesser-known Cambridge sights, including a bar on King's Parade where I was later told you could at lunchtimes sometimes hear a gaggle of red-faced English dons, C.S.Lewis among them, percolating on schooners of sherry and boasting to each other about which well-known works in the English Literature syllabus they regularly taught but had not actually read. Ian also took us for our first punting afternoon on the Cam, offering a raffish commentary on the College gardens and the curious customs of the dons who inhabited them. So involved was he in delivering this polished routine that he committed one of the cardinal sins of punting. At the conclusion of his stroke he held on to the pole for a second too long, lost his footing on the greasy deck, and then, with the sorrowful countenance of a Buster Keaton, slid slowly down the pole and plopped gently into the waist-high waters of the Cam. Ann and I hooted with unsympathetic laughter. But Ian rose above it and, nothing daunted, half-strode and half-swam back up to our craft, scrambled aboard, shook himself all over us, resumed the pole, and continued his commentary as if nothing untoward had occurred.

We also called on an old Merchant Taylor's school chum of Ann's, who was holed up in the all-female fastness of Girton—though on that occasion our reception was considerably less cordial. The lady in question was (rightly) proud of her achievement in getting to Cambridge, but obviously considered that graduates of the University of Leeds had no right to invade Girton's sacred portals. We were quizzed, like illegal immigrants, about what our motives were in coming to Cambridge and eventually given a weak cup of Earl Grey and a thin biscuit, but never invited again. This, we gradually realised, was the other face of the university.

The fissures within Cambridge society soon became apparent. It was not simply that the various Colleges kept up a constant propaganda barrage about themselves and each other—ranging from the insinuation that the white wine in such and such a college was regularly diluted with urine for unpopular visitors, to the statement made by Downing's F.R. Leavis that Peterhouse could no longer be taken seriously as it had appointed a pornographer to a fellowship! At the time this was presumed to refer to Kingsley Amis, recently appointed to Peterhouse. Amis replied disarmingly that he thought his books were if anything rather chaste. He had recently read of someone who got their rocks off by tearing paper into strips and hitting themselves with it, and that if some people wanted to use his books for that purpose, he could have no reasonable objection . . . .

It was not just the bitchy old male dons. Ann found that her new women acquaintances were also infected. From the start, as we were setting up home, they would apparently grill her about where she had bought her tea towels, or cups and saucers—with the implication that the location of the purchase, rather than quality of the goods, was the significant cultural indicator. She quickly discovered that any casual suggestion that the girl friends might meet up for coffee would be followed by a longish examination of which Cambridge venues were currently 'in', and who had been seen with whom in another coffee house—now by association irredeemably disgraced.

The main dividing line was of course between town and gown, and it was in this respect that my new berth, the Cambridgeshire College of Arts and Technology, occupied a position rather like a small neutral state locked between mutually antagonistic power blocs. Originally formed from the amalgamation of the local Tech and the Angela Ruskin School of Art, the college's clientèle then ranged from well-heeled undergraduates studying for University of London degrees and floating around in twee little gowns, to day-release bricklayers on whose studded leathers you could strike matches. The Department for which I worked—Liberal Studies— serviced both ends of the college spectrum, offering lectures on a variety of esoteric subjects to the academic high-flyers, and (rather less happily) what was thought of as the trace of a liberal education to the more practically-minded souls.

It was in this latter area that I, and a few others, thought that the College failed. There was a considerable distance between the rather tentative attempts made to keep the day-release students amused, and (this being Cambridge) the fulsome claims that were regularly made for the educational 'outcomes' involved. One of my new colleagues was a well-known contributor to the *Education Guardian*, and we regularly read in that worthy journal that not only had the sensibilities of the CCAT day-release students been expanded and their moral polarities refined, but that their core creative selves were being nourished by his efforts. On occasion he even published, in the *Guardian*, writing which he claimed had flowed from the day-release students—entirely because of his ministrations of course. Very occasionally his published pieces mentioned his colleagues. But while it was flattering to read that some of us were at the forefront of educational practice, I knew that this bubble reputation was undeserved. I suspected that the students were in their turn humouring the staff, having realised that sitting in the warm was a sight easier than toiling on a freezing building site—even allowing for the shame involved in having their (heavily edited) hopes and wet dreams published in a national newspaper.

I felt that one of the basic mistakes we all made was trying to lever our way into the minds of the day-release students by using some of the approved texts of the liberal establishment. We went into the lecture rooms armed with novels such as William Golding's *Lord of the Flies*, which to our students, wholly untutored in the arcane niceties of lit crit, seemed to describe a group of repressed public school kids throwing off their shackles, allowing themselves to behave naturally for once and then enjoying a bit of a rumble. Some of my colleagues tried earnestly to get the day release lads and lassies to see its wider metaphorical meaning. They failed. As a result the gulf between the pieties of the liberal establishment and the lives of the day-release students would inexorably widen. Nor were the lecturing staff encouraged to meet the day-release people on their own cultural ground of rock, pop music or film. I recall that one luckless young tutor did make the attempt, but was promptly sacked for the crime of *playing the guitar* (in the early 1960s the instrument of the devil) in a Liberal Studies class.

Fortunately, there is no need to spell out our antipathy to *Lord of the Flies* in any more detail, for it is already the stuff of record. On the day I joined the CCAT staff, I walked in to the college with another new staff member, six years older than me, by the name of Tom Sharpe. Tom, a lanky snuff-taking Pembroke graduate, had just been deported from South Africa for sedition, having already written two searing comic indictments of the Apartheid régime, *Riotous Assembly* and *Indecent Exposure*. His reaction to the cultural apartheid at CCAT was no less extreme. He soon began work on a series of farcical novels set in a ficticious Cambridge college, in which the staff were expected to teach from the wrong kind of material, such as *Lord of the Flies* . . . .

The resultant novels—*Wilt, The Wilt Alternative* and their five successors—eventually became not just best-selling comedies, but for those of us who had worked with Tom and knew him well, they also worked on another, more scurrilous, level. Not to put too fine a point on it, many incidents in *Wilt* were heightened versions of real life occurrences in and around CCAT. All of us who were on the staff were able to recognise ourselves in parody form in the books, a fact which generally brought us pleasure. However the question of who was represented by which character remained a matter for debate. I found myself, some years after *Wilt's* publication, denying that it was me who, after a drunken orgy, had got his todger trapped in a suddenly deflated sex doll. That did sort of happen, but not—I repeat *not*—to me!

Meanwhile Ann was enjoying her bucolic sabbatical in Burwell. Each morning her bus wound its way to the Village College calling in on a number of grim fenland hamlets with *Carry On* comedy names such as Gripe's Bottom or Clap's Fen. Her pupils, after the relative sophistication of Nottingham, were refreshingly rustic in outlook—a number of them had aunts or uncles in the same class as their sisters and brothers, and seemed in general none too certain about their family ties. But whatever entanglements there may have been in their immediate ancestry, and whatever shortcomings there may have been in their scholastic attainment, they were kind and loving, hugging her each day as they came into her classroom, and regularly bringing her gifts of rudely-shaped, soil-encrusted vegetables.

*   *   *

Soon we were entertaining a stream of visitors—old university friends, former colleagues and of course our respective families. And here there was an unexpected bonus. Although I had expected Ann's parents to like Cambridge, I had imagined that mine would find it impossibly affected—prone to indulge in the kind of abstract theorising about life that my father's family in particular had always held up to ridicule ('Yer 'ed 'll explode!'). But I had got it wrong. My parents, my father in particular, loved the place, making immediate contact not with the transient parade of dons but rather with the down-to-earth landscape gardeners that tended the centuries-old College lawns and gardens. I was once walking along King's Parade behind a tour guide who was assuring his flock that nobody, and most certainly not a casual visitor, would ever be allowed to set foot on the college greens, when I saw my father wander casually on to one of the immaculate lawns, deep in conversation with one of the ground staff and, bending, plunge his pocket knife into it. I hurried on and never mentioned it to him. He would have been worried that he had somehow let me down in front of all my brainy friends— whereas in truth I took pride in the way that he had ingratiated himself in a more elemental Cambridge.

Visitors flowed in to our Parker's Piece home in such numbers that occasionally we found ourselves having to apologise to the neighbours for the din that emanated from our house. And here again we were lucky, for the couple that lived in the flat above us—the scholarly Reverend John Habgood (later to become Archbishop of York) and his agreeable young wife—were smilingly tolerant of our occasional excesses. Only once do I recall them being a little nonplussed. The usual way out of their flat (unless they were to use the shared hallway which for them involved unlocking and locking three separate doors) was down a rear fire escape and out through the small walled garden into a lane at the back of our shared property. Now Ann and I, still young, had found a romantic way of enjoying the leafy delights of Cambridgeshire. Being conveniently close to the river we invested in a two-seater kayak, which was capable of navigating the upper reaches of the Cam, where punts could not go. It had quite an amount of storage space. So we had also purchased a small bivouac tent, thinking that when we had some free time and the mood was on us we would simply up sticks, paddle up the river for a few miles, and pitch camp overnight. We even did it, on a few occasions

On that particular summer's afternoon we decided to try out our new tent in the walled back garden. We blew up the inflatable mattresses, flung the canvas over the poles, tightened a few guy ropes and, naturally enough, dived in and made love—with a certain amount of squeaking and giggling, I do not doubt. After about half an hour I emerged from the tent, looked up, and saw John and his wife frozen at the top of the fire escape—with him earnestly pointing out to her interesting features of the nearby roof guttering. They had probably been there, petrified with embarrassment, for some considerable time. Years later, when we met him by chance in Cannon Hill Park in Birmingham, he unsurprisingly made no mention of it.

Even people as far down the social ladder as ourselves were sometimes invited out to Cambridge dinner parties. Some of these, it has to be said, were quite bum-clenchingly awful. Not only were College dinners stuffed with ancient rituals (loving cups being passed around, Latin prayers, discreet table-spanking, that sort of thing) but some of the private dinner parties were also absurdly formalised. The winners in this category were undoubtedly the well-dressed young couple who prefaced dinner with a long, alcohol-free, tour of their terraced house, so that we could be shown, and could handle, the pieces of ceramic pottery they had recently picked up (or stolen) in Turkey. They then offered us a pre-prandial glass of wine whose contents were barely visible to the naked eye. Dinner was even more of an ordeal, involving a lot of thoughtful chewing of each dish, accompanied by fact-filled discussions about where and when this or that ingredient had been procured. The whole grisly business was finally topped off by the Hostess indicating to Ann and the other female guest that ladies should now leave the table (so that, as custom had it, the gentlemen could fart and tell dirty stories). It might have passed off as gracious living had not the lady guests discovered that they were to gather in the only other available ground floor space, which was the built-in garage.

A wonderful exception to all this stale flummery were Sydney and Gia Bolt, who became friends to us both. Sydney had taken his Double First before the war and, like many of his eminent Cambridge contemporaries, had joined the Communist Party. At the outbreak of hostilities he had been recruited into the Intelligence Service and been sent on a mission to India (this at the time of the short-lived German/Russian Pact). For this he was briefed in conditions of the greatest secrecy and told that he was to join the Embassy staff in Delhi, go to as many social functions as he could, talk to everybody and try to put a name to all the Communist sympathisers in that region of India.

This Sydney could have easily accomplished, as his branch of the UK Communist Party had helpfully supplied him with a list of his Comrades he might like secretly to contact there. But as the authorities in the UK had not troubled to delve into his affiliations— assuming, as they did in those days, that any previous political interests of a Oxbridge graduate could be put down to youthful indiscretion—he decided he would indeed be busy socially, but would 'discover' nothing. That resolve was strengthened when he saw that a youthful activist on the list was the dazzlingly beautiful and intelligent Gia.

In any case as the war progressed the Russians came over to our side, and so his mission lost its urgency. After the war Gia came over to Britain and she and Sydney married. By the time we knew them Sydney had given up his post-war career in industry and had settled back into a senior position at CCAT. They had two sons (one of whom, Ranjit, is now well-known as an adaptor of foreign drama classics, Molière in particular), lived on the Newmarket Road and kept a most welcoming table. One always cherished an invitation to dine with them for, apart from anything else, Gia was a superb cook who as a bonus taught us how to choose and prepare pukka Indian ingredients.

Around the table would be an eclectic mix of CCAT staff and families, university dons of the Bolts' acquaintance and a surprising leavening of writers, artists and (usually left wing) politicians, whom Sydney would interrogate relentlessly. His brother Robert, who was by then a well-known playwright and script writer (*A Man for All Seasons, Flowering Cherry, Lawrence of Arabia*) was a frequent visitor, and on occasion brought with him his second wife, the actress Sarah Miles. If Sydney and Robert were outspoken, Ms Miles was little short of outrageous. She would explain to anybody that she had not met before that she attributed her delicate skin tone and general good health to the fact that she drank her own urine—which (as she both drank copiously and visited the bathroom quite often) would raise all sorts of images in the newcomer's mind which it might have been better to leave dormant.

At other times the Bolts' dinner table would become a political debating chamber, at which the conventional view was invariably absent. It happened that we were due to dine there on the night President Kennedy was assassinated. I rang Sydney to find out whether, in view of the suddenness of events, he might prefer to postpone. 'Oh no. It will give us something to talk about.' And sure enough, by the time we had got there, he had added to his guests a visiting Republican journalist who had published a swathe of anti-Kennedy articles, and who certainly did not view the President's assassination in the same light as the rest of us. It was a lively evening, as usual.

★　★　★

Having been uncomplimentary about one aspect of CCAT, I must now redress the balance. When it came to the performing arts, the staff found themselves—despite the wretched facilities on campus—extraordinarily well supported. The Principal, Derek Mumford, was a keen musician and sufficiently interested in the theatre to hail you in the corridor and ask you your opinion of something opening in London, or of that week's offering at the Cambridge Arts Theatre. When in due course a proper theatre came to be built on the campus it was only fitting that the auditorium should bear his name.

In the meantime College productions, whether of drama or opera, were generally presented in an old-fashioned College Hall, bounded on three sides by a raised corridor, on whose balustrades the lighting was rigged. Sets had to be constructed elsewhere and then erected in the well of the hall on the day of the dress rehearsal. Yet such was the skill of the College carpenters that the result was not just structurally sound but visually dazzling. One of the first shows I produced there was an English adaptation of Molière's *The Miser*, for which the College carpenters produced a three-quarter-size, sumptuously gilded, model of the stage at the Salle du Petit Bourbon, where Molière had first presented the play.

The Deputy Principal, John Irwin, was equally helpful. When I first saw him hovering at the back of the rehearsal rooms I thought he was probably engaged in some sort of managerial assessment of my teaching skills, but when I got to know him better I realised that the real reason was that he was himself a fledgling playwright and was drumming up courage to ask me for help in placing his scripts. Eventually he showed me one of his pieces, a light comedy and, under the grievously mistaken impression that I would know everyone in the theatrical world, asked me to whom he should send it. Off the top of my head, as the leading male part was a debonair sort of chap, I suggested Tony Britten, then well-known in such roles. I had not of course claimed any personal acquaintance with Mr Britten, but in his covering letter John Irwin must have mentioned the fact that I had recommended him. I was surprised, and in a slightly guilty way relieved, to see that when he returned the script Tony Britten had, either as a precaution or as a simple politeness, sent his 'Best Wishes to John Pick', even though he didn't know me from Adam. John was duly impressed.

In turn John was extremely helpful with what was my biggest dramatic project in my time at Cambridge, when I wrote and directed a full-scale adaptation of Charles Dickens' *Hard Times*. He made himself responsible for the budget—so I was able not only to set and dress it well, but also to have stylish posters and programmes featuring prints by Gustave Doré. That production turned out to be something of a *succès d'estime* and I was secretly flattered to see twenty years later that the Mumford Theatre on what was now a university campus was still using photographs of my production in its publicity material.

In addition to directing, and taking part in, college productions, I also ran drama classes to introduce what were then fairly new notions of improvisation, mime and documentary theatre. And I found time too to take part in one or two other Cambridge productions. I played the Inquisitor in Anouih's *The Lark*, the storyteller in *Peter and the Wolf* at the Corn Exchange, and waggled a foppish handkerchief as Tattle in *Love for Love*. Although I did not really notice, or care, about the development, I was inexorably moving into middle aged roles—Azdak the Judge in *The Caucasian Chalk Circle*, and when CCAT staged a sumptuous *Romeo and Juliet* I played Juliet's cantankerous old father, Capulet.

Indeed, playing a harassed father might have been something of a portent. One evening, when I got in from rehearsal, Ann told me she was pregnant and, in almost the same breath, that we would have to move from our central Cambridge flat to a more suitable dwelling in the suburbs. Though delighted with the news, I was apprehensive about all the new responsibilities those pieces of news seemed to place on us both. We set out to find a house, albeit in circumstances very different from today. Houses, even in Cambridge, were very much cheaper then, but we had no savings, and any mortgage would be granted on my income only—in any case Ann's income would stop before the baby was born. So we had to find somewhere that was affordable—but not *too* derelict. After a few weeks' frantic searching, we found a semi-detached dwelling in Orchard Avenue which was, as the agent put it, 'in need of some repair'. In appearance it was pure Addams family, but it had three bedrooms, a garage, an unusually large back garden (part of the orchard which had given the avenue its name) and the asking price—incredibly to contemporary eyes—was just £2,350. By pointing to all the repairs that needed to be done, we even managed to get that price reduced by a further £75! After a nervous visit to the Building Society I discovered that my salary—just over £1,000 p.a. if memory serves—was sufficient to get a mortgage.

We moved as soon as we could, in early January 1963, and this time our luck deserted us. The first three months of 1963 comprised one of the coldest winter spells of recent record. Although Orchard Avenue was only just over a mile from the city centre, the journey to and from work each day was horrendous, while Ann was left in an icy house which had no central heating of any kind, just two or three open grates in which at weekends we could try to burn frozen logs. Each day she had to sally forth to buy fresh groceries (we had no fridge, either). The only room we could attempt to heat in the evenings, with a plug-in electric fire, was the kitchen. This was less than satisfactory because although I had attempted to fill in the cracked and broken windowpanes with cardboard, it proved a poor barrier against the weather, and even the kitchen was racked by stabbing gusts of icy wind.

So, the scene is set for our greatest ever social débâcle. For a reason I have long forgotten, Ann had made the acquaintance of a lady whom I shall call Holly. They had got on well and (no doubt expecting the cold snap would pass) Ann had invited her to supper, accompanied by her husband of course. However as the chosen day approached it became clear that this was one of those cruel once-in-a-century winters, intent on breaking all known records. It was if anything even colder on the day of the dinner than in the weeks preceding it. Knowing that Holly and her husband would probably expect the temperature in their hosts' house to be above freezing point I nailed a few more sheets of cardboard over the broken windows, and took the unusual step of turning on both bars of the electric fire two or three hours in advance of their arrival. Ann by then was not drinking so I thought the visitors could be fobbed off with a pre-prandial sherry, a reasonable Chardonnay with the grub, and a warming glass of brandy with the after-dinner coffee. So, on that fateful February evening, all unaware of what was coming, we numbly laid our kitchen table, prepared to hide our mittens, and waited.

The front door bell rang precisely on the agreed time of arrival, and I rushed to open the door to reveal two muffled figures stamping their feet in the icy gloom of the front porch. Holly introduced her (seemingly rather older) husband, who passed me a bottle of red wine which I could see immediately was several notches up from anything we normally bought, or drank. As I shut the door I explained that we had just moved in, and so I hoped they didn't mind but we should be eating in the kitchen. At that same moment Ann opened the kitchen door and for the first time flooded our guests with light. In a split second we realised the enormity of what we had done.

For Holly's husband was at that time one of the most famous, and most easily recognised, men on the planet. His picture had recently been prominently displayed in every newspaper and magazine as well as in TV news bulletins. The previous year he had (with others) been awarded the Nobel Prize. Fêted everywhere, he was currently engaged in a further period of intensive

research at the Cavendish Laboratories at Cambridge—
from which dedicated work his second wife had no doubt
insisted that he must absent himself in order to attend
this social treat. Holly (being a nice unpretentious lady)
had of course not told Ann who her husband was, having
no doubt assumed (as wives of the famous will) that
everybody knew who she was married to. It was also
possible that Holly had assumed that Ann was playing
the same modest game, and had thought that *her*
husband (probably an up and coming young scientist)
would have a lot in common with Holly's, which was why
she had issued the invitation . . . .

Thoughts such as these somersaulted through our
minds as the four of us shuffled the few paces into the
kitchen, together with an immediate shared understanding that we couldn't possibly trawl through the
various misunderstandings that had led us to this
freezing impasse. Instead we sat around this cramped
Formica-topped table. Everyone smiled uncertainly. I
uncorked the chardonnay, doled out the paella, and said
nervously that it was very good to meet him.

And—may his memory be forever blessed—that great
and good man, who must have been inwardly seething
at the pointlessness of it all, said that it was very good to
meet me, and what exactly did I do? In the silence that
followed my answer (he knew as much about drama as
I knew about the DNA Molecule) Holly explained how
Ann and she had met, and a determined, very British,
sub-zero evening was had by all. At his departure our
visitor (I never got to call him by his first name) even
said, albeit without much conviction, that we must go
round and have supper with them when the weather
improved.

Of course it never did improve sufficiently for that
to happen, but by late April a few signs of spring could
be seen. Putting that inglorious evening firmly behind
us we eventually found workmen to put the house to
rights—sufficiently for Ann to have a trouble-free labour
at home, and for Martyn John Pick to make his first noisy
appearance in to this world on June 3rd, 1963.

❋7❋
Nottingham

MY FATHER was not alone in regretting our move back to Nottingham. Our Cambridge friends could not understand either why we should contemplate quitting the centre of the academic universe for a city in the dank Midlands. Yet we had no doubts about moving. In our four years there, Ann had never really taken to the clannishness and sense of willed isolation that seemed to characterise so much of Cambridge life. As for me I have to confess to a common failing, knowing that such bogus confessions are of course a symptom of inverted narcissism. The base truth was that I looked forward to being a bigger fish in a small pond. There were other reasons. The work (i/c Drama at Nottingham College of Education) looked, and indeed would prove, to be more interesting.

Nottingham itself was undergoing yet another cultural renaissance. The Playhouse, under its glittering triumvirate of John Neville, Peter Ustinov and John Dexter (from which first Ustinov and then Dexter soon detached themselves) twinkled across Wellington Circus facing the new Midland Group Gallery, which then showed interesting non-representational modern work (the leaders of the visual arts world had not by then substituted 'conceptual art' or 'art installations' for the real thing).

Meanwhile Notts Forest were holding their own in Division One, while at Trent Bridge Clive Rice, Richard

Hadlee and Derek Randall* were reviving Notts' old
glory on the cricket field. There were local novelists—
Alan Sillitoe, Stanley Middleton—a few not-too-precious
poets and a thriving pub jazz scene. Best of all Ann and
I already knew people there. From our previous time
in Nottingham we already knew Kate and Ian Little,
Robert, who was still at Bilborough, Eddie Wainwright,
who was now at Clifton College—and of course Ken
Rowat who, despite now working with his soulmate Jeff
Nuttall at Leeds College of Art, had kept the house in
Cranmer Street in which his wife Audrey still lived and to
which he returned at weekends to paint and play his part
in their amicable divorce.

Ann was pregnant with our second child and so,
mindful of our growing family, we bought a detached
house with four bedrooms and a walled garden in 'Bread
and Lard Island' as West Bridgford was, none too
affectionately, known. This gave easy access to the city
centre, and was on the same side of Nottingham as the
college. At first I essayed my daily journey to work on
one of the newfangled Moulton bikes. But after a couple
of months battling the wind and rain and enduring the
jeers of the students gliding past me in the South Notts
bus ('Come *on,* Sir John, *pedal!*) I reverted to the less
healthy, but more dignified, family car. For her part, while
awaiting the advent of Cath, Ann pushchaired Martyn to
coffees and teas with other young mothers, discussing (so
I was told) the long-anticipated advent of the 'house
husband'—a concept much bandied about in the pages
of the *Guardian,* but not yet visible in West Bridgford.

The College of Education (destined soon to be caught
up in the doleful machinery of educational reorganisation,
expensively grafted on to the local Tech and the College
of Art and renamed 'Nottingham Trent University') was I
think quite untypical of what the public then thought of as
a 'Teachers Training College' (i.e. a darkly cloistered single
sex institution). Clifton was in fact a modishly unfettered
environment in which the inmates—fine specimens of both

---

* Derek Randall, a Retford lad, had been taught by my mother. As
Derek became internationally famous, and my dear Mum became
correspondingly demented, she claimed to have taught him how to bowl,
field, square cut, etc., etc., etc. and would, when she saw him playing on
the telly, shout technical advice to him.

sexes—roamed freely. It was also distinctly uncloistered, largely because of its jolly Principal. Thanks also to him, it was also awash with alcohol, from the well-used sherry decanters in the SCR, through the musty ales of the nearby *Man of Trent,* to the wines which accompanied the weekly formal dinners. Its brand-new College buildings were set in rolling greenery, on the banks of the River Trent —hard by the spot where, according to D.H.Lawrence's *Sons and Lovers,* his lusty young hero had apparently had his wicked way with his doxy. This led a mischievous colleague, no lover of David Herbert's literary skills and no great fan of his sexual prowess either, to assure his more gullible students that if they looked carefully, they could still see the scorch marks on the trees.

And so Ann and I settled in to our different routines and quite soon Catherine Ann Pick (always to be known as Cath) entered this world. This time I wasn't present at the birth, and it was Ann's mother (staying with us to help with the event) who telephoned the college with the news. My drama class was rapidly terminated, and I rushed home to greet the proud Mum and my lovely new daughter. Everyone rejoiced—except for Martyn, who for a while seemed a little wary of the prospect of sharing things with this new squalling bundle. However he soon came round and since those first days the four of us were destined, through all kinds of trials and tribulations, to remain in friendly and regular family contact (which is, I'm led to believe, a comparatively rare achievement in these tumultuous times).

Following the excitement of Cath's birth it was not long before I plunged back into the hectic schedule of the College drama world. Hectic it certainly was. Its stage productions read like a list of productions at a major repertory theatre—as a list of the full-length plays and operettas produced there during my time might suggest;

A Man for all Seasons, The House of Bernanda Alba, Romanoff and Juliet, Next Time I'll Sing to You, Othello, Oedipus Rex, On the Brink (Revue), *Iolanthe, The Beggar's Opera, One Way Pendulum, The Crucible, Patience, Over the Brink* (Revue), *The Devils, Little Malcolm and his Struggle Against the Eunuchs, Don Juan, Love for Love,*

Blood Wedding, Lysistrata, Beyond the Brink (Revue), *The
Importance of Being Earnest, St Joan, The Diary of Ann
Frank, Luther, The Long and the Short and the Tall* . . . .

The quality of production was variable but we were
generally good enough to attract an audience from
beyond the college walls. I was not of course directly
responsible for all of these but, as actor, director or
designer I was involved in a majority of them. Some
were directed and led by the students themselves, and
others were produced in cooperation with the Nottingham Theatre Design School, newly set up by Nottingham
City Council and the Playhouse, and led by Patrick
Robertson, Rosemary Vercoe and Stephen Doncaster. In
my academic role I was responsible for the training of
would-be drama teachers, and for the children's theatre
we sent out to schools. But I still found time to act
occasionally (in Pinter's *The Lover* and *The Birthday
Party*) or to direct (Chekov's *Three Sisters* and Vanbrugh's
The Relapse) elsewhere in the Midlands.

As will be obvious from the foregoing—with performances, rehearsals, teaching and what is euphemistically
referred to as 'networking' (that is, boozing in Nottingham's numerous drinking dives)—I was spending far too
little time with my wife and family. In other words I had,
to use an old-fashioned Northern phrase, become far
too full of myself. It should not therefore have come as
a great surprise to me that, early one morning in bed,
drinking our customary cup of tea, Ann said that she
had something she wanted to share with me. She then
told me quite calmly that as I was now so much involved in my own affairs, and was leaving her so much
to her own devices, she had taken a lover and that lover
was Ken.

I was dumbfounded, although my other reactions were
—if I can recall them aright—not the conventional ones
of cheap literature. I did not rant or swear vengeance. I
felt no anger towards Ken and certainly not towards Ann.
On the contrary I felt renewed admiration for her, and
the cool and honest way she had brought things into the
open. I was also filled with a growing shame that I had so
taken my wife for granted, and had selfishly fallen into

the laddish cliché of leaving the missus at home to mind the kids while the husband caroused in the local fleshpots. But, as I bring that poignant morning back to mind, I should be dishonest if I did not add that amongst my confused emotions the morally disgusting thought that this could lend a new piquancy to our marriage was also edging itself into my mind.

As our tea cooled we cautiously explored this new and unfamiliar territory, looking over our new relationship with something akin to awe. I only remember that Ann said that for her part she had no wish to stop being with me or to break up our family. She had no wish to break with Ken either, and hoped he would remain a family friend. I in turn promised to be a better and more understanding husband. We agreed that we did not want to be in a meaningless 'open' marriage. Equally we did not want to be drawn into a cynical tit for tat series of extramarital affairs. Our new fidelity meant that we would try, difficult though it may be, to be as honest as we could with each other about our respective temptations and occasional indiscretions.

There are no doubt better ways of repairing a marriage than being cuckolded, but I had been given a salutary lesson, and determined to act more like a grown up. Certainly the following weeks, months and years were happy ones. We saw no need to redraw the terms of our understanding, and for several years we smiled happily together at our foibles and those of friends and acquaintances—including those we (temporarily) fancied and, from time to time, those who fancied us. I eased up on the intensity of my work, which pleased my students and colleagues, who had in any case grown increasingly mutinous over the manic, unresolved quality of too much of it.

At about the same time I had an insight into my own jumbled character, which seemed so obvious that I convinced myself that I'd always known it. I do not know whether it was our new relationship which had brought it into my conscious mind but I realised that for me dramatic performance was much more than an entertainment, an educational tool, or even an occasional form of therapy. I began to think that performing was not something extrinsic to my life, it *was* me. My attempts to role play—whether as poet, peasant or *bon viveur*—were less a sign of delayed adolescence than acknowledgement of the fact that there was no one John Pick, just a cluster of instincts, memories and attitudes, an entity who in his time, in daily life and in the dark recesses of his imagination, played many parts.

For some people this is a commonplace. For others, I could see that the thought might prove troubling. But it need not do so. All it meant was that my existence was not bounded by one skin nor confined to one unidimensional character. I recalled a lesson from my student philosophy days: *cogito ergo sum* ('I think, therefore I am') is clearly a fallacious argument, because in the initial premise it posits the entity 'I' that it seeks to prove the existence of. All one can logically assert is 'There is some thinking going on'.

To some degree (she was also a much better philosopher than me) Ann shared this way of looking at things. At all events, she seemed happy to play with the strings that moved my disjointed parts and, by slow degrees, we became more firmly bound together in a new and deeper relationship. I stopped being so desperately involved in my work. We spent more time together, and enjoyed our time with the children—picnicking in the garden, walking in the park, playing indoor games, or shopping in the local supermarkets. We took family holidays in the Dukeries, in the Yorkshire Dales, in the Welsh mountains and with Ann's parents, who had retired to Eastbourne ('God's Waiting Room') on the South Coast—though at that time we had of course no inkling that we should end our days in that strange time capsule of a resort.

Nottingham still had much to offer. There was plenty to enjoy in the visual arts, and in the writing of local authors. However it was the Playhouse which dominated the city. John Neville, now its sole director, was successfully persuading well-known friends of his to work with his company for absurdly low salaries. So, in addition to Mr Neville we had performers of the calibre of Judy Dench, Michael Craig, the Hollywood star Robert Ryan, Leonard Rossiter, Wilfred Brambell ('Old Steptoe') and others, mixing as casually with the local townspeople as the regular company did and (a bonus for me) frequently involving themselves with the drama work at the college.

It was not dissatisfaction with the city that led us once more to consider moving. Far from it. In suburban Nottingham, just like every other place we lived in, we found a number of congenial, mildly anarchic, left-leaning couples, who tended to live in houses with colour-supplement dining kitchens (complete with the obligatory Agas) and whose children made friends with ours in the sandpits and slides of Bread and Lard Island. At various times we played bridge with Kate and Ian, discussed poetry with Vernon and Lillian, talked novels with Robert and Margaret, boozed with Susie and Stan, and continued our easy, multifaceted relationship with Ken and Audrey. It was not from any feeling of cultural poverty that we thought of moving on.

It was rather that Martyn was already coming up to school age. Indeed—and at that time there was no parental choice in the matter—our address meant that he was already down to attend a rigidly old-fashioned West Bridgford School, with school uniforms, strict discipline and an old-fashioned Wackford Squeers sort of headmaster who believed in regularly caning his little charges. Unless we moved, or paid for them to attend a private prep school (which would perhaps just offer more of the same) Martyn, and Cath after him, would spend his formative years in this mean and repressive environment. So I started to look around, and (sure sign of someone on the move) started once more to take the *Times Higher Educational Supplement* and the *Education Guardian*, which were gratifyingly full of advertisements seeking the kind of dynamic and inspirational teacher that I fondly and foolishly imagined myself to be.

So I started to make applications. In a rash moment I even applied for the post of Head Teacher in a well-known private 'progressive' school. What finally put me off was receiving a garbled telephone enquiry asking when I would like to be interviewed? (When I would *like*? Were there no other candidates?) Though even before their call I had begun to have doubts, as the particulars for the post had said that the successful candidate would be solely responsible (there being neither governors nor trustees, only an advisory board of doubtful provenance) for recruitment of pupils, for their daily, and nightly (this being a boarding school) well-being, for the syllabus, the discipline, the hiring and payment of staff, maintenance and for *keeping accounts* . . . . I could imagine only too well the regular conflicts with students, staff and parents, the accusations of professional and managerial incompetence, the well-publicised appeals to my predecessor (the school's founder, an amateur child psychologist who enjoyed an enviable reputation amongst the *Guardian*-reading classes) to return to save the school, my sacking, and my ignominious banishment to some far-flung British Council post, together with the stigma that inevitably attaches itself to such a fate . . . . No, it was not for me. I announced I was not available for interview and formally withdrew my application.

Ken (with whom I played a Friday afternoon round of golf) suggested that I might enjoy a post as a 'Complementary Studies' tutor at Leeds College of Art, then much admired for its avant garde educational practices. Ken gave me some examples of these. Yoko Ono, having taken a fee to give a public lecture, sent instead a cardboard cut-out of herself and had it set up on stage while repetitive sitar music was played for an hour (Ho hum!) Ken's friend Jeff Nuttall had entered himself for one College show as a 'living sculpture' which turned out to consist of him, stark bollock naked, gyrating in an outsize goldfish bowl (Ha!) Ken added that he had been forced to give counselling to one deranged boy who had come to Leeds in order to learn to paint representationally (of all things!) and who thought that the Oko/Nuttall notions of art were a waste of his time . . . . So, however kindly Ken's intentions were, by the eighteenth hole I was determined not to put myself at risk of being appointed to that kind of establishment. True, I wanted occasionally to kick against the pricks, but not to work alongside a lot of pricks who were kicking meaninglessly out at everybody and everything.

I applied, unsuccessfully, for a job in Leicestershire, where the admirable Village Colleges scheme was getting under way, and (over-ambitiously) for a director's job in radio, but eventually, with my new-found philosophy in mind, I cautiously accepted a post as Head of Drama at the old and venerable St Peter's College in Birmingham. Its hearty Principal, the Reverend 'Marty' Buckmaster (always known to staff and students alike as Farty Fuckblaster) told me at interview that as the college had only just started to recruit young gels, they thought they'd better have a Drama Department to occupy 'em, eh what?—but as none of the staff knew what such a department looked or sounded like, it was up to me to show 'em! Well, that was fine by me. Though come to that I wasn't sure what a Drama Department should look like either, but it was comforting to know that we were all working in the dark together.

I had gone by train to Birmingham for the interview, but now I had to drive the family there on scouting missions, to see where we might live, find a good school for Martyn, find our way around the shops and so forth. We were invited to stay with Robert (who had taken up a post in Birmingham). It was then I discovered the awful truth about driving a car around that curious and fractured city. The problem was, and is, that Birmingham's motorways are set, as in a historical theme park ride, over and above the remnants of the old Victorian city. This meant that when one saw a sign from the Bull Ring pointing to some desired destination, and turned off, one found oneself shedding a century and being confronted by a maze of dingy side streets. On our first such visit we attempted to find our way to King's Heath, where Robert and Margaret now lived. We had a slightly out-of-date map, from which Ann, through the sound barrier of her husband's screams, was attempting to direct us to Robert's house. Twice I pulled off the Expressway, thinking I recognised signs for one of the suburbs through which we we had been told we should pass, twice we had found ourselves lost in a labyrinthine Victorian underworld, and twice we had to manoeuvre gingerly back on to the Expressway. Never the most skilled or most patient of drivers I found myself morphing, like a character from a graphic novel, first into the Wolf Man and then into the Incredible Hulk. Goaded by the non-stop giggling of my passengers ('There's that bus stop again, Dad') this slavering green-tinted, muscle-bound beast stopped the car, howled twice, turned off the engine, got out and announced through clenched fangs that if sodding Birmingham couldn't be arsed to signpost itself properly, it was going to leave the car where it was, and walk the rest of the sodding way. Which outburst, I am sorry to report, led to renewed hilarity inside the stationary vehicle.

It was I believe James Thurber who said that he was quick to rouse and then impossible to calm down. In this, James and I are polar opposites. I hardly ever get angry, and when I do it is all over in a moment, as I immediately want to apologise to everybody in sight for having momentarily lost my cool. So it was on this occasion. I shed Hulk's mantle, said sorry to Ann and the children, and mouthed apologies to the phlegmatic Birmingham bystanders who had gathered on the opposite pavement in the hope of seeing me go completely berserk. Disappointed, they drifted away from the scene. Deep breaths all round. A few minutes later a crumpled and humiliated loser climbed back in the car. This time he kept silent and humbly followed his wife's directions. In less than fifteen minutes they were knocking on Robert and Margaret's door.

We did a certain amount of house-hunting that weekend, and a lot of eating, drinking and giggling with our old friends, but what I recall more clearly than anything was Ann and I enjoying a wonderful evening at Peter Dewes' blissful production of *As You Like It* at the old Repertory Theatre in Station Road. Robert had kindly got us tickets for Saturday evening, suspecting both that we might enjoy it and that it might demonstrate, *ex pulvere palma,* that in spite of its dreadful road systems and general air of hopelessness, there were many good things in Birmingham. He was right on both counts.

Before curtain-up at the rep the Theatre Manager appeared, in full fig, and informed the audience that they may have read that the city authorities had threatened to close down the production. This was because Mr Dewes had directed the wrestling match between Orlando and Charles in such a way that the vanquished wrestler fell off the front of the stage, in contravention of an ancient

Birmingham bye-law which decreed that neither actors nor audience should pass through the fourth wall and invade each other's space. He assured us solemnly that there would be no such transgression in that evening's performance, bowed stiffly and left. His solemnity gave an extra edge to the evening's entertainment, leading as it did to ripples of suppressed laughter as the players teased onlookers and management throughout the performance by wandering at unexpected moments dangerously close to the front of the stage.

It was an enchanted evening. We left the theatre reconciled to living in Birmingham, with the previous day's fracas near the Bull Ring banished to the back of our minds. Now all we had to do was find somewhere to live.

in France: Ann, Martyn, JP

aboard in Cairo: John, Ann, and Denis

❖8❖

Birmingham

ST PETER'S was at the opposite end of the educational spectrum from Nottingham. Whereas Clifton considered itself at the forefront of educational thought, St Peter's prided itself on bringing up the rear or, as they would have put it, remaining firmly rooted in the finest teaching traditions. When I arrived the male students still wore woolly cardigans, had partings in their hair and did not take umbrage when one of the older staff members stopped them in the quadrangle and told them to clean their shoes. A daily service, albeit one in which the clergy regularly outnumbered the congregation, was still read each day in the College Chapel. And when students went out on teaching practice they were still instructed in 'blackboard technique' (although virtually all classrooms now had whiteboards) and were commanded to wrap their working folders in cling film so chalk dust would not sully their pristine lesson plans.

But, for better or worse, such old-fashioned habits were rapidly changing, not least because two years previously the college had for the first time in its long history chosen to admit women to its musty precincts. It was partly to cope with this disturbing new influx that it had also decided, in defiance of its own well-ingrained traditions, to found a Drama Department. The reason for this was that modern young women were rumoured to be more interested in the arts than in technical drawing

and metalwork. However, many of the College Elders
had been unimpressed by the argument that having a
Drama Department would almost certainly attract a
large number of these exotic and fee-paying creatures.
To them it was all an offence against the natural order,
as if a monastery had decided to modernise its image by
offering membership to Pussy Riot.

That comparison is not altogether inappropriate as the
Elders also feared that young women might not just be
of the modern world but also *interested in it*. By which
they did not just mean that the new cohort might read
radical magazines, or want to explore the question of
mass immigration or the problems of the Middle East,
but that they would probably also take a lively interest
in the youth culture of the day, in pop music, in drugs,
in underground films or how they might safely engage
in regular sexual congress. The truth was that *any* kind
of engagement with the world outside the college walls
threatened the Elders' well-ordered world.

When they arrived the drama students turned out to
be interested in all of the above, and more. They were
colourful, lively and as interested in social justice and
sexual experiment as anybody else in the early seventies.
Yet they did not draw the ire of the Elders. Largely this
was because the ancients had rather shot themselves in
their feet, prior to my arrival, by adapting one of their
ancient lecture rooms as a blackoutable Drama Studio in
readiness for the coming of the new department. A
happily conceived gesture—which nevertheless offered a
perfect illustration of the law of unforeseen consequences. For it was behind the drawn curtains of the new
Drama Studio, out of sight of the more censorious of
the College traditionalists, that the students would
perform their various seditious, blasphemous, filthy—and
occasionally drug-fuelled—works.

However, from time to time, and in conventional
theatre spaces, the students redeemed themselves by
presenting more formal dramas—a dark and smoky
Macbeth, a delicately poetic *Blood Wedding*, and a sturdy
Romeo and Juliet in which the feuding Montagues and
Capulets shaded into the Protestants and Catholics of
war-torn Ireland. Yet the most significant works,

whether improvised, sung, danced, expressed in shadow puppetry or whistled in the dark, were all staged in the seclusion of the Drama Studio. Once a week at the regular *Wednesdays at One*, interested staff and students went in to watch or take part in the latest student offering—although as we opened the Studio's doors it was rare for any of us (myself included) to know what we were, literally, letting ourselves in for. Work in the Studio ranged from the brilliantly innovative to the limp and predictable, but it was almost always hostile to theatrical and political conformity.

It was entirely fitting therefore that during a brief lull in their bookings, the decidedly unpredictable Ken Campbell and some of his (probably sectionable) Roadshow company should have kipped down there, in return for meeting my students and taking a few improvisation classes with them. Those classes were as memorable as they had threatened to be, but they also had a less predictable outcome. A member of my third year class, a soft-skinned and voluptuous blonde who was rumoured to enjoy a bit of rough trade, entranced by the Ken Campbell Company's weird glamour, threw up her course and ran away with its leading man, the ape-featured performance artiste Marcel Steiner. This outstandingly hairy fellow—in addition to performing his regular Roadshow role as a sexually predatory gorilla—also ran 'The Smallest Theatre in the World', which edifice was housed in the sidecar of his oily old motor bike. As the reader may readily imagine, it was love at first grope, though the relationship was not to last long. In later years I ran across Marcel occasionally—the last time being when he was unleashing a giant motor-driven rat with a throbbing phallic tail amongst middle-aged blue-rinsed ladies at a Harrogate conference—and once I even glimpsed the blonde ex-student, clad in a diaphonous nightie and with her throat bleeding prettily, rising from the grave in a Hammer horror movie.

But the St Peter's Drama Department was far less concerned with imitating the professional theatre than had been the case in Nottingham. Its main visible strength was in Children's Theatre, and in this we were all indebted to John Coultas, the star lecturer of the department. John, after a short career on the conventional stage (much later, I realised that I had in fact seen him playing a supporting part in a Jessie Matthews comedy), had turned to educational drama and had for several seasons played with Brian Way's Children's Theatre Company. He knew many techniques for involving audience and performers in dramatic experiences, and instantly understood and sympathised with my own, still hesitant, beliefs about the parts we all play in real life. We worked together well, and I was delighted when, a few years later, we found our professional relationship unexpectedly extended. Of which more anon.

★   ★   ★

Back to the domestic story. After two or three abortive weekends trudging around Birmingham's extensive suburbs, Ann and I had finally chanced upon our new home. It was certainly not our usual style. For the first and only time in our lives we put down a deposit on a new house in a 'development' being built on what had been private parkland in Harborne, a leafy suburb of Birmingham. It escaped being an 'estate' (with all of that term's derogatory associations) only by virtue of the fact that the houses were arranged in little clusters rather than in straight rows, and that parts of the site—those bits too wet or hilly to build houses on—were landscaped. The landscaped bits included a nearby copse set around a pond—now designated a 'water feature'—on which (we learned much later) Martyn and his minute friends were wont to sail on homemade rafts lashed together with sellotape. The development would also contain a little collonade of shops and, most pertinently, in the nearby village there was a good school to which first Martyn, then Cath, would go.

According to the tasteful drawings in the sales catalogue there were three different kinds of houses, ranged according to size and price. We chose the best we could afford—i.e. the cheapest—at £7,500. For this price our (just) detached home would have three small bedrooms, a midget-sized downstairs loo, a garage and a steeply sloped back garden. The houses on the development all had standard fittings, except for the kitchen and bathroom tiles, which the purchasers could choose from a (strictly limited) range. But the house promised to be easy of upkeep, and the developers—who predictably turned out to be a firm of shysters—solemnly promised us that they would definitely have our house all ready, with chosen tiles in place, by the end of August. This was excellent news. It meant that Martyn could begin his new school term on the appointed day.

Except that their solemn promise was not kept. When we returned from a camping holiday in the middle of August our plot was still at the stage of being 'pegged-out'. We were not, at the time, unduly troubled by this discovery. We extended the time our furniture would be kept in store and agreed to wait another week, which we were told was the time it took them to 'run up' these desirable residences. When it became clear that second deadline would not be met either, and having vacated and sold our Nottingham house, we found ourselves homeless. However Robert and Margaret kindly came to our rescue and arranged for us to stay for two consecutive weeks with neighbouring Kings Heath families with whom they were friendly.

It was with considerable annoyance that we learned, as the end of that fortnight drew near, that the house was *still* not ready. Our Kings Heath landlords now had other things to attend to, so where on earth could we lay our heads? We had no other friends, or friends of friends on whose goodwill we could batten. We had not got the boodle for a stay at even the crummiest Birmingham hotel. Ann and I discussed the situation earnestly, but a problem shared is a problem doubled, and we got nowhere. It was Ann alone who hit upon the solution, which may have been unconventional, but it worked. As we still had all our camping equipment with us in the car, she hired the nearest open pitch she could find— which happened to be in a site adjoining Dudley Zoo— and we resolutely set up camp there. So it was that, for several days, having been awakened by the roaring of hungry lions in the nearby enclosure, we got dressed in one of our two available changes of clothing, made a simple dreakfast on our calor stove, zipped up our tent and drove Martyn to school.

It was only a brief interlude, for the evil developers (perhaps goaded by us drawing up our car each day on the site and fixing a baleful stare on the workmen) now told us that our house was ready for occupation. Quickly, we arranged for our furniture to be brought out, blinking, into the autumn sunlight and then watched the removal chaps trying to fit it into the unaccustomedly small spaces. We also, having begun to grasp the secret of the Birmingham traffic systems, ventured into Birmingham's teeming shopping malls to buy bedclothes and towels. Finally we set ourselves to fit our personal belongings into our new home, driving screws into the drying plaster and putting up shelves in every miniscule alcove. All seemed set for a new, well-ordered, life, albeit somewhat shrunken in scale.

Then the nocturnal visitations began. At our Dudley camp site we had become used to the nightime roars, grunts and farts of the zoo's restless inhabitants, but the strange nocturnal howls that we now heard were of another order. Their source was a mystery, and there was no pattern nor discernible rhythm to the cries. At unexpected moments during the night our marrows were chilled by a sudden eerie howling borne towards us on the autumn air. We quailed. Had we slipped unawares into another dimension and, all unknowing, entered the Realm of the Undead? Was there a frightful fiend lurking beneath a nearby viaduct? Could a brand new house possibly be *haunted*? We lived in mortal dread until finally the truth emerged. When we confessed our night time horrors to a neighbour who already knew the area, she was able to offer the explanation. Our development it seemed had been built close to the rear boundary of the Birmingham Botanical Gardens, in whose well-trimmed grounds there roamed a proud colony of peacocks . . . . It was then that we began to understand.

Now I for one yield to no-one in my admiration of the male peacock, both for its glorious multicoloured plumage, and for the way it proudly struts its stuff amongst the dowdy and shoddily-accoutred females of the species. I had imagined, on the comparatively few occasions I had given any thought at all to the reproductive habits of big birds, that the peacock beaux were actually saying to their blousy belles something like, Look love, I'm not making any promises, but if you get yourself a new dress, put on a bit of lippy, smarten yourself up, you might get yourself a bit of the other. But apparently I was wrong. The male peacocks like their women just as they are, and can't wait for night to fall so they can make the air glad with their mating calls. And although that strangled cry of passion sounds to us like the rusty clutch of a pre-war motor lawnmower, to the peacock hen it is a warm declaration of love which suggests nights of unbridled passion and endless connubial bliss. Each to their own. After receiving this comforting intelligence Ann, I and the children quickly got used to the peacocks' unearthly shrieking—though for many months afterwards badly shaken guests would greet us at breakfast with the worrying news that during the night they had been woken by the screams of a witch being burned nearby.

But our lives were now once more on an even keel. I spent far less time in St Peter's College than I had at Nottingham, took a much less frequent role in play production, and (to no-one's particular distress) rarely acted. I liked my new colleagues well enough, but there was really only one outstanding character, the smooth-talking, velvet-jacketed Barry Grayson, poet, bon-viveur and Head of the Music Department. Amongst much else Barry was both a keen party-goer and giver, and just occasionally hit the sauce rather too hard. One such occasion was when he was due to play the narrator in a production of *A Soldier's Tale*. An hour before curtain up he arrived in full evening dress, but plainly (in his own fruity terms) 'thoroughly bladdered, old boy'. However, under his direction, we undressed him, lay him on his back and shoved his head and torso under a cold shower. After twenty minutes or so he levered himself upright, towelled himself dry, combed his hair, reassumed his formal dress and strode off to give what I was assured was a flawless performance. Though, much as I loved him, I couldn't bear to watch.

My new position (Head of Department, no less) coupled with a marginally enlarged salary meant that with our move to Harborne we were moving inexorably into the lower middle classes. We bought *The Guardian*, and would have read *The Observer* on Sundays, had not its weight and bulk defeated us. With the children we took vaguely educational packaged holidays ('The First World War Trenches', 'Castles of the Rhine', kind of thing), in addition to making weekend trips to the Cotswolds and nearby Stratford on Avon. Our neighbours tended to be (in the dim social docketing of the time) 'upwardly aspirational', ranging from accountants to suburban bank managers. Their children mixed with our children. We had competitive little supper parties. When we went out for the evening we could even afford responsible grown-up baby sitters, which meant that Ann could on occasion come out to College events, and even see some of our College shows.

One of the few occasions on which I did take charge of a production was of a fairly ambitious reading of *Murder in the Cathedral* which played first in Birmingham Cathedral, and then went on to the Thomas à Beckett Festival at Sutton-under-Brailes in the Cotswolds. It was quite well received, though privately I have always felt the piece too ritualistic and wordy to be truly dramatic. Ann was able to come out to Sutton to see it. She sat in the Thomas à Beckett church alongside Robert Speaight, who had played the Archbishop in the original Canterbury production. He had been invited to the Sutton Festival as an honoured guest, but unfortunately seemed to be so well stricken in years that he did not appear capable of recalling anything about the play's pre-war première, or indeed about the play itself. Ann noticed that he slept soundly through our performance. He then awoke, smiling beatifically around him, as if he were waiting to be told why these people had kidnapped him and released him in this strange enclosure. Although it has to be said that now, at this distance, I tend to think it was his long experience of attending similar festivals, and being obliged to watch productions such as this, rather than a failing memory, that led Mr Speaight into the tactful arms of Morpheus. I now believe that feigning sleep absolved the actor from the embarrassing duty of having to congratulate a group of unknown players on their performance of a play which, as he well knew, had once been very much better done.

Our stay in Sutton, in the homes of local theatre lovers, was otherwise delightful—save only for the fact that on a morning stroll through the nearby lanes one of our actors, used to the regular thrum and throb of Birmingham traffic, became so disorientated by the countryside's silence that he failed to register from which direction a farm vehicle was approaching, and as he ran distractedly from one side of the lane to the other, was run into by a large tractor driven by a small dumb girl wearing thick dark sunglasses. I'm told that the crash, followed as it was by a frantic mime show, resembled nothing so much as the opening scene of a Hitchcock movie, though fortunately in this case none of the participants was seriously damaged.

Apart from that, the chief daytime interest of Sutton was that the veteran actor Hugh Griffith lived there and was an enthusiastic supporter of the village pub. At lunch-times he would sit crumpled at the bar, regaling my young actors with well-honed stories of his long film and theatre career, and of his fellow actors' drinking habits and unusual sexual liaisons. In return for these scandalous reminiscences, the actors bought him copious amounts of beer. The arrangement worked rather well until the young thesp who had collided with the tractor suggested that as Hugh was obviously a man of great discrimination the cast would much value his opinion of their work. Would he like a ticket to see their *Murder in the Cathedral?* At this Mr Griffith did a full bodily recoil for the length of the bar, and screeched 'No, bloody hell! No!!' before roaring out the memorable line, 'I like sex boy, but I'm buggered if I want to watch other people doing it!'.

* * *

At Birmingham I became increasingly interested in another aspect of the arts, best described as arts politics. It was then all the rage, with sixties 'arts lovers' supposedly united in the belief that, as proof of its thriving cultural life, a civilised country needed a state-funded Arts Council to dish out 'subsidies' to worthy, state-approved clients. So far as I could see, this was a simple confidence trick, with the aim of aggrandising the role of the Council rather than the arts themselves. The arts did not in my view divide into the worthy and the unworthy. And in any case some of the ACGB clients weren't worthy at all, just smooth-talking chancers who had mastered the art of filling in grant applications. As for the Arts Council itself, it could not pretend to be a disinterested critical body. More than anything it resembled the UK banks—too dependent on keeping its clients in permanent debt as a means of prolonging its own existence.

Those clients who enjoyed regular state support were told that they were the 'high arts', whereas commercial organisations were 'lower' arts or demoted to the ranks of mere 'entertainment'. At that time this false division was even enshrined in law, with 'entertainment' organisations being forced to pay an 'Entertainment Tax' on their tickets, while state-subsidised 'arts' clients of the ACGB paid no such tax. This strange fault line ran deep through British cultural life, doubly disadvantaging any cultural organisation deemed unworthy of subsidy. And (in my opinion) this corrosive but well-ingrained practice meant that the Arts Council, in spite of its pretensions and for all of its talk of the 'Arm's Length Principle', had become a political tool of the government of the day. Not because the ACGB imposed a state *diktat* on the arts, but because it accepted a state bribe to free the government of any responsibility for taking such matters seriously. Ministers could now shrug off any number of awkward questions involving education, allocation of physical resources, civic development or public celebrations by simply pointing to this secretive, unaccountable Quango—'Ah now, *that* is a matter for the Arts Council.'

Because I had voiced these heretical views I was invited to join the Drama Panel of the regional arts association, West Midlands Arts. I was, said the Director, to be the official dissenting voice, but I soon discovered that my new colleagues were every bit as cynical about the new artspeak as I was. The panel comprised play-wrights, designers, critics and the Director of the new Birmingham rep, Michael Simpson. It was to suit Michael's convenience that we sometimes met in the theatre's green room.

It was there, one fateful winter's afternoon, that our panel gathered. On that occasion we shared the green room with an alarmingly colourful parrot, borrowed from the Mermaid theatre, and currently appearing in *Treasure Island* in the main auditorium downstairs. The parrot had been trained by Sir Bernard Miles himself and, by all accounts, was acquitting himself well on stage, hitting his marks and squawking 'Pieces of Eight' bang on cue. What we did not then know was that during his training the bird had been allowed free rein backstage at the Mermaid where, as was widely known, Sir Bernard was liable to let rip with some fruity language. The result was that the bird's conversation was salty in the extreme. It was a potty-beaked parrot.

To be fair, before we began our deliberations Michael had asked panel members whether we minded having the parrot's company and, being then unaware of the parrot's bar room vocabulary, we had murmured no, no, not at all. One or two of us had even smiled at his cage and made vaguely encouraging clicking noises. And when the meeting got under way we rather forgot about the parrot, and started as usual to argue about how the Arts Council's latest dicta might be bent and applied to our various random actions. Before long one of the panel's members topped his argument by shouting—sarcastically—the injunction, 'Remember the Arm's Length Principle!' At this the parrot stirred, fluffed its feathers and rent the air with a window-shattering cry of 'Bollocks!', adding in a suspiciously familiar West Country burr, ''Tis all bollocks.' As soon as the panel had recovered from its surprise, and by a substantial majority, minuted the fact that it agreed with the parrot, it continued its deliberations. As the meeting went on, however, we could not help noticing that the parrot reacted in like fashion whenever anyone gave voice, however ironically, to any one of the Arts Council's toe-curling mantras, 'Few but roses', 'The best for the most' and, top of the bill, 'Centres of Excellence', which last drew from our feathered companion a blistering volley of paint-stripper oaths, topped up by the terse advocacy of a sexual vengeance which should, in the parrot's opinion, be wreaked upon the Arts Council's Secretary General.

On a less enjoyable level my involvement with WMA in its turn led to my having some early experience of helping to set up an Arts Concil tour—in this case the Royal Shakespeare Company's touring production of *The Hollow Crown*. This popular piece was to be produced by John Barton, and performed by a group of well-known RSC actors. It was, we planners thought, bound to be very popular. The tour was financed by an Arts Council grant, conditional upon the production playing to 'new audiences', thus bringing 'the best' to people unused to visiting the ACGB's 'centres of excellence'. I realised that this meant that the production should be offered in new venues, but rather expected that it would also play to 'the most', i.e. the largest possible audiences, which meant booking the largest and most accessible arenas. But I had reckoned without the window-dressing involved in such 'tours'. The venues were to be chosen less for their ability to house large new audiences than for the impression they gave to the powers-that-be of subsidised companies bravely going where no man had gone before. Thus the Ye Quaint Olde Forge at Grimpen Under Sludge (say) was much more politically acceptable than was the spacious and well-equipped Dumdown Town Hall—in spite of the fact that the latter could have accommodated twenty times the number of interested first-time theatre-goers.

Taking advantage of this political absurdity for my own nefarious ends (and hoping to get in well with the College Elders, who had heard of the RSC) I suggested that *The Hollow Crown* should begin its tour in darkest Saltley, with a performance at St Peter's. Passed *nem. con.* I then suggested that they should play in the heavily curtained Drama Studio, but this was a step into obscurity too far. Instead their PR man settled for the College Hall. So, one dark and foggy Birmingham afternoon, John Barton arrived with an intrepid company which included Alan Howard, Sara Kestelman, Barry Stanton and a man with a lighting chart. I showed them their 'dressing rooms' (the Drama Department staff's offices), gave them a series of chits to the college bar for their drinks and snacks, introduced them to the two students who were to operate the new 18-way fingertip control lighting board, and retired so they could hold their dress rehearsal in secret.

By seven thirty a satisfactory audience had assembled and was regarding the bare stage with cautious apprehension. On the half I had slipped into the makeshift dressing rooms to find the other actors trying to console Alan Howard, who was shaking with nerves at the prospect of being so near to, and being actually able to *see* members of the audience. I was able to assure him that those out front were much more terrified of him than he was of them. And indeed, he need not have worried. *The Hollow Crown* went like a dream.

Until its conclusion, that is. *The Hollow Crown* ends with the central character, crown aloft, speaking its final words. During this last soliloquy, Mr Howard's noble form was to be framed in a pool of white light which gradually narrowed, until finally his crowned head was picked out only by a pencil-thin spotlight. After his concluding words that pinpoint of light must be held there for one second only, then abruptly cut out. Darkness. Tumultuous applause! Cue curtain call.

At the afternoon dress rehearsal all this had worked perfectly. Yet on the night the finger tip control failed. The student lighting man slid it up on cue but nothing happened. The finger tip slider failed to engage. Meanwhile the spotlight continued to pick out the detail on the crown and on Mr Howard's increasingly nerve-racked features. During the ensuing pause the audience stayed their hands, suspecting that the actor's noble visage, now furrowed with terror, meant that he had something else to utter, some further nugget of timeless wisdom to impart. But in the merciless glare of the spotlight Mr Howard was silent, his face congealing into a perspiring death mask. Up in the lighting galley the students were desperately jiggling the board, to no avail. Then, belatedly, they realised that they could override the stuck fingertip control by throwing the master switch. Which they did. The spotlight went out and the stage slumped into a relieved darkness. A tentative ripple of applause. Then light once more flooded the stage and on trouped the company for their call. Applause redoubled! A general loosening of nerves, and in the happy hubbub the backstage inquests begin. The lighting boys reckoned the hiatus with the lighting had only been of 'a couple of seconds' duration, so no worries. Against this however must be set Mr Howard's breathless testimony as he limped off the stage. His estimation of the pause— judging by his accusing expression—was nearer to twenty minutes.

But we now approach another turning point in my narrative, and with it another confession. Nearly all auto-biographies, and virtually every biography, has a decisive turning point after a chapter or two. It will usually come about because the subject 'suddenly realises' that his true vocation lies in figure skating, investment banking, growing orchids, or whatever. This revelatory moment will be underscored by testimony from some neighbour, teacher or distant relative who will have 'always known' that he/she would be a whizz on ice, or in the City, or up to his/her elbows in compost. Not in my case. I have to confess that not only did my neighbours and teachers fail to offer any prognostications about my future but that later in life, even when I was passing what would later be regarded as a 'turning point', I had no inward sense of being at one.

In fact I could quite happily have gone on for many years at St Peters, had not the government intervened to prevent it. The educational world was just then going through one of its periodic fits of collective insanity. This time it was the weird belief that any schoolchild capable of tying their own shoelaces and of understanding some pop lyrics not only had the right to a university education, but also to a good degree. In pursuance of which nonsense the government had set out to create, from art colleges, technical colleges and media outlets, fistfuls of new 'universities' to accommodate this expansion. Coupled with this was a second belief, intertwined with the first, that any activity at all—from sheep shearing through candle making to water skiing— could be made the subject matter of this new sort of degree.

Teacher training was not spared from this mania. A former High Master of Manchester Grammar School, Lord James, was asked by the government to produce a report into teacher training. Needless to say, the *James Report* advocated that teacher training should now become the subject of new degree courses and that for the most part colleges such as St Peter's should be subsumed into the new universities' new 'education departments'. The writing was on the wall. For all its deeply-rooted traditions, St Peter's was doomed. Though it has to be recorded that this news did not greatly distress the senior staff. The College Elders settled comfortably back in their common room armchairs and waited to be told the size of their retirement pensions and lump sums. Young sprogs like me—youths still in their thirties —had no such expectations and would have to find another berth.

Then came a stroke of luck. It appeared that the county authorities in Somerset wished to revamp Dillington, their Adult Residential College and Arts Centre. They had advertised nationally for a Director, who would combine responsibility for developing their arts centre (whose facilities included craft and music rooms, a Gallery and a small theatre-cum-cinema), their programme of short courses and especially their residential adult courses (it had seventy student beds). The College it appeared had some thirty permanent staff variously to attend to secretarial duties, cooking and ordering food, running and stocking the bar, cleaning, bedmaking, maintenance, gardening and booking—but no staff to programme or teach either the educational programmes or the arts centre. The Director and his Deputy were to be responsible for all of that—plus the fact that teachers for all of the courses, and all of the visiting artists, had to be separately contracted, and their transport, accommodation and marketing arranged.

In summary, it seemed the new Director had to be expert in hotel management, inward with all levels of further and adult education, conversant with all the intricacies of music, theatre and visual arts administration, a good personnel and office manager, and capable of reshaping and giving new impetus overall to an organisation which had become far too well-set in its ways. To say the least, the prospect was daunting. However, a photograph of Dillington House—built of warm ham stone and set in the luscious Somerset countryside—decided me. Although I had none of the required skills, I was arrogant enough to believe that I was nevertheless the man they wanted. I would, I told myself, make up in style what I lacked in application.

But the immediate hurdle to overcome was getting myself an interview, for once there I would surely impress them all with my winsome chic. I carefully applied, and by various devious means—which I do not at this stage propose to reveal—I made sure my name was put before the Somerset authorities with some emphasis. In due course Mr and Mrs John Pick (why did they want to see us both? Didn't they kmow my wife was a crypto feminist who held very strong views about women being treated as mere appendages of their husbands?) were invited to Dillington for a weekend to be interviewed. In time some might come to say my time at Dillington was a turning point in my life—but it was surely created by circumstance and luck, rather than by any inherent qualities I possessed.

Dillington House

❧9❧

Dillington

THE INTERVIEWS at Dillington revealed everything that needed to be known about that magical and maddening place. After lengthy negotiations, lines having been drawn in the sand about the role of wives in a modern marriage and no-go areas having been agreed, Ann and I arrived for the weekend's events in time for Friday supper, with Brahms playing softly on the car stereo and the House's gothic exterior glowing seraphically in the warm evening sunlight. That first dreamlike impression, of being transported into the pre-war world of an Agatha Christie whodunnit, was reinforced when a maidservant, whom we were later to know as a member of the college staff, answered the bell, led the way upstairs, showed us to our quarters and told us that at seven a gong would summon us for dinner in the dining room (after which, presumably, the body of one of the candidates would be discovered in the Library, stabbed by a dagger of curious oriental design). Wondering vaguely whether I should not have brought evening dress I glanced at Ann who, reading my thoughts, brought me down to earth, telling me that I should wear the clothes I had driven down in, while she intended to wear the one dress she had brought with her on this and *every* evening and that if they didn't like it they could lump it. I did not demur, even though I wasn't sure what 'lumping it' might involve.

At dinner the candidates were joined by a few local
bigwigs who arranged themselves around the room so
they could keep an eye on us—presumably checking
whether we knew which knife to use and didn't neck
wine straight from the decanter. I was introduced to my
fellow shortlistees (all white, all male) who proved to be
a likeable and impressive bunch, ranging from a fairly
senior university chap to the successful Principal of a
Further Education College. They all looked confident,
as if they'd already been privately offered the job
but had agreed to go through with the interviews for
form's sake. We were told that after dinner we should
be meeting the Warden and could ask him 'anything
we liked', so we kept our powder dry and engaged only
in small talk. The real battleground was on the distaff
side. Except for Ann, the candidates' wives wore British
Council bunfight fatigues (dusty magenta gowns with
craft jewellery dangling from ears and neck), and two
of them, presumably to prove that they had suitably
catholic interests, artlessly placed their 'current reading
books' beside them at the table. One of these was a book
about Leibnitz, and I listened as Ann, who was genuinely
interested in the history of ideas, attempted to engage
its owner in a conversation about the philosopher. It was
painfully clear that the lady had never read a word of his
writings, and didn't know a monad from a nomad.

However, it was the meeting with the Warden that was
to define the problems that would face the first Director.
He would be the first Director because Dillington, like
most other Adult Education Colleges set in old country
houses, had previously had a 'Warden' at its helm.
Wardens in residential colleges had traditionally been
responsible not only for putting on the residential short
course programmes, but also for the upkeep of the house
and grounds. The County authorities now wished to
appoint a Director with a much wider remit. However,
it soon became clear that the rip-snorting Captain Hines
(RN Retd.) who greeted us in the library after dinner
had seen his Warden's role in a traditional light. He
told us at length about the shrubs he had planted in the
arboretum, and his renovations of various outhouses in
the grounds. Turning to its residential role, he told us

with some emphasis how proud he was of the way he had continued to run Dillington like a proper country house. Staff used only the kitchen door and then, under the eagle eye of the Bursar, for the most part stayed below stairs out of sight. The cooks enjoyed cooking fine dinners for 'the right sort of people', but used up packages of processed food when they had to cook meals on in-service courses—for teachers, social workers and 'that kind of person'. The country house routine of bells and gongs was paramount, so actors who came to play in the theatre in the evening were a 'demn'd nuisance' because they didn't choose to get up for breakfast at the appointed time. Most worrying of all, when asked what advice he would give his successor, he said that he would advise them to have as little as possible to do with the County Council. (As little as possible!! Surely it was the County Council that underwrote everything, and with ratepayers' money?)

At this point it is worth inserting a note on Dillington's history, and the role of the County Council. The present house was built in 1838 by Charles Barry, the architect who just previously had worked with Pugin to rebuild the burnt-out House of Commons. George III's infamous Prime Minister Lord North had then, through marriage, acquired Dillington, and so it had become for a short while the Prime Minister's country residence. It had continued to flourish as a Country House until just after the Second World War, when the Cameron family, its owners, had decided they were no longer able to afford its maintenance. They therefore rented it out for a hundred years and at a peppercorn rent to the Somerset County Council, for use as an Adult Education College. The consideration was that the Council would maintain the fabric of the Main House, Stables and Mews, and keep the immediate grounds (including its croquet lawn, ice house and arboretum) in good condition.

Plainly the tension was between maintaining Dillington as a fine country house, and ensuring that it was fully used to meet the multiplying demands of adult education and arts centre. The latter would mean making full use of the lecture rooms, gallery, theatre, craft rooms and grounds for residential courses, in-service training, lecture series and day courses—and for arts activities which might range across instrumental and choral groups, drama, crafts, creative writing, photography, film, pottery or landscape painting. Such full programming would make house and grounds satisfyingly busy, and be good for the balance sheet, but would make it much harder to maintain the peaceful tranquillity that residential students might reasonably expect from their stay at an English country house.

It was clear from the Warden's introductory talk, and clearer still when we talked to the staff the following day, that until then the emphasis had been firmly upon maintaining Dillington as a country house. The whole place shut down for staff holidays. Students were forced to accommodate, particularly over bedtimes and mealtimes, to the staff's convenience, and the Warden expected to be treated as the Lord of the Manor. Now the County authorities wanted to change this radically, to programme it more intensively, to reach a much wider clientèle, and better to justify the considerable portion of ratepayers' money which was being spent on it. This much was clear to me—as it was to the other candidates. The only remaining question was, which one of us would be best able to achieve this minor revolution?

As we continued next day on our rounds of the staff and bull-necked bigwigs I became more and more convinced that I should like the chance of doing the job, but also that any of the other candidates would probably be better at it than I should. Ann disagreed with me on the latter count. After spending the day with the other candidates' wives (who had adopted for daytime wear the regulation National Trust uniform of cotton smocks with matching green anoraks and little wellies) and hearing them talk approvingly of their husbands' virtues, she had decided that they were all yes-men, who would dance to the authorities' tune.* My secret weapon, she told me sweetly, was my smooth-talking, back-stabbing nature, my well-known ability to be all things to all men—and in any case there were so many contradictions inherent

---

* At that time, Dillington was still owned by Ann Cameron, who lived in a cottage in the grounds with her son Euan, now Lord Cameron, the present owner. His second cousin David is currently Prime Minister.

in the post that the ideal person to fill it would surely be a chameleon like me. I thought little of it at the time but after the unexpected events of Sunday, after I had indeed been offered the post and Ann had spoken her mind to the appointments committee, I would see the truth of her remarks.

So let me set the scene. On the Saturday evening, after we candidates had spent the day strolling the grounds with studied nonchalance and talking informally to the various interested parties, the powers-that-be posted the schedule for the following day's interviews. We were to be seen in alphabetical order by a carefully-chosen clutch of the p-t-b. But while the other candidates were to be scrutinised during the morning, I saw that my own interview was scheduled for two o'clock in the afternoon, after a final buffet meal. And that (the timing of the interview, not the buffet) turned out to be my salvation.

★   ★   ★

As our presence was not required on Sunday morning, Ann suggested that we might usefully while away the time by going for a drive and taking a closer look at a county we knew only by hearsay. Of course we had ulterior motives. The specification for the job had said that the County would provide the Director with a house in the grounds suitable for his family, but we had taken a crafty peek at the present Warden's quarters—a flat-roofed prefab looking out on a wonderful view across the Deane Valley but with a depressing and cramped interior—and had decided that it would be a useful precaution to size up the local housing market. And we also wanted to see if we could find some evidence of ordinary Somerset life beyond the rarified confines of the college—surely the entirety of the county was not locked in the same feudal time warp as Dillington? In the event we found neither house nor evidence of contemporary life—though we were later to discover that in one respect at least Somerset was bang up to date. A smartly-dressed lady, wife of a local bigwig, had called one day to welcome Ann to the neighbourhood and after chatting amiably about who was who, which shops to patronise, which walks were worthwhile and which local schools were thought to be sound, had smilingly asked her whether she and her husband would be interested in joining the local wife-swapping club.

But on that fateful morn, unaware of any consequence yet hanging in the air, we drove innocently out into the mysterious heartland of Somerset. The country, when we were able to glimpse any of it above the grassy banks which skirted the roads, looked verdant and lush. From time to time we came upon clusters of thatched-roofed cottages clustered around a village green or a whitewashed pub. Our spirits rose. Above the verdant hedgerows we glimpsed orchards dappled with blossom, while in the roadside vegetation insects lazily wheeled and whirred, the sun shone from a cloudless sky, and a mellow haze hung over all. No traffic intruded upon us (which I remember thinking was a good thing as the Somerset lanes did not appear to have passing bays). And so we meandered quietly along, wrapped in our timeless nirvana.

We neither saw nor heard the coming of the lorry. It reared up suddenly over the brow of a hill and rattled blindly down towards us, indifferent to everything in its path. I had just time to wrench the steering wheel over and jam our car into the bank. But it was too late. The lorry hit the car's rear end with a long retching thump, before bumping on down the lane. There followed one of those long apprehensive silences that will be familiar to anyone who has ever been in a car crash. We looked dazedly at each other and started to take stock. The car's bodywork may have been badly dented, but at least we were unscathed. I began to breathe again. I levered myself slowly out of the car and looked along the lane to where the lorry had crunched to a leisurely halt, watching mesmerised as its driver unwound himself from the cab, ground out his fag and ambled amiably towards us.

'You all roit then?'

His geniality was enervating and the blistering Brummie rejoinder that I had been preparing died stillborn on my lips. He beamed ingratiatingly, then looked up to where Ann had clambered out of the car and was looking palely down on the scene.

'You all roit there ma'am?'

She assured him, rather coldly, that she was. It then began to dawn upon me that it was the lorry driver, the perpetrator of the outrage and not us, the innocent victims, who was taking the moral high ground. He was employing none of the shifty body language that contributors to car smashes usually exhibit. Indeed he appeared to be feeling no guilt at all. I tried unavailingly to make sense of this. Then I realised he was a *local*, a son of Somerset who no doubt felt that he held *droit de seigneur* over his own county's byways. So, in his eyes, it was Ann and I who must bear responsibility for the incident. We were plainly a pair of grockles, who should a' known that he always came down that road every day, reg'lar as clockwork, at midday near enough. And we should a' known that in them parts cars get out of the way of lorries, if they know what's good for 'um. Having given us a few moments to appreciate the absurdity of our position, he essayed a compassionate glance at our battered vehicle.

'You'll not be droiving yon agin terday. You wants the garage.'

'We have to get to Dillington by one o'clock.'

A long wondering look at Ann and me. So, *thats* the kind o' people we was.

'Adrian'll see you roit. Oi'll get Adrian, don't 'e worry.'

After he had gone it occurred to us that we had not even got his name, never mind his address. We waited there for about twenty minutes, during which time we removed our few personal possessions from the boot and glove compartment and wandered disconsolately about, occasionally fingering the raw metal exposed on the side of our crumpled vehicle. We were marooned in the countryside, and at the mercy of an unnamed lorry driver who for all we knew might have been a well-known local tearaway who regularly terrorised the back roads. And who was Adrian? Come to that, *where* was Adrian? The only sound to be heard was the purposeful buzzing of the insects among the tangled hedgerows. And, as if to underline the unreality of the experience, for the whole of the time we waited not a single vehicle passed us by.

Yet the unnamed driver turned out to be as good as his
word, for eventually we heard in the far distance the faint
but unmistakeable thump of an approaching motorcade.
Then there clattered into view a muck-spattered pick-up
truck followed by a smart-looking taxi cab which, with a
deftness no doubt born of long practice, its owner parked
up on the grassy bank, before bounding across to greet
us. This would be Adrian.

He was young, smartly dressed in tie and a well-cut
suit (had he been called from his Sunday devotions?),
with sunglasses rakishly pushed back on his tanned
forehead and sporting a jet black pony tail. He shook
my hand briefly and muttered some sort of rural curse
before turning his undivided attention to Ann, asking her
smilingly whether she was quite sure she felt up to going
back to Dillington? (So if she wasn't, where did he intend
to take her?) Meanwhile the pick-up truck men, who
judging by their oil-stained boiler suits had decided to
give Matins a miss, were yanking practised chains into
place around our crumpled Sirocco.

Ann said that yes she was up to being driven back
and I added that we should like it if we could be back
by one o'clock as I was meeting an interview panel at
Dillington. At this further mention of the College, he
furrowed his brow, and flashed me a sly smile. (I later
learned to decode that kind of signal; Dillington, with
its daily comings and goings from Taunton Station, was
soon revealed to be a prime source of income for local
cab drivers.)

'I rang the College like Mr Oswald said.'

After which gnomic utterance, he motioned me to get
in to the rear of the car, and opened the front door for
Ann to take her place. He raised a farewell hand to the
toiling truck drivers, smoothly insinuated himself into
the driver's seat, pulled down his shades, switched on
the air conditioning and set off. Throughout the ensuing
journey he gave Ann a customised commentary on the
various beauty spots, crime scenes, country estates and
ancient battlefields through which we were passing. It
was indeed a rich tapestry. Somerset was on the surface
quite different from any place I had previously lived in—
lusher than the Dukeries, wilder and less curated than

Cambridge and of course much more sparsely populated than Nottingham or Brum. Yet its essential difference did not only lie in such quantifiable matters. Even from the cab's rear window Somerset looked mysteriously *other*. On that balmy Sunday morning it was slowly revealing itself to be nothing less than a foreign dominion, with its own mythic history, its own language and customs and its own languorous climate . . . .

My reverie was cut short by the realisation that we were now pulling on to the gravel in front of Dillington. It was ten minutes to one. The participants in the morning interviews were straggling towards the main house for the final bun struggle of the weekend. As I saw their faces turning towards the cab, and saw them nudging each other and pointing, I realised that fate had dealt me a trump card. A detachment of solicitous suits hurried towards us and gingerly opened the car doors, telling us they had heard all about the accident (from Adrian's phone call?), had been dreadfully worried about us and couldn't apologise enough for the state of the county's roads. It was scandalous and something should be done about it, but never mind that for the moment, were we all right? Shouldn't we see a doctor? Go to outpatients for a check-up? As I took in their practised anxiety, with Adrian's smile all the time hovering in the car mirrors like Alice's Cheshire cat, I saw my opportunity. I climbed stiff-legged out of the cab, breathed in deeply as I had seen released hostages do on the television news, and twisted my face into a brave little smile; 'No, no, I'm quite all right, just a bit shaken, that's all.' My chosen voice was breathy and low, rather like the one I had, years before, used for Iago's soliloquies. There was a respectful silence. Out of the corner of my eye I saw the Chairman of Ways and Means ushering Ann purposefully towards the bar; 'But if I could, perhaps, have a drink of something?'

I dominated the buffet lunch. Sitting on a comfortable chair in the Library, glass in hand, a plate of lamb kebabs and prawn vol-au-vents on a low table nearby, I gracefully received anxious supplications from the interviewing panel ('Are you quite sure you're up to being interviewed, old chap?') and rather less sympathetic comments from my fellow interviewees ('Well you've certainly got everybody interested in your activities'). Even those who did not seek audience with me could be seen glancing and occasionally gesticulating in my direction. After which, to cut a long story short, the interview was a breeze. From the start the panel was obviously impressed by the fact that this candidate had dragged himself from the wreckage of a truly terrible accident and somehow struggled back to base for the interview. That he was now disporting himself so bravely and was able to answer the panel's piffling and impertinent questions—albeit in an strangely low and breathy voice—was further proof of his essentially brave and heroic nature. So they could not possibly come to any other conclusion. Would I please consider accepting the post of Director of Dillington College? Yes I most definitely would—that last sentence uttered in a haughty, yelping voice (not unlike the imperious tones I had adopted in the Cambridge Arts Theatre as Julius Caesar).

There was just one thing. They would—if I didn't mind—like a few words with Mrs Pick. I said huskily that would of course be fine. After a few seconds a bejeaned Ann was brought in, and cushions found to line her chair. The world—or at least my portion of it— held its breath. They apologised abjectly for subjecting her so soon after the dreadful crash to such a merciless interrogation, but would she mind saying, if it were not too much trouble, how she felt about moving to Somerset with me, and her family? She replied softly that she was very happy for me, and for our children, and would enjoy living here, *but* (more firmly) that she had no intention of playing a purely decorative role as the Director's wife. She would find work in the neighbourhood, and hoped they were happy with that. After the briefest of pauses, they declared that this chimed perfectly with their deepest wishes. *And,* she continued, I have to say I could not possibly bring my family to live in the Warden's house in its present state. Bless you my dear lady, you mustn't worry about that, they cried, we will have it completely rebuilt! A Dillington Director must have guest rooms (though until then we had put guests up on our stained and battered sofa) and a Dillington Director's wife could not possibly share a bathroom with her children (until then we'd all shared the same loo and loofah) and Mr and Mrs Pick must of course have their own dining room and their own study. Ann nodded, adding that her growing children must each have a bedroom and their own wardrobe space. ('Of *course*, Mrs Pick, of course!')

So there we were. All in a day we had survived a car crash, I had been appointed Director of Dillington and thanks to Ann's intransigence we were having a house built looking out across one of the most beautiful valleys in England. And so, contentedly, to bed.

* * *

In that same summer Ann, I and the children spent our summer holidays in Greece and the Greek Islands, as we were to do for several years thereafter. This involves backtracking on my story, and introducing the extraordinary Professor Denis Donegan.

I first ran across Denis in the late sixties. I only know that he seemed to know folk I knew and that I ran into him quite often, almost always in pubs. They were his natural habitat. Ensconced in a bar he would always begin the session by listening to the general *craic*, but would later contribute a series of improbable anecdotes from his blurred past, which *inter alia* included qualifying as a psychiatrist (he was by then a Professor of Education at Pittsburgh University), a spell in uniform in Vietnam, a brief spell in the slammer, arranging dance performances for the National Endowment for the Arts and working as a member of Bobby Kennedy's campaign team. He had been married at least once, and carried with him photographs of two youngsters, a boy and a girl, whom he claimed were his children—though he was as reticent over details of his domestic as of his working life. His ostensible reason for being in Britain was, on behalf of a US Consortium of Universities, setting up and recruiting staff for their English Summer School held annually in London University premises.

Quite early in our acquaintanceship he invited me to teach Drama in that same London Summer School. I much enjoyed this. The school was probably a good immersive experience for the students, but for the staff it was nothing less than a Bacchic revel. The mornings were very properly given over to teaching, but later in the day Denis would lead the English staff through a wildly indulgent progression of drinking clubs and exotic Soho restaurants—meeting on the way a weird assortment of grizzled poets, boxers, designers and disgraced politicians, all of whom seemed to want to party and gossip with Denis. Even the sinister George Wigg, at that time the enforcer in Harold Wilson's political entourage, whom we encountered one evening in Brewer Street, greeted Denis like a brother and indulged in a whispered exchange of (presumably classified?) information with him.

It isn't easy to account for Denis's quirkily magnetic character. He was muscular, good-looking in a vaguely oriental kind of way, narrow-eyed with high cheekbones and a perpetual five o'clock shadow. He smiled a lot, and talked incessantly. He would naturally insinuate himself into any conversation anywhere (as I discovered in Turkey when he companionably joined a group of thugs plotting a political outrage at a nearby café table). In any social gathering he always insisted on being the host, ordering for the whole company in a quiet Bronx drawl. As a committed epicure he refused any invitation to a meal unless he was told in advance what was on the menu. Finding London University breakfasts not to his taste he hightailed it to Denmark in the early hours of the morning 'for something decent to eat'. Refused a last drink in a West End pub, he told the Scottish landlord that he was thinking of buying the business and was hustled into a back room for a business conference over a large dram. Everything he did was suffused with a curiously puckish sense of humour. When years later he and I were joint partners of a small travel business, he insisted it should be called 'Bertree' (a conflation of 'Bermuda' and 'Triangle'—a code which, happily for us, our customers did not decipher).

For the reasons given above he was very popular with his male friends, but it was hard for any of us to account for his extraordinary success with women. Yet every woman he met seemed to adore him. There's no mystery about it, Ann told me one day as she was sewing new buttons on to one of his jackets, women want to mother him. Whatever the reason was, when I moved to Birmingham he was somehow still about, often staying with us during his frequent visits to the UK. For my part I genuinely enjoyed Denis's company, carefully insinuated myself into the Consortium's good books, and as a result enjoyed a number of short teaching jobs in the States, Rome and the USSR. So it came to pass—to bring us up to date—that in the summer of '73, before I took up my post at Dillington, Denis had invited Ann, me and the children to accompany him to Athens, where I was to teach drama (what else?) at the Consortium's Greek Summer School.

This made our move from Brum to the South West very much easier. As the accommodation in Somerset would be rent free, we did not have to worry about how quickly our Birmingham house sold (a good job, as the sale took eighteen months). So all we had to do was to drive to Heathrow, park the newly-repaired car and get on a plane. And it proved to be an idyllic holiday, the beginning of my family's lifelong love affair with Greece. Even the teaching—with the students presenting their Greek drama extracts on stage at Epidaurus, and engaging in Socratic dialogue in the shadow of the Acropolis—was wonderfully enriching. As on subsequent summers, staff and students stayed together in the Hotel Akademos in Athens for the length of the Summer School before relaxing into long self-indulgent days cruising around the Greek islands.

All of which explains the euphoric mood when on September 1st the Picks' family jalopy, released from its convalescence in the airport car park, drew up outside their newly rented house in Ilminster. This is a critical moment, so let us pause, pan out and take a long shot. Look, the Pick family is disembarking, sandy and sun-tanned from their weeks of Hellenic frolic, with their T shirts, straw donkeys and beribboned sun hats cutting an unexpectedly colourful dash in the monochrome of the town's main street. Are the passers-by smiling or pursing their lips at this unseemly spectacle? It is too early to say. For now the keys that the Picks have been sent open the front door first time and they troop inside. They find that someone has thoughtfully put basic provisions in the fridge, and has left a note on the hall table welcoming them to Somerset. They had not been used to that kind of treatment.

* * *

The house suited us very well, and it turned out to be a well-disguised blessing that we were forced to live for a while in the local community, and get to know some of the local customs before we decamped to our newly-enlarged home at Dillington and, as it were, pulled up the drawbridge. Ilminster itself contained a number of surprises, not the least of which was the annual Ilminister Carnival, which erupted almost as soon as we arrived. Until then, following attendance at a number of depressing gatherings in my youth, I had understandably fallen into the habit of confusing carnivals with funeral processions. In Retford any use of the term 'Carnival' brought to mind grey rain-sodden gloom. A Carnival involved watching a troupe of surly infants trudging alongside a farm cart shrouded in damp bunting with a 'May Queen' or similar forlornly draped athwart its bows.

But the Ilminster Carnival procession was utterly different. Professional in its execution, its thirty or so colourful floats punctuated with marching bands wound noisily round the town's streets, followed by a sparkling entourage of vividly-dressed pantomime characters—including the local policeman dancing about in glam drag waggling his truncheon suggestively at the salivating crowds. If it were not such an alien concept to Britishers, one might have said that during carnival, Ilminster was *en fête*.

On weekdays Ann learned the ins and outs of local shopping, Martyn and Cath started their new schools and each morning I made my way up from our temporary Ilminster home to Dillington, where members of staff were enjoying what was to be their last collective Summer holiday. I met my deputy, the pleasantly-disposed Bruce Dick, an under-gardener, two of the cooks, various chambermaids and cleaners, the two secretaries, as well as the dreaded Bursar who had hitherto been responsible for keeping the staff in their proper place 'below stairs'. She haughtily announced that she was going to continue to do that. Because of this, and her other intransigences, in due course I sacked her. I then announced to a staff meeting that from that time on, the Centre would be open every day except Christmas Day, that we should be serving a much wider range of people, and that we were going thereafter to treat all types of visitor in the same manner.

Some parts of this new policy proved easy to implement. It was for example a simple matter to abandon the practice of having a 'high table' in the dining room at which previous Wardens had presided. Less easy was shedding the way in which Dillington had traditionally kowtowed to favoured coteries by giving over its premises for their exclusive use (and moreover at specially reduced rates). I caused an early rumpus when I refused to allow a famous Somerset Regiment to continue to book their annual reunion dinner at Dillington (with full military paraphernalia and mess bars) on what was a publicly-funded teaching weekend. I could deal with the outraged phone calls from furious colonels, but I was uncertain what the response of the County authorities might be to this new radical thinking. They might after all have relations in the ranks! So I was relieved when I received their somewhat incredulous congratulations; 'Start as you mean to go on John, eh what?'

Meanwhile Bruce and I got on with planning the Spring syllabus, complemented by a broader range of artistes in the theatre programme—Janet Baker, Alan Aykbourn's Scarborough Company, Peter Pears, Robin Hall and Jimmy McGregor, the Burslam Puppets—new shows in the gallery and some innovative one-day courses—car maintenance with the RAC, Chinese cookery with Kenneth Lo, cleaning oil paintings with Ken Gribble. Hardest to expand was the residential course programme. The well-established courses each had their own coterie of followers and it would have been churlish and counter-productive to cancel them all outright, so we interleaved the most interesting ones with new attractions such as 'Ghosts of The South West' (for which I recruited my old university friend, David Fontana, who had developed an interest in the supernatural), one on 'Gardening' (led by Cyril Fletcher and Bob White, who were at that time fronting the ITV Gardening Show) one on 'Elizabethan England' led by Bristol University staff, and (with my erstwhile Birmingham colleague, John Coultas, now Somerset's Drama Adviser) acting courses aimed directly at young adults. The new enlarged programmes demanded that our recruitment net be cast wider. So we raised the numbers on our mailing list, expended a lot of energy on getting into the newspapers and on to the telly, accepted any invitation to talk to anybody anywhere and in general made a lot more noise about what we were doing. And, by and large, it worked. The numbers gratifyingly rose. In time, even a few sceptical staff members were won over.

My new post did not however seem to involve much teaching. For half of the time it consisted of planning, and for the other half of greeting, and ensuring the welfare of artists, lecturers, demonstrators and some of the forty-five thousand members of the general public who were now coming annually to Dillington. I became more practised in my welcoming speeches, getting the required laughs ('This is Dillington and you're welcome to it') and including just enough of the place's history to interest the majority without alienating the minority who already knew more about Lord North and the Cameron family than I did. And Bruce and I became increasingly ambitious in our planning, for example housing an edition of the BBC's *Face the Music* for which Bruce, a knowledgeable music lover, was asked to join the regular broadcasting panel and, embarrassingly, easily outscored the professionals. On Bank Holidays we opened up for a 'Dillington Day' with sideshows and free-fall parachute displays in the grounds, and 'tours of Dillington House' undertaken by the Director. The National Theatre brought down their production of *Romeo and Juliet,* with the irrepressible Beryl Reid playing the nurse (their specialist stage crew spent two days arranging set and lighting only to have us discover when the curtain finally rose that it was all being played in black curtains). We staged a *Son et Lumière* on the lawns at the rear of the house, narrated by an ailing but courteous Sir Michael Redgrave. We had the *Dolmetsch Family* in residence and, prompted by the ubiquitous Denis Donegan, promoted a US Summer School, which was not only profitable but highly enjoyable, as the American visitors happily accommodated themselves to the mystic vibes of nearby Glastonbury as well as the more tangible delights of Somerset scrumpy.

It was an extraordinary time. Enough of Dillington's former glamour attached itself to its new Director for him to be invited to act as a local nabob, opening fêtes, sprouting at speech days, crowning May Queens, speaking to local societies and so forth. And my hitherto unrecognised talents as an after-dinner/ladies-luncheon-club sort of speaker were, surprisingly, recognised by Cyril Fletcher who enrolled me alongside the likes of Michael Parkinson, Harry Wheatcroft and David Jacobs in his *Associated Speakers* agency—though at a much lower fee. Speaking gigs of course had to be accommodated within the Dillington timetable, as did my teaching with the US Consortium—though, truth to tell, I still felt myself to be underemployed.

This I had not expected. Yet, when not engaged in programme planning, or smilingly welcoming visitors, I really had too little to do. This feeling was strongest during the day when the Director's House was often empty, the children either being at school or cavorting with their friends in the grounds, while Ann had taken a job teaching in the County's Adult Literacy Programme. So I elected to fill up my hours firstly by enrolling for a part-time MA with Birmingham University, and then by joining up with our new Ilminster friends, Malcolm and Sonya Young, to present a series of three-handed stage shows under our chosen banner of *Menander Productions.* Malcolm and Sonya were well-known performers—Malcolm had spent several years in *Crossroads* and in tribute to this feat their marital bed rested on piles of discarded scripts—and it was no doubt their reputation which got us a remarkable number of bookings, ranging from an appearance in the Dartington Festival to a short US tour.

In the day-to-day operation of the college there was of course no shortage of comic material. Such as the time the staff discovered a wooden leg had been left under the bed in one of the rooms. They were used to finding various items of underwear hurriedly stashed out of sight, but a *wooden leg* . . . ? How would he or she explain its loss to their significant other? Why hadn't we noticed its owner hopping dejectedly out to the car park? Did he or she carry a *spare*? And then there was the morning when some of the students appeared to have turned blue in the night, which turned out to have been caused by an over-zealous staff member marking a line around the students' baths to show the depth of water the government recommended during Mr Heath's 'Three-Day Week'. She had unfortunately used soluble ink. Finally there was the night when after his theatre performance I passed the time playing table tennis with Richard Stilgoe, who was waiting for his phone to ring to say that his wife had given birth. But the hoped-for call didn't come, and so about 4 a.m., we jacked it in. A fortnight later Richard wrote to say that the new baby *still* hadn't arrived, adding mordantly, 'I think she must be a different species.'

In retrospect Dillington was like taking an extended and luxurious sabbatical, before returning to the rigours of real work. In our different ways we were all discovering and reinventing ouselves. It was at Dillington that Martyn had his first cine-camera, and there that Cath gave us our first glimpse of her literary and performance skills. After brief flirtation with running the Dillington gallery, Ann turned to working with Romany groups for the Somerset Adult Literacy Services, so beginning a new phase in her career. As for me, I developed my growing interest in arts administration, first through my work with the regional arts association, South West Arts, and second (having finished my MA) through the enquiries I was making in preparation for my doctoral thesis. It was a contact I made while doing this who, out of the blue, suggested one day that I should apply for a newly-advertised university post for which I would, apparently, be eminently suitable. I hadn't seen the job and hadn't therefore considered applying. A day or so later, somebody else phoned and suggested exactly the same thing, so this time I took the hint.

10

London

WE CAN THIS TIME dispense with all that repetitive stuff about interviews, house moves, cupidity of builders and so on, and cut to the chase. As things turned out, our time in London became the defining period of our lives, and incidentally saw the rise and decline of my career. From the start Ann and I felt at home, and soon convinced ourselves that although we had until then publicly carried the flag for the provinces, secretly we had always aspired to be citizens of the great wen. Indeed long afterwards, when we had left it all behind us and no longer even worked in the capital, we did not describe ourselves as being inhabitants of Sutton or Eastbourne, but rather as retired Londoners. We spent only fifteen years actually living there, but the metropolis nevertheless dominated and defined the second half of our lives.

The autumn of 1976 saw us rattling about in a spacious old North London house which extended over nine stories—if you included the small subterranean dungeon we grandly termed the 'wine cellar'. It allowed us to have discrete rooms for Cath and Martyn (in which, we later learned, their friends sometimes enjoyed extended hospitality) and a spare room for Denis, with a wardrobe in which he was able to leave his 'English' clothes. From there I set out each weekday to my new post at City University, while Martyn and Cath were able to walk round the corner to their new London school. Ann, waiting to apply for a place on an MSc (Social Science) course at LSE, took a part-time job as a social statistics interviewer and buzzed off each evening in her Mini to ask householders in the East End how often they had sex or which was their favourite opera. It never occurred to either of us that this could, one way and another, have been a dangerous undertaking.

The house was in Minster Road in West Hampstead, a neighbourhood set within the dishevelled suburbia that lies between Brent Cross Shopping Centre, the greenery of Hampstead and the Irish drinking houses of Cricklewood—in some of which collections were still being taken for 'our boys' in the IRA. A street or two away from us lay a tumbledown row of old shops and wheezy boozers, which perfectly exemplified the cosmopolitan character of the neighbourhood. At the Northern end of this row the Alliance pub abutted an aromatic Greek deli where on warm summer's evenings the proprietor and his family would gather on the roof and play balalaika music on their crackling radio, punctuating the recital with sudden bursts of what may have been a chorus from a Greek folk song, but which sounded more like an insurrectionist call to arms. On the other side of the pub was a microwave shop run by a loaf-faced Irish comedian who was destined, for reasons I shall later explain, to play a part in my life.

It was all a world away from Somerset, and though Ann and I revelled in this grimy, litter-strewn but non-judgemental environment, and our friends were delighted to be able to doss down in the smoke for nothing ("But we *must* take you out to dinner, we *insist*") Cath and Martyn did not immediately take to their new life. And though they later accommodated well to its apparently casual but highly-strung ethos, Hampstead Comprehensive at first appeared to be very different from the ordered world of Ilminster Middle School. In Hampstead, staff and students were on aggressively first name terms, and amongst the pupils Jews, Muslims, Buddhists and Born-again

Christians took their places among the freethinking offspring of the Hampstead intelligentsia. Yet however offbeat it may have appeared, from that school flowed an impressive stream of writers, musicians, television producers, artists and the like (including our own talented progeny). In later years we became used to hearing Martyn or Cath casually say, as the image of some new personality appeared on the telly or in the newspapers, 'Oh, they were at school with me.'

The inter-denominational, multi-cultural mélange that London had become was clearly evident as I drove each day to work, past churches of God the Prophecy, the blinding gold dome of the Regent's Park Mosque and the classical pillars of London's Grand Masonic Temple. (Those who know London well may be surprised that I took such a circuitous route to the university campus, but at the time the IRA were thought to be intent on blowing up the City—there were various roadblocks barring entry to it and my convoluted route avoided them.) After that, with just a brief glimpse of the lowering skyscrapers of the newly-built Barbican, I would turn into Islington and creep through Finsbury Square, singing tunelessly:

> Up and down the City Road,
> In and out of the Eagle,
> That's the way the money goes,
> Pop goes the weasel!

By then no smoothing irons were pawned in the vicinity, and although the Eagle was still there, few people seemed either to go in or out of it. It lay defeated, like the other pubs scattered around the neighbourhood, between modern office blocks and the few terraced houses which had escaped the scavenging maw of the inner city re-developers.

Each day, after arriving at my office (with 'Director of Arts Administration Studies' forbiddingly stencilled on the door) I would read my mail—if I had any—then spend a little time catching up on the University gossip with Joyce Morgan, my knowledgeable secretary, before finally turning to the major questions of the hour. In the early days the most important question was who I was to lunch with, and what my tactics were to be. City was essentially a commuter university. Few of the staff lived in central London. Mornings and late afternoons were for the majority spent jammed in tubes or commuter trains, leaving all the important business to be transacted over lunchtime. On some days I took a long lunch with my new university colleagues, who would take the opportunity scornfully to deride the secretiveness and illogicality of the Arts Council of Great Britain. However, as the courses in Arts Administration were at that time still partly funded by that same Council, on other days I took a less libidinous luncheon with senior ACGB officers, who in turn deeply deplored the arcane illogicality of City University regulations. All of which pointed to the fact that any problems with the courses in Arts Administration could be characterised in terms of academic bureaucracy versus professional practice. So— no change there then.

From the start I set out to make Arts Administration a proper university subject, with its own history, a full international dimension, and its own language and method of inquiry. They were absurdly ambitious goals and, inevitably, I failed to reach them. However, in the short term, so far as external trappings were concerned, I seemed to enjoy some success. After a few years of backstairs conniving, I had been appointed the world's first Professor of Arts Management and was Head of the new Department of Arts Policy and Management, offering a range of master's degrees in the subject. The burgeoning APM Department was housed in a sumptuous new suite in the Barbican comprising staff offices, resource centre and teaching rooms, all strategically sited above the offices of the LSO and the RSC.

Intriguingly, valued at cost per square yard, the new APM Department occupied what was the most expensive university space in the UK. Equally surprising however was the fact that a generous external body, the Mercers' Company in the City of London, was paying the ground rent. This meant that the new Department of Arts Policy and Management was, on paper, highly profitable—as our fee income exceeded our remaining outgoings. So DAPM, without its academic standards being scrutinised at all, immediately moved near the top of the Thatcher

Government's 'cost-efficiency rankings' of university departments—which absurdity in turn led to me being invited to a Reception for Thrusting Young Turks at Number 10—the one and only time I met the lady. Nothing to report there. We stood about madly smirking, waiting for our senses to be bludgeoned to pulp by our steely-eyed hostess. It was like being a crowd extra in a satirical exposé of rampant capitalism.

I could pretend that this sudden elevation to the rank of Turkish Thruster was part of a Machiavellian scheme to gain entry to the Establishment, but it would be a lie. As the reader may already suspect, I had neither the wish nor the mindset to join the Establishment. My translation to Thruster status had come about by a mixture of bad luck and happenstance. I had been peripherally involved in negotiations between City University and the notional 'Gresham College', which had been founded in 1597 by Queen Elizabeth Ist's Chancellor Sir Thomas Gresham, and which was in the throes of being re-established by the Mercers' Company. So the Mercers, who were very rich, were temporarily willing to fund my department against the possibility that it might one day be a constituent part of a revived College. A further gesture by the Gresham Council had rather surprisingly been to appoint me to one of the College's ancient chairs, which involved giving five public lectures a year for what was a very handsome reward. All of which meant that for a brief period in the early eighties I was City University's Professor of Arts Management *and* Gresham Professor of Rhetoric.

It was revealing to see the differences these important-sounding titles made to the respect I was accorded. My students for example, who were bright and street-wise, on the whole treated me with rather *less* deference than when I had been plain John Pick. They were more eager than they had been to lock horns with me both over my general beliefs and, more irritatingly, over matters of detail. I found that now, even at the interview stage, prospective students would go to the trouble of bringing in a book or a paper of mine in order to highlight what they perceived as erroneous—so the interview became less about whether they should be admitted to read for a higher degree than about my suitability to teach them.

But in the wider academic world things were different. Doors of which I had no previous knowledge now swung invitingly open. I was invited to pontificate on radio and on television, to write newspaper articles, to discourse learnedly at other universities and to take a central part in that mutually-congratulatory activity which is such a staple of modern university life—the academic conference.

I cannot recall when I completed my PhD, but then the fact that I became (the wrong kind of) doctor did not make any difference to the lack of respect I was accorded. Friends and enemies alike began to use the term 'Doctor' sarcastically, as a means of drawing attention to the absurdity of it all.

However, in the perusal of my leisure pastimes—for example talking to Rotarians and Ladies' Luncheon Clubs for *Associated Speakers*—my new titles were of absolutely no use. Those audiences were not impressed by letters before or after the speaker's name. What they required was an audible talk with a certain amount of name-dropping, two or three mildly risqué jokes (though with some ladies' clubs, I discovered that risqué was simply not rude enough) and a morsel of advice to chew upon—all flavoured with self-deprecating personal anecdotes as appropriate. Those eminent Associated Speakers who were regularly on the telly or in films (Esther Ransom, say, or Robert Morley) didn't need the name dropping, being sufficient names unto themselves. But unknowns like me who had no hope of interesting audiences in their life stories had to deploy their dog-eared pack of jokes and then drag in, often at right angles to the subject, their few encounters with the famous. That is of course one reason why Mr Morley and Ms. Ransom were paid scalper's money to speak, but non-entities like me were not.

Though my dual life as a university don and Associated Speaker did provide me with one luminous insight into the differences in pay different kinds of orators attract. One day Dabber Davies, in his office role as a front man for *Associated Speakers,* rang to say that the agency had a job which was right in my line. The organisers of some international gathering or other were prepared to offer a fee of £5,000 (I think it was) plus first class travel and hotel for a high-profile engagement, if the speaker could deliver a 'stimulating' keynote lecture. Unfortunately I had to decline as I had already agreed on that date to speak, for expenses only, at an international conference in Vienna. I could not break my word to the organisers—academics' honour, and all that! But out of interest I asked Dabber the location of this fabled gathering at which the organisers would pay such a humongous sum for what, in all honesty, sounded like a walk in the park. 'Let me look at their bumph,' he murmured down the phone, 'Ah yes . . . .' (and you can guess what's coming). 'Vienna.'

My titles were of even less use to me in my other spare-time hobby, in which I had spasmodically indulged for some years but which, now I lived in London, I took up with renewed gusto. This was acting as Chairman for various professional Music Hall companies—among them the Players Theatre and its various offshoots, Rita Triesman's Gaslight Gaiety Company, and the Bee and Bustle Show which was run by the microwave-shop-owning loaf-faced Irish comedian, Eamonn Jones. The role of Chairman was a coveted one, not least because it allowed you to drink on stage, but also because you were permitted—indeed expected—to mock the medium in which you were performing—which brought together the two warring sides of my character which John Allen had so kindly drawn attention to.

I achieved this artistic duality by means of an affected distaste for the milieu in which I was being forced to operate. After a flamboyant entry in full Victorian fig, I would raise up my gavel and sonorously announce; 'Ladies and *Gentle*men, Good *Evening*!' (await audience response). 'Tonight we are proud to present *forty-five minutes* of sparkling entertainment' (droop shoulders, adopt tone of world-weary resignation) 'spread out over the next friggin' two and a half hours . . . .' (recovering) But our agents, Burke and Hare, have left *no stone unturned* in their search for talent. Tonight you will be amazed by our speciality act, Conan the Human Cannonball. You don't often see an act of his calibre. Also appearing is . . . . (etc. etc.).' Corny stuff of course, but if solemnly delivered with a slightly desperate, easily-punctured stage dignity, it helped create a framework of pastiche Victoriana within which speciality artistes (who were often very good indeed) could flourish. When I recall the music-hall work of such as Chris Beeching, Bernard Cribbins, Peter John, Doreen Hermitage, Johnny Dennis, Peter Charlton, Barry Cryer, Rita Triesman and that doyen of chairmen, the incomparable Michael Kilgarriff I am recalling genius—of a particular kind, but genius nonetheless.

I achieved some small notoriety within that restricted world as a Chairman, though the general run of my university students, I like to think, had little notion that I indulged this secret vice. However as time went on various graduate students, by then engaged in running their own arts centre or theatre, would be surprised to find that a company that they had booked sight-unseen contained their former university mentor masquerading as a music-hall artiste—but when that situation arose we hid our mutual embarrassment, behaved like grown-ups, and just got on with it. Only once did an ex-student express a strong opinion about my performance. The lady, who had as usual been surprised to see her sometime professor togged up like a Victorian dandy, and exchanging lewd insults with a drunken audience, rushed bright-eyed into my dressing room after the show and gushingly told me that I was superb and should do this kind of thing full time!—as everybody agreed I wasn't much good as a university don.

The only occasion, so far as I can recall, that students-in-training actually paid to watch a music-hall performance of mine was at the King's Head in Islington when I was coming to the end of quite a long residency, during which I had slyly congratulated myself that my students, pursuing their studies only a mile or so away, had remained in ignorance of my evening job. I had enjoyed the engagement as a pleasantly relaxed antidote to the rigours of the university day—until that fateful performance when the magic curtain was crudely torn aside and it all came tumbling down.

You should know that at the beginning of the second half of cod music halls there is a 'Chairman's Spot' ('No madam, not a medical condition!'). With the house lights half up, the Chairman chats to members of the audience, celebrating their birthdays and anniversaries, asking them where they come from, what they do for a living and so on, hopefully topping their answers with apparently impromptu (but in practice well-rehearsed) comedy put-downs. On this occasion I shaded my eyes and peered out at a couple sitting huddled in shadow at the back of the small theatre. 'I can see what you're doing now,' I quipped leadenly, 'but what were you doing during the hours of daylight?' 'Finishing your essay, professor!' came the reply. This brusque mention of my day job shattered the fragile illusion that we had all time-travelled together back to the nineteenth century. The audience withdrew their suspension of disbelief not only from me but from the other performers, and a frost descended upon the proceedings. So, although moon-lighting in illegitimate theatre didn't usually harm my credibility as a professor, mention of my university position in the theatre certainly destroyed my stage act.

Let me briefly add one other music-hall story. I had been asked to chair a music hall composed of Players Theatre stalwarts in Brussels which, I was told, would attract an English-speaking audience. On the opening night, in my accustomed sardonic style, I swung into action, only to feel the audience's sympathy ebbing from me. The rest of the bill they loved, but me they did not. After the show I was having a disconsolate drink when I was approached by a smiling man. 'I enjoyed the show very much.' 'Thank you, but I'm afraid that I wasn't very good.' 'No, you were not.' 'Why? What was the reason?' 'Because, you were not like the man on the television.' 'Of *course!* The music hall they knew well was *The Good Old Days,* endlessly repeated across Europe! The following night and for the rest of the week I offered a carbon copy of Leonard Sachs' dictionary-swallowing style, 'Indefatigably and ineluctably *incandescent* . . . . Mechanical, lifeless, and stylistically bogus. It went like a bomb, of course.

But enough of this petty self-indulgence. Let me widen my focus and describe the most consummate lecture performance I ever witnessed. Quite early in my time at City I had instituted, in honour of Lord Alport (a staunch supporter of my subject), the 'Alport Lecture in Arts Administration'. This annual event was widely publicised, well-attended and, I like to think, added a little lustre to the speaker's reputation. In the early days of Mrs Thatcher's reign, when her attitudes to the arts seemed a touch phillistine, we invited the Tory Arts Minister, Norman St John Stevas (who in spite of being a member of the Iron Lady's cabinet, had retained the confidence of most of the arts world) to deliver the Alport Lecture and clarify his and Mrs T's position. On the appointed evening a full house had assembled and I stood waiting on the steps in front of the university's main entrance in order to welcome him, certain that nothing could now go wrong.

The first intimation that I was mistaken in this belief was when a furtive-looking Civil Service type in a long raincoat, who had been standing alone and palely loitering on the far side of the steps, sidled up to tell me that Mr St John Stevas might possibly be a little late this evening. This was quite unlike the Minister, who had a reputation for strict punctuality. Then I noticed that the Civil Servant chap was also carrying a folder of typed A4 sheets which, I surmised, might be the lecture that St John Stevas was going to deliver that evening. That again was quite unlike him. The Minister was not usually a man who read verbatim from scripts. I had myself on occasion felt the lash of his slightly waspish tongue, and he had a reputation in the House as an excellent impromptu speaker.

I hopped from foot to foot for a quarter of an hour or so before speeding back to the lecture theatre to announce that the Minister had been delayed (I knew not why) but that the lecture was certainly going ahead. Then I scuttled back to my vigil. A few of the assembled audience, having given up on the evening, stumped huffily past me down the steps and out into the night. The Speaker was now half an hour late. One of my colleagues, coming outside to enjoy a quick fag, offered to go back in and organise a sing-song to keep the remaining crowd amused. But just then, at long last, the Ministerial car nosed silently into the square, and St John Stevas slithered out. He tip-tapped fastidiously up the steps towards me, wordlessly taking the folder from the Civil Service Spook (who then, as befitted his calling, disappeared into the night), brushed aside my polite suggestion that he might like to visit the washroom, strode into the lecture room, patted away the spatter of ironic clapping, and sat down. I introduced him. He then with considerable panache delivered the lecture he had been given, and sat down to well-deserved applause.

Though somehow the lecture was not quite what I had expected nor, I confess, hoped for. It had consisted of a *defence* of the candle-end savings in the arts then being forced through by Mrs Thatcher. However, in the question-and-answer session he opened up rather more, and in the ensuing reception answered the students' questions clearly and listened courteously to the gripes of the professional administrators who had attended the lecture. Then, as things were winding down, he motioned me to go into a huddle with him away from the milling throng, and murmured that he was sorry to have been late but—as I would in any case read all about it in the papers the following morning—he wanted to tell me the reason. At six thirty that evening the Prime Minister had called him in and abruptly sacked him from his Ministerial post. Taken aback, I first expressed my admiration for the professional way he had delivered his talk. Then, taking advantage of our momentary intimacy, I asked him whether that evening's lecture had, as I now suspected, been foisted on him by the mackintoshed Civil Service apparatchik—the whispering man on the steps? It was a step too far. St John Stevas was a politician to his beautifully-manicured fingertips. In the wincing phraseology of the red-top press, he smiled graciously, made an excuse and left.

Mention of these extra-mural excitements is not of course to belittle the importance of the daily routine of full-time university teaching, which was at the heart of my work. For it should never be forgotten, in spite of the modern trend for universities exclusively to focus on government-funded 'research', that the main function of any university is to teach. In arts subjects such teaching used to take place in 'tutorials' when one student (or

a small group) refines opinions under the supervision
of a tutor. Then there was the seminar, in which staff
and students work together to examine one tightly
focussed topic. A third means was the lecture. Because
the realignment of funds now makes funding staff for
tutorials and even seminars a problem, the lecture (aided
and abetted by the pervasive use of Google) performs a
pivotal role in modern university teaching.

Unfortunately many university lectures are appalling,
sometimes by virtue of their content, but more frequently because they are very badly delivered. After a
lifetime spent trying to practise it, I have come to
believe there are four simple rules for good lecturing.
The first is one which my technically-minded colleagues
at City University (who believed that a lecture was just
a means of transmitting information) never seemed to
comprehend. It is that *teaching and learning do not take
place simultaneously*—the lecture itself is only one part
of a teaching sequence, and students must not only
prepare for it but must be given the means further to
explore the lecture's subject after its conclusion. The
second rule for lecturers is *not to fill the allotted time with
a continuous ribbon of verbiage*, expecting your listeners
fully to concentrate *and* to make notes throughout its
undifferentiated length. At the very least the lecturer
should vary his or her pitch and tone, and there must be
clear pauses, so the listeners can re-order their thoughts
before the speaker moves on. Personally I also found it
useful to distribute printed handouts in advance. These
not only listed the main points to be covered in the
lecture, but usually contained relevant passages which
illustrated and expanded them.

The third rule is that none of the foregoing is wholly
effective unless at the very beginning the lecturer has
*properly 'set up' the relationship between speaker and
audience*. This particularly refers to the moments when
the speaker first meets his listeners. A lecture's meaning
goes for nothing if someone creeps anonymously into
the room, puts on a pair of spectacles and starts reading
from a script—as I am told used to be the case at Oxbridge, when clerks would sometimes be deputed to read
the dons' lectures. In such a case students might just as

well read it 'on line' (which, like 'distance learning', is a poor substitute for live teaching). A good lecturer must first establish eye contact with listeners, and then use that subliminally-effective 'travelling eye' throughout—a technique employed by a host of effective public speakers ranging from Jo Brand to Justin Welby to Bill Clinton.

Alas, I wish I could lay claim to have followed my own rules and always to have offered my students fully-considered lectures and a full learning experience. But I too often fell short of the mark, even with the fourth rule of good lecturing, which is that *the lecturer should finish strongly, preferably by posing a question.* Sometimes as the lecture period was running out I found I had not really got enough material. Then I would take refuge in the 'bogus summary' technique to pad out time, knowing I had nothing new to offer. I would try to retain the listeners' attention by saying something like, 'In conclusion, I have just four points to make.' Then I would realise too late that I had set myself an impossible challenge. Flustered, I would reiterate, with different phrasing, three points I had already made and then finish by declaiming, with broad gestures and furrowed brow, a platitude of such mind-numbing banality that it simultaneously anaesthetised and insulted the intelligence of my listeners. 'And fourthly,' I would thunder, staring wildly out at the apprehensive audience, 'I want you always to remember—a stitch in time saves nine!' (or some other cloddish lump of parish-pump wisdom). Deeply embarrassed, the students would gather up their belongings and, avoiding eye contact even with each other, silently shuffle out. Oh shameful memory! Oh *mea* ever so *culpa*! Although, on the plus side, they do say that confession is good for the soul . . . .

I do not want however to give the impression that either I or my colleagues were over-much concerned with style. It was the substance which (mostly) concerned us—the ever-fluctuating tension between artists, critics and audiences and the ways in which the law, technical change and government policy continuously bore upon it. But, unlike established university departments, we were developing our subject area from scratch. We had no body of work to fall back on. Neither the study of Arts Policy nor of Arts Management had agreed boundaries, a fully-realised history or, significantly, a properly attested body of publication. It was true that libraries contained shelves-full of histories of art, histories of music, histories of drama, lavishly-illustrated accounts of various cultural epochs and thousand upon thousand of 'management' texts (university libraries, and indeed universities them-selves, by then contained a veritable infestation of *those*), and nearly every book of every kind seemed to toss off generalities about the way the 'the arts' were created, and about the way 'the arts' reflected a 'society'. Yet such assertions were never underpinned by serious research, nor subjected to even the most primitive linguistic analysis. So, in summary, we had to begin from nothing the all-important task of deciding upon the terminology, the methods of enquiry, and the bits and pieces of existing scholarship and publication that could be called into the service of this new subject area.

For us, there was a further problem. In its early days the Department perforce worked closely with the Arts Council, which had its own publication programme con-sisting of cultural surveys, annual reports and the like. These contained a series of propagandist slogans about the nature of the arts. And sadly those who mouthed them most often—in this case the senior officers of the Council—had come to believe in them as self-evident truths. But such slogans were, as often as not, wholly spurious. Some were deliberately misleading; the much-quoted 'arm's length principle', for example, was neither a scientific nor a legal *principle* but simply a rule of etiquette which the Council used to shield itself from impertinent suggestions that they should be accountable, either to prying Government Ministers or, worse, to the general public. Other ACGB axioms of the time, such as 'The Best for the Most' or 'Few but Roses', were fortune-cookie mottoes dressed up as profound political axioms. Yet officers of the Council seemed to believe that in the new Department I and my colleagues ought, like evangelists for some arcane religion, to ignore all the available evidence and instead impregnate our students' minds with these mystical, unexamined commandments.

By far the most corrosive element in all this was the Arts Council's underlying belief that 'the arts' had to be defined, not by any inherent meanings they may possess, but by whether or not they were state-subsidised. The giving of state aid was the ACGB's 'Seal of Approval'. The Council thus saw itself as sitting in Olympian judgement, permitting certain works to be funded and to bear the title of art, while condemning others to be cast into the outer darkness. 'At the Arts Council,' wrote one ACGB apologist, 'We pondered long and hard over whether Jazz was an art or not . . . .' That way of defining 'the arts'—as an epithet capable of being bestowed by a committee sitting in Piccadilly—is rendered nonsensical by the numbers of poets, orchestral musicians, craftsmen, visual artists, novelists, pop singers, broadcasters, playwrights, architects, singers, showmen, sculptors and directors who throughout history have been accorded the title of artist by critics and the general public but who have not, ever, received Arts Council support. For it cannot be too often repeated that it is the readers, listeners and the general public that finally determines what constitutes 'the arts'. A picture is just paint on canvas until it has been viewed; a poem does not exist until it has readers. And no authority on earth has the right to tell the public in advance what they *ought* to think of a creative work.

Yet the officers (of those days) went on believing in their unique ability to make critical judgements which were inherently *superior* to those of the general public. Popular taste was invariably conflated with lowbrow taste. I recall for instance a senior member of the Council's Art Department, in the course of a general discussion at the ACGB's headquarters, suddenly spitting out, with real venom, 'Oh—*sod* the public!' And, as if just sodding the public were not enough, the Arts Council developed another method of ignoring the public's voice—grant-aiding chosen artists or arts organisations to work on an 'arts project', in *advance* of its completion. After that the privileged ones were well advised, if desirous of staying on the ACGB payroll, to produce 'art' that was obscure and 'difficult'. So when the public was eventually brought in to the equation and failed to respond to the work, or found it embarrassing or just plain silly, the Arts Council could loftily take pride in saying that was because it was 'cutting edge', and 'ahead of public taste'. Yet anybody who has followed the vicissitudes of the subsidised arts world over the last forty or fifty years will be able to compile their own lists of 'cutting edge' visual artists, composers, lunatics, lovers and poets that the Council has in this fashion falsely elevated to the status of 'artist'. On the other hand they might also ponder the fact that over the same period it is difficult to think of one real and undeniable work of art that the Arts Council's patronage has produced.

I did not at first realise the lengths the Subsidised Arts World was prepared to go to in order to protect its own interests, but that was to change with the strange Case of the Sensitive Censor. Because of my modest reputation as a prick in the Arts Council's side, I had been invited, alongside other dissidents, to take part in the making of a BBC *Panorama* programme on arts funding. I gave a longish interview for it, and wrote and delivered several links. The programme was duly completed, and flagged up in the *Radio Times* for its scheduled Monday evening showing. However, at the last minute, it was cancelled without explanation. A dusty old compilation about the long-ago miner's strike was dragged out of the vaults and shown in its stead. Shortly afterwards I learned, to my mounting alarm, that the programme's able young Director had been summarily dismissed from his post. Eventually it emerged that the mastermind behind all this manipulative villainy was the sinister William Rees-Mogg, Deputy Chairman of the BBC Trust, whom Mrs Thatcher had also just appointed Chairman of the Arts Council. The upshot was that the 'arts funding' edition of *Panorama* was banished to Room 101. It has never been shown, and by now it will almost certainly have been erased, Soviet fashion, from the public record.

★ ★ ★

Once they were bedded in, my family prospered in London. Ann gained her M.Sc. at UCL, and soon made her mark on the Social Services. Her first stint was in Westminster, when the head of the Council there, a

Lady Shirley Porter (whose family business was Tesco) was busy 'cleansing' Westminster of rough sleepers by the simple expedient of closing down all the hostels and refuges in the borough that were trying to help them. The lady was also, in homage to the views of her friend Mrs Thatcher, selling off all the rented housing so that the accommodation could be given to its rightful owners, the deserving rich. This was subsequently known as the 'Homes for Votes' scandal, and led to Shirley being dubbed the most corrupt politician in UK history*. Her actions did not endear the lady to her Social Services Department either. Ann and her colleagues took a keen interest in her subsequent harassment and prosecution, and when she was finally brought to book some years later they reunited and held a shamefully vindictive celebration.

The title 'Westminster' perhaps gives a misleading impression. Ann herself pointed out that although her patch did include the House of Commons (and there's plenty to interest a social worker in that establishment!) it also extended to Raymond's Revuebar, situated hard by the Social Services Headquarters off Brewer Street. Indeed Mr Raymond's heavies were of a great deal of use to Social Services, carrying food, washing and medication up to the large number of elderly clients who lived in the upper stories of Soho's tenement blocks. After that Ann's next job was in the London Borough of Brent, which was certainly less glamorous and had its own problems. There she had first to overcome a certain amount of (under-standable) racial prejudice from the largely black population: 'I don' want no white social worker lookin' after me!' But after the murky politics of Westminster, she found in Brent that needs and remedies were much easier to discern, and her bosses and clients very much more straightforward.

Martyn and Cath meanwhile proceeded through Hampstead School, gaining all the necessary exam results and, more importantly, interesting friends. Martyn went

* Lady Porter first lived in Israel. When she eventually set foot back in England she owed the Courts £42m. She claimed to be skint, with 'only £300,000 to my name', but was able eventually to cough up £13,500,000 in partial payment, *and* buy herself a pad in Mayfair for £1.4 million.

almost immediately on to St Martin's College of Art, where he studied film and met his first wife. For a year or two after her school-days Cath immersed herself in theatre, playing in venues as varied as the Cockpit, the Shaw Theatre and the Tricycle; most memorably playing the beautiful but anguished Christine Keeler in Vince Foxall's *Listen, Do You Wanna Know a Secret?* before herself setting off to read film studies at Harrow College of Art. By this time Martyn had married and he and his young wife were spending their first months of wedded life in a small flat which we had fashioned in our Minster Road House. After graduation Cath also began working on TV productions while Martyn, having secured a prestigious year-long BFI grant, started work (in his new East London flat) on *Signature,* the first of his several richly-layered animated films.

Such a blurred canter through those crucial years can only give the vaguest idea of the ups and downs and highs and lows of our family lives. There were occasional tensions of course—deriving as much as anything from the inadequacies of the parents as from any transgressions by our children—but we remained, always, on speaking terms (not invariably the case with highly-strung families) and as often as not our frictions dissolved into laughter. Our children faced challenges— drugs, rock 'n' roll, the tyranny of teenage fashions, the collapse of deference, the pill, Aids—of which we had known nothing. I think our generation was poorly equipped to offer moral or practical guidance to theirs, in this newly permissive but perilous world.

An old-fashioned psychologist might have said our children were left too much to their own devices, but somehow they came through it all, and became the creative, warm and colourful people they are today. And it may be that I am looking back through the rose-tinted spectacles of old age, but family gatherings in retrospect seem to me to be happy rumbustious affairs; wine-charged evenings at the dinner table, enjoying one of Ann's lamb roasts or one of the New York steaks which Denis had brought over (illegally) in his hand luggage, the feasts at Christmas when Ann's sister and the cousins would sometimes join us, the parties of course, and the long evenings at the Shama on Cricklewood Broadway. Then there were the Spring family holidays with my parents from which Martyn and Cath eventually, and understandably, excused themselves, feeling that they had more interesting things to do than shiver in a damp cottage with only car trips through the sodden countryside to look forward to.

More congenial were family visits to London theatres; the excitement of *Evita,* the disappointment of *Cats,* Brook's *A Midsummer Night's Dream, Tamburlaine the Great* at the National, *My Fair Lady,* Nureyev and Fonteyn. In the realms of music and the visual arts however we began to recognise the cultural divides which were beginning to open up between the generations. We occasionally shrank from the works which Martyn and Cath thought significant, as they sometimes pulled back from our wizened cultural icons. Minster Road was testament to this generational battle, its walls covered with an uneasy melange of rude photographs, political murals and abstract art, while the record player alternated between Mozart, Gilbert and Sullivan and the Sex Pistols' *Never Mind the Bollocks.* It was the best of times. It was the worst of times. It was the human menagerie that was London.

★　★　★

This cultural bifurcation had an impact on my own work, and that of my new department. Some of my colleagues stayed cautiously within the art forms they knew well. Others tried to embrace the whole spectrum of all those varied activities, once divided between entertainment and the arts but which were now increasingly bunched under the generic title of 'culture'—gardening, computer games, architectural design, film, TV, pop culture, circus skills, folk music, religious ceremonies, sport, fashion and interior design—to name but a few. This new definition of 'culture' did not involve making value judgements, and concerned itself only with a Gradgrindian accumulation of fact.

There was in addition another and more insidious trend that went hand in glove with the adoption of this new terminology. This was the insistence by the

Thatcher government that the arts should be regarded as nothing more than an *industry*. Art works must no longer be valued for their intrinsic worth but for their *profitability*. This robotic new creed, which absolved its adherents from making any genuine critical judgements at all, was soon endorsed by politicians and bureaucrats of all stripes and, more shamefully, by those many artists and arts managers in Tory Britain who were openly on the make. The Arts Council, wilting before Thatcher's verbal assault, excused its compliance by limply insisting that it was speaking in 'the only language the Government understands'*. Worst of all, the UK universities prostrated themselves before this rampant brutalism. Soon university arts departments such as mine were being swallowed up in horrible new Faculties of 'Cultural Industries' which in turn were quickly eaten up by the all-conquering Departments of Management. Everything in life—truth, art, beauty, love or worship—could now be *managed*. All semblance of liberal education was wiped out by this new Utilitarian advance, together with humane and liberal values in daily life, until at the end civilisation itself collapsed and . . . . But, stop! I must pause, take a deep breath and let my anger cool. A sober

Martyn with a rhino-ceros

and more considered account of the spread of this inhuman dogma which has wrought so much destruction on British life must, together with the unavailing attempts made to counter it, await a later chapter. First I shall describe some of my travel adventures, before I return to this explosive topic in a calmer frame of mind.

---

* But I see I am falling into the common trap of inflating Mrs Thatcher's reputation by blaming her for everything. So let me redress the balance by pointing out that by far the most mean-spirited and destructive book ever written about the arts was penned by Mr Blair's first Culture Secretary. See Chris Smith, *Creative Britain* (Faber, 1999).

11

Travel

THAT HOARY OLD MAXIM, 'It is better to travel well than to arrive' no doubt has some kind of deep metaphysical significance but, taken literally, it is surely nonsense. Travel of any kind must always have an end, a point of arrival, in view. It cannot be an end in itself, unless a traveller who tumbles out of a moon rocket and is left spinning pointlessly in space can be said to be travelling. Nor have I any patience with those parish pump mystics who characterise life itself as a journey, for that too implies purposeful movement, and that you know your intended destination. Yet when and where you might end your life is always—unless, for example, you are facing a firing squad—a matter for speculation. You cannot know what triumphs or tribulations may await you, or where and in what state of grace you may meet the grim reaper. All you can know is that just as you were born somewhere, so you will somewhere and at some time die, and in Hamlet's words enter

> The undiscover'd country, from whose bourn
> No traveller returns;

which may indeed be our common destination, but it offers no guidance about when and how you will enter it.

On a more mundane note, I now view virtually all travel as a tiresome necessity—an uncomfortable and cramped humiliation that must be endured in the hope, at best, of a pain-free arrival at my destination (although I do exempt seaborne craft from these general strictures, and seaports too, which though chaotic by nature are nevertheless places with a human dimension). But I do not care at all for airports or for aircraft. Neither have I any love for trains or railway stations. In all of these environments, static or mobile, human beings seem to me to be reduced to the status of cargo, and are forced to suffer indignities which in other circumstances they would never countenance.

The termini for rail and air travel are particularly depressing. The echoing fastness of a city railway station calls to mind the grim satanic mills of the nineteenth century, while the similarity of airports to crematoria— the acrid tang of air freshener, the piped music, the hushed movement of the automatic walkways—cannot be accidental. When I have walked at night through the hushed passageways of a near-deserted airport, past the taped-off departure lounges and the shrouded service desks, glimpsing uniformed cleaners on their silent machines removing all traces of human habitation and re-scenting the stale air, I can never escape the feeling that I am witnessing hygienic preparations for some secret state-sanctioned holocaust.

In spite of such thoughts, in past times I confess I have—albeit with steadily diminishing pleasure—undertaken quite a lot of travel. There have been business trips, academic conferences (may I be forgiven!), holidaying with Ann and the family, teaching at overseas universities, acting in stage productions and combinations of all of these. Though combining these purposes has its hazards. One Summer term time I was down to speak at a conference in Italy. Ann came with me. Rather than fly straight back to London, as we had a few spare hours and as the sun was shining we thought we would take a day's break in Venice. Nemesis was lurking. We took the tourist boat trip along the Grand Canal and as we were gliding serenely along I suddenly espied Charles Arnold-Baker (the law professor in my London department) standing on the balcony of his Venetian flat. At the same moment he saw me, waved gleefully, and shouted 'Hello, John!' so that the other passengers, together with a number of people on the banks, looked at me enquiringly. Then, using all of his considerable lung power, he bawled at full throttle, '*Breaking Term???*'

The most frequent and most desirable destination for all of us was Greece. I have described our first summer there when we travelled to Athens by air, but subsequently we decided it would be more fun for all of us— Ann and I, Martyn, Cath and the ubiquitous Denis—to drive there in our family car. Denis and I would share the driving. On the first day we would belt across France, skirting Paris, and aim to arrive in Auxerre by evening, where the memory of the first leg of the journey would be erased by a sumptuous fondue. Next morning we passed through the tunnel and, pausing only for meals, eventually driving down through Italy, and ending up at Brindisi. We then (after a light supper) boarded the overnight ferry and disembarked in Greece in time for breakfast (melon and peaches) followed by a leisurely car ride over to Athens, and a triumphant feast of roast lamb. The journey passed like a dream, cost less than travelling by air, and the food was far better than the airlines' rehydrated roadkill. The only time we were less than happy with travelling by car was the year we decided by way of variation to drive back through Yugoslavia. There were only two routes through that country, the pretty coastal road, which meandered pleasantly through the hills, and the other one. We took the other one, the so-called motorway, and were pulled over every few miles by the state cops. Those Soviet capitalists, having clocked our GB plates, issued us with a series of on-the-spot 'fines' (payable in pounds or dollars or, when you'd run out of ready cash, packets of Marlboroughs) for 'traffic violations' of their own invention.

Sometimes it was the hotels rather than the motorway police that operated their own black economy. I knew that in the cheap hotel I habitually used in London there was a thriving trade, run from the front desk, but I was surprised to see the same kind of operation in a tourist hotel in Leningrad (as St Petersburg was then called). But nothing could equal for cold-blooded efficiency the Las Vegas hotel which had a catalogue by the bed detailing the kind of companions one could buy into one's room, and the

practices one might care to indulge in with them. My
pretence of worldly wisdom dropped away. It wasn't
just the blatant commerce which repelled me. I didn't
know what on earth was being offered. I was caught in
the same dilemma as the couple in the well-known
limerick:

> A subaltern out from Khartoum,
> Took a lesbian up to his room,
> > But they argued all night
> > Over who had the right
> To do what, and which way, and to whom.

But it is not seemly to affect innocence. I was of
course fully aware of the meaning of the discreet tap
on the door in certain hotels when one had retired
for the night. I recall one night in Warsaw, after I had
turned in early and had already refused the services
of three heavily-scented ladies, being awakened by a
fourth knock, and upon scrambling out of bed yet
again, being confronted by a smiling youth, with a
Ruby Wax hair-do. 'Look,' I half-shouted, 'I do not
want *any* kind of sex. I have to be up early in the
morning to deliver a lecture, and I want to *sleep*!!' 'I'm
sorry to have disturbed you Dr Pick; I'm coming to
your lecture of course,' said the crestfallen sex worker,
whom I now recognised as a young Cambridge man
of my acquaintance, and who was also giving a paper
at the Conference. 'I've only just got in, but I thought
I'd say hello.'

★   ★   ★

One-off lectures abroad and contributions to
international conferences had of course—as at
Dillington—to be fitted into my schedule. Timing
was often tight and made tighter by having to stick
to commercial airline schedules. The cities which I
visited in this way—Rome, Oslo, Athens, Paris,
Helsinki, Bruges, Maastricht, Berlin etc. etc.—may
sound interesting or even exotic, but my memory
of most of these destinations is a confused *compote*
of airport taxis, snatched meals, obsequious but
hopelessly inaccurate introductions and rows of

puzzled-looking listeners (did they understand English?) acknowledgement of whose polite applause would be followed by a surreptitious glance at my watch to make sure I was in time for the plane home.

I do not know what, if anything, such international sorties achieved, then or now. Certainly in each country there were respectable scholars who could have delivered at least as good a lecture as I did, if not a considerably better one. And I soon formed the opinion that, as nothing was required of most attenders at international conferences save that they deliver a 'paper' (which nobody would read) in attending them any fool could pass for a scholar. I eventually decided that being asked to talk at such moribund *kulturfests* was less a sign of academic distinction than of a sad grubbing for academic notice. After a time I stopped accepting invitations to them altogether.

But not before I had unwittingly caused a minor diplomatic incident. I had accepted John Perlin's invitation to visit Newfoundland and offer training to the province's theatre and arts centre managers. I was to stay with John in his comfortable country house outside St John's, where I enjoyed sumptuous hospitality. I liked working with the managers; they seemed satisfied in turn and even though I felt a little fraudulent (surely there was no need to fly in a foreign 'expert' to teach what were commonplace managerial skills?) I did not demur when John suggested it be repeated annually. On a subsequent visit Ann joined me. We landed, for reasons which now escape me, quite late in the day at St Johns. For once we were intercepted at customs, and I was taken off to be interrogated by what looked and sounded like a young schoolgirl on work experience filling in for the regular staff. Grasping her pen in both hands she went laboriously through the predictable questions. Was I Dr John Pick? Yes. A pause while this information was recorded. Was I employed at the City University, London. Yes, I was. Was I bringing any meat or fresh fruit in to the Country? No, I wasn't. Was I going to pass on currency or bonds? Hell, no. The questioner painstakingly plodded on. Was I bringing a sample or samples into the country? I didn't know that was a requirement . . . . Then after cleverly uncovering the purpose of my visit (by asking me 'What is the purpose of your visit?') she put the question which is asked of every working person wishing to enter that country. Was there any Canadian citizen who could do the work that I was being hired to do? Thinking of the bright young scholars that I had met on my previous visits, and bearing in mind my increasing doubts about the efficacy of these international jollies, I answered with mock modestly, 'Yes, I'm sure there are. Hundreds!' The interview was over. A bare five seconds after I had mouthed these words my young interlocutor was registering a look of barely concealed triumph and was writing 'YES' in big capital letters on her official form.

There were no immediate repercussions and I rejoined Ann, who had been patiently waiting for me in the lobby. However when we arrived at John's house we found that Customs had already been on his phone, explaining that he was now harbouring an illegal immigrant and telling him that for the length of my stay I would have to attend the Police Station each morning at ten and report to the local fuzz. On hearing this I chuckled indulgently and said that such a friendly country as Canada could not possibly pursue such a trivial misunderstanding. I added that as he, a member of the Civil Service, had invited me, my entry into the country could hardly have been more legal! I had no intention of trolling down to the cop shop each morning.

That said, we sat down and tucked into the lobster which had been provided as a treat for the English visitors. (Lobsters are an everyday food in St Johns, being brought ashore by the potful, but as the province lacks deep-freezing facilities by the harbour, they cannot be frozen and packaged for export). My host, worried by the turn events had taken, said he thought I should obey the authorities and turn up the following morning but, foolishly, I continued to make light of it. In the following days the course went well, and in the breaks I even retold the Customs story once or twice for laughs. Not until we were sitting at the airport in readiness for the return journey did I hear more of the matter. Then a keenly-shaven young man carrying a determined clipboard called me over, and told me that as I had broken the terms of my probation (huh?!?) I should not, ever, be allowed into the country again. I tried to take the news calmly, pleased that in his rush to pronounce my banishment he had failed to notice the boxes of fresh lobster we were illegally carrying on board.

My banning was, perhaps, a blessing in disguise as I had earlier fallen foul of another powerful section of Canadian society—the Enforcers of Political Correctness. I had been asked to speak in Vancouver at a 'World Conference' devoted to the question of 'Public Patronage versus Private Philanthropy' in the arts. At one point in my opening talk I was reckless enough to characterise the UK Arts Council's fawning acquiescence to Mrs Thatcher's demands by quoting a well-turned line from a Henry James novel;

> 'He would have raped her, had she not prevented him by her timely compliance.'

I was then intending, as if it were not sufficiently obvious, to point out that you had to reverse the sexes to make sense of the little joke (I was talking, you see, about the UK Arts Council's spineless attitude to the government). But before I could labour the point a woman in the audience, having heard the word 'rape' brazenly uttered by a male person, stood up and said, 'Professor Pick, I think you should apologise to all the women present!' A murmur arose from the audience, which at first I believed to be irritation at the untoward interruption. So I replied, with what I hoped was polished irony, 'On behalf of Henry James, I apologise.' That went down like a cup of cold sick. Afterwards it became clear that the majority feeling was that this preening, sexist Brit had been deservedly put in his place.

At all events, following the airport mishap, I was, perhaps mercifully for all concerned, never allowed back into Canada. Afterwards the Association of Canadian Dons (or some such) wrote to say that it was a disgrace that such a distinguished academic as me (huh?!?) should be excluded from their shores. I had only to say the word and they would inaugurate a high-profile

campaign to reinstate me. But I said not to bother. My
Canadian friends could still visit me in London and
there was in any case a good deal of truth behind my
little pleasantry—there *were* many Canadians who could
undertake training courses at least as well as me. Having
said that, some years later the permanent ban did briefly
rise up to embarrass me. I had been invited by Ruth
Bereson to visit the NY University at Buffalo. A party of
her colleagues and students were driving over the border
to the Shaw Festival in nearby Canada. Though I should
have liked to go, I had to cry off, fearful that I should
not be allowed through the border Customs or, if I were
by chance allowed in, I should be stopped on the return
journey and be left stranded on the Niagara bridge like a
stateless spook in a John le Carré novel.

I did spend longer periods in some places—in
Moscow for instance, to which (thanks to the British
Council) I returned several times. During those early
visits—Brezhnev was still leader and the Cold War still
being waged—Moscow, and the USSR as a whole, did
genuinely feel foreign. It wasn't just the Russian language
which made it seem so different, but the many surprises
of everyday city life—the fact that even in the depths of
winter the Soviets ate tons of their (admittedly delicious)
ice cream in the street, the sophistication of their
films, the readiness of everybody to laugh at the fabled
incompetence of Soviet bureaucrats and the cool beauty
of many of the hotel and GUM store girls.

Moscow in particular seemed full of peculiarities.
Some were immediately apparent—such as the disson-
ance between the blankly stuccoed buildings squatting
above ground, and the ornate grandeur of the Metro.
Another oddity was the contrast between the constant
scenes of public drunkenness and the orderly management of the city's few public bars. Any visitor to Moscow
quickly notices that quite a large proportion of its
perambulating citizens are half cut. A few will be hog-
whimperingly hammered—in winter the authorities
considerately provide an insulated van into which, as
the drunken ones collapse into Moscow's gutters, the
paramedics roll them before they freeze to death. But
alcohol fuels Moscow society. In any private gathering—

unless things have changed radically—the visitor will be offered a sticky slug of viscous liqueur, which friendly gesture can quickly spiral into a full frontal piss-up, with hearty toasts to world peace coupled with the injunction to knock back increasingly generous tots in one gulp. So after your introduction to such alcoholic freedom it is doubly astonishing to discover that in order to enter Moscow's public bars you have to queue outside and then wait for a seat to become free! Within these official bars the sober revellers sit primly at tables perusing a drinks menu while waiting for a waiter to serve them that day's state-approved cocktail. It is all very different from the drunken brouhaha of the Moscow streets.

But, in spite of its occasional irritations, I liked being in Moscow. It seemed, in my time, to be orderly and safe, and if nothing else it was good to be in a foreign city where the drunks were not British holiday makers. I liked the great ornamental park that is the Kremlin. I liked to walk along the banks of the Volga. I loved the theatres. I even liked the steamy fastness of GUM the great arcade-cum-department-store in the middle of the city—in spite of discovering that they didn't stock a fur hat big enough to fit my head. But in particular I thrilled to the two Moscow State circuses (no longer functioning as they were, alas) though I confess to a partiality for the older one's richly colourful auditorium and brassy orchestra. Its acrobats were breathtaking (in spite of performing, to the disapproval of Western circus owners, with safety wires), its Cossack riders magnificent and (most shocking of all) it had clowns that were actually funny.

It was however in the new circus building, which has all the necessary technology for such things, that I saw the most astonishing illusion I have ever witnessed. At the announcement of the act the orchestra fell silent. The magician bowed once and then threw a handful of glittering confetti at his showgirl assistant, who had been standing in the ring in plain view of the audience. As the confetti fluttered downwards, she simply disappeared. Without pause the illusionist then, apparently at random, threw another fistful of glitter at a quite different spot in the ring, some twenty feet away, and she just as soundlessly reappeared. Yes, yes, I know how it was probably done—but the sheer blinding speed of it! And all in a circus ring overlooked from all sides, and in stillness and in silence, and without black drapes, artificial fog or covering music.

Yet I still haven't mentioned the most memorable thing—the reaction of the audience. I have seen many stage illusions in America and in Europe. Some, like David Copperfield or Siegfried and Roy in their Las Vegas show, were spectacularly good but, although they may sometimes have raised a gasp from their sophisticated audiences, I never saw or heard a reaction like that of the Muscovites to the illusionist's act. The sound was compounded of childlike screams and a stunned exhalation at the sheer wonder of it all. True, I once heard a similar sound in Moscow's puppet theatre —but that audience was composed almost entirely of children, whereas the circus audience contained a majority of supposedly rational adults. The moment can only be described by a term which can hardly ever be applied to the staging of Western drama. Although it occurred in the most material society on earth, that circus illusion was a moment of pure *theatrical magic*.

It would be silly to pretend that even in the 1980s all was fun and comradeship in the Soviet Union, but it did seem to me that the sinister picture painted of the USSR in the Western press was at least partially misleading— as was the picture of the West which the Soviet media presented. I recall a bright young student at Moscow University looking at me with alarm when I told her that my wife was half-Irish and that she often travelled in that country. My interlocutor just *knew* that the English were still brutally oppressing the brave Irish freedom fighters, and asked me earnestly 'Why do you let her go there, into such danger?' Useless to protest that Ann spent her time in Ireland visiting relatives and peaceably drinking Guinness with her sister. As it was equally useless for my young student friend to protest that Soviet citizens had choices about where they worked, went on holiday or what they did in their leisure time. Like so many of our contemporaries on either side of the iron curtain, we had both been relentlessly brainwashed since infancy by all that we had heard, seen and read. So in spite of my apparent friendliness she still saw me at core as a mindless oppressor, and in spite of her youth and obvious intelligence I still found myself at some level pitying her as a deluded cog in the Soviet machine.

My saddest glimpse of Soviet life was in the year of the Moscow Olympics. In an act which seems in retrospect to have been hypocritical in the extreme, the US and Britain had decided quite late in the day to boycott the Olympic Games because the Soviet Union had invaded Afghanistan (the West's own invasion of that luckless country came later). I was paying a brief visit to Moscow. On the journey out all was friendly bonhomie but the mood had soured by the time of my return journey. I flew back to London in one of the luxury jumbo jets that the Russians had got ready to transport their Olympics visitors, with only a handful of passengers scattered about the aircraft. I briefly engaged the sad-looking stewardess in stilted conversation, to say that I for one was very sorry the politicians had got everything round their necks. So when we were fully airborne and after she had attended to her other duties she asked me whether I liked caviare, as they had taken a full load on board. I said yes, I did. With that she brought out plates, blinis and a great vat of the black stuff, asking if she may sit down by me. We tucked in, with both of us near tears for the tangled idiocy of east-west relations. So it transpired, O best beloved, that on that mournful day I flew back into London, marooned in the fastness of a luxury jumbo jet's near-empty cabin, spooning down caviare and weeping in unison with a depressed *Aeroflot* hostess. As one does.

* * *

The longest period I ever spent abroad came about entirely through my capacity for self-delusion. I had been asked by the British Council to visit Hong Kong and write a 'training programme' for their arts administrators. In my report I had suggested that my London Department could usefully link in with the University of Hong Kong, and that we should annually send a specialist teacher there for a full term. My colleague Caroline Gardiner had done the first stint and had been a resounding success—so much so that the Hong Kong

directorate had written to ask whether she would go
again. We agreed internally this was not a good idea, and
thinking (mistakenly) that anything Caroline did I could
do equally well I decided, heedless of my known hostility
to the UK's colonial-style governance of the Colony, that
I should be their next academic visitor.

This decision was greeted with modified rapture by
the University of Hong Kong, but by the time I arrived
they had more or less adjusted to the fact that I was
not Caroline. I was greeted politely enough and given
a pleasant air-conditioned apartment on the Mount.
Each morning when I stepped out on to my balcony the
heat would hit me like a damp bolster, and I would be
confronted by a line of unusually shaped and brilliantly
coloured birds staring accusingly from my balcony rail.
At first I thought this was a tropical hallucination but
later learned that these were the inbred descendants of
the Governor's aviary, whose original inmates had been
released into the wild when the Japanese invaded in 1941.

My Hong Kong students were less exotically dressed
than the parrots but considerably better-mannered.
They refused to look at me at all and slavishly wrote
down everything I said while politely refusing to answer
questions ('You already know answer, so why you ask
us?'). Amongst the university staff as well I made few
friends, and I became used to being unfavourably
compared with Caroline Gardiner. My plummeting
reputation may also have been because I found that on
your way in to the steaming campus you could, for next
to nothing, buy a bottle of pink champagne from what
must have been the world's last surviving NAAFI. As
a consequence I was regularly seen carrying a clinking
carrier bag as I headed for my office, which had a lovely
little fridge in it.

Let's turn to the colony's other good points. The
food in Hong Kong was as good as the champagne.
And while there I made some interesting acquaintances,
most memorably the former War Correspondent of the
Daily Telegraph, Clare Hollingworth. Clare, long retired,
had poor eyesight and although the Hong Kong Press
Club was her natural stamping ground, could no longer
comfortably read the newspapers. However she loved

to talk about politics and regaled me with scurrilous stories of Messrs Churchill and Heath, and the tangled love life of Lady Dorothy Macmillian. She was a lady of indomitable spirit* who just before the official outbreak of World War Two had famously ridden into Poland on the front of a German tank, before telephoning her editor to let him know that the invasion had begun. So I was flattered when she offered me the chance of staying with her in the *Telegraph's* flat in Shanghai, and even more so when she said she would pilot me there on her personal plane. Though I confess that when, a few weeks later; she told me crossly that we could no longer fly there in her plane as the idiots had refused to grant an extension on her Pilot's Licence, I did feel a certain relief, as by then I had noticed that she could no longer cross a room without bumping into the furniture.

Yet in spite of the food and drink and friendships, I did not take to Hong Kong any more than I have ever liked being in Singapore. Partly it is the relentless presence of the sun. That which so many of my friends adore is to me a punishment, torturing me with a cruel mixture of brilliant light, darting black shadows and drenching sweat. Perhaps it is because I suffered from Hay Fever in my youth, but more likely it is because I am basically a Northern child, always happier in frost than in searing sunshine. Once, on a midwinter visit to Finland, when the ice lay so thickly in Helsinki harbour that buses could safely drive across it, I thought I had found my ideal holiday destination, but then I visited during their brief summer, and found it as disappointingly sun-drenched as the Far East.

But there was another reason for my dislike of Hong Kong and Singapore—the strutting self-righteousness of the British ex-pat communities that infest both places—the grisly 'old China hands' who in their own imaginations still wear helmets of the purest pith, while ordering coolies to agitate their fans for them. Whenever I met one of those mothballed fossils I knew in advance what questions I should be asked: 'Where in London did I go for treatment now the NHS had collapsed?', 'Would dear Mrs Thatcher succeed in seeing off the Unions?',

---

* Enough of the past tense already. I am told that Clare, now 104, still daily regales her friends in the Hong Kong Press Club.

'Which school did my children go to now that UK state education was in such chaos?'—and when I jibbed at that last question, 'But had I not *seen* what went on in *Grange Hill!!?*' Ex-pats carried two contrasting pictures of Britain in their minds—the green and pleasant land where everybody still left the front doors of their thatched cottages ajar, waited for letters from their sons serving in the Colonies and drank home-brewed ale as they watched the workers morris dancing—contrasted with the hated Welfare State, whose drugged and dumbed-down citizens lived in mortal fear of black terrorists, gobby gangs of pregnant teenagers and marauding Union leaders. Meeting these ex-pats I knew how my cultivated American friends felt when confronted abroad by their own brightly-coloured, over-opinionated compatriots—a deep feeling of shame, coupled with an unrealistic wish to resign from the human race.

A third reason for my unease in the hotlands of the Far East may have been that I am obviously identifiable as a Male Westerner (I could even, Heaven forfend, be mistaken for an *ex-pat!*), who in foreign climes will naturally attract the hostility that this prototype engenders. But whatever the reason, my distaste for Hong Kong was more than equalled by their dislike of me. I was seen as a poor advertisement for true Britishness who, apart from carrying clinking carrier bags around, had *twice* been seen heckling a troupe of ex-pat morris dancers as they jangled their bells and waved their silly hankies about in the Hong Kong shopping arcades. Caroline, on a later visit to see friends in the colony, said tactfully on her return that she had been surprised by the venom with which people spoke of me there. Oh dear! Whereas most academics on teaching trips abroad will get their egos inflated, in Hong Kong my ego —no doubt quite deservedly—suffered a slow puncture.

I found Australia much more compatible, not least because I could wander anonymously in the streets, as in that well-fed land I was if anything slightly *below* both average height and girth. But it is the greeting you're given on arrival which makes travelling to Oz so distinctive. As incoming planes whine to a stop on the tarmac and the passengers wait to disembark, masked officials enter the body of the aircraft to spray passengers with disinfectant as a precaution against them bringing any foreign insect life into the country. Fair enough, but once free of the airport and upon venturing into the great outdoors the same visitors will of course find themselves being relentlessly stung, bitten, poisoned, scratched and murderously dive-bombed by buzzing hordes of Australia's many and varied killer insects. Indeed one longs for the homely wasp.

The reader will by now have realised that alcohol and laughter are high on my list of favourite things, and I have memories of enjoying both in Australia. But other moments also stay with me. The first was blithely agreeing, in a gallery where it was on display, to put Ned Kelly's huge armoured helmet on my head ('Of course I can wear it—I'm not a whingeing pom!') and then sinking ignominiously to my knees under its weight, gibbering pitifully. A second was being welcomed to Melbourne by two polite young gentlemen who took me to the flat which they had prepared, and told me of the exciting programme they had all ready for me. It was touching to see the polite way they gradually accommodated to the fact that in spite of being British, limp of gesture, arch in manner and from the arts community, their visitor was not actually homosexual. A third showed that the fates sometimes do smile on me. I had been scheduled to visit Townsville, in order I think to view the barrier reef. Instead I found myself talking to Ruth Bereson, the young administrator of the local theatre company. We had a series of lengthy conversations during which she impressed me considerably both with her grasp of the paradoxes of state 'support' for the arts and her ability to argue laterally. To cut a long story short, I suggested that Ruth should read for a doctorate. She agreed, registered, moved to Paris to develop her studies (on state-run international opera houses), was in due course awarded her doctorate and after occupying a number of prestigious university posts in the USA and Singapore, is now back in Australia as a Dean at Griffiths University. During all this time our conversation has continued seamlessly and even now, when and wherever we meet, we simply take it up where we left off last time.

As for the USA, I have visited it so often, for work and for pleasure, that it has at times seemed like a second home. The externalities of US life are, through films and television, well known to virtually everyone on the planet, so I will only mention a couple of the Americans' less obvious characteristics. First is their extreme ignorance of abroad. It was for instance reported that at the time of George Bush's invasion of Iraq, fewer than half of the State Department staff had passports. It was also said that after he had ordered the mass bombing of Vietnam, Mr Macnamara asked for a map of the region to be brought into his office, because he had never visited the country and knew nothing of its topography. As for my own experience, I was sometimes nonplussed when someone told me they had 'visited Europe', and would watch their eyes glaze over when I asked which country or countries they had visited? 'Whaddya men? Country? Is Edinborrow a country?'

A second characteristic is their readiness to go to law, even against their nearest and dearest. I was staying for the weekend with a friend of a friend in Pennsylvania. I and the family had been told on Sunday to get up in our own time and make our own breakfasts. I rose around nine o'clock, feeling a little guilty at being so late, but found I was in fact the first to appear. I made myself toast. I was eventually followed down by a young man whom I had briefly met the previous evening. He busied himself with the waffle-maker. After a few minutes there entered a girl who looked about eight years old but, this being America, was probably much younger. They briefly greeted each other and after a few minutes the man wiped his lips and left—leaving plate and used napkin, I noticed, to be cleared up by the hired help (who came on Tuesdays). When he'd departed the little girl spoke to me for the first time. 'That was Mel,' she said, referring to the waffle man who I later learned was her step-brother, adding casually, '*We're suing him.*'

★   ★   ★

Ann and I once spent a few days in California with the laconic Bert Burns, Academic Vice Chancellor of the University of San José, and his wife. Mrs Burns had been born and brought up in the Deep South. Ann asked her one night at supper what her childhood had been like. She sighed and closed her eyes, before murmuring in her soft breathy voice, 'Oh my, there was blossom everywhere!' At the time we assumed that this, which sounded like a well-rehearsed parody of a Tennessee Williams belle, was a family joke revisited for the delectation of foreign visitors such as ourselves. But we were quite wrong. Mrs Burns was not only a natural poet but also sharp as a tack and, unexpectedly for a US citizen, she habitually spoke (as in this case) with a gentle self-mocking irony.

It was her sharpness that she demonstrated the following morning by smilingly refusing to join us when a neighbour said he would take us out to lunch, aboard his private plane. We thought it a good, if unexpected, idea. We drove to the university airfield (*sic*), got into his decidedly wonky-looking aircraft and rattled off into the clear blue sky. We skimmed noisily over various Californian golf courses, and rambling mansions with vivid-blue swimming pools, before landing on another private airfield down the coast. There a hired limousine awaited us and away we went, bumping along pitted side roads before pulling up in front of a dusty roadside shack, decked out as a restaurant and with an upside down union flag nailed incongruously to its front. Our pilot/host waved a well-tanned hand towards it. 'There y'all are,' he said expansively, 'A fish and chip shop! *And* there's English beer!' And so there was—Watney's Brown Ale, in a rusty-looking keg above the counter, just where it caught the Californian sun. Knowing this had all been lovingly arranged as a special treat for the English visitors we dutifully sipped a paper cupful of the gruesome fluid as we chewed our chips and lumps of rubbery fish, saying how lovely it was to have real English food again, instead of the beautiful rump steaks, with predictably perfect salads and those cool carafes of Californian wine....and if we harboured thoughts of taking them, when they next visited the UK, to enjoy a deep-fried beefburger in a bun (with Pepsi) at the greasy spoon on Cricklewood Broadway as a 'special treat for our friends from the States' we kept them firmly to ourselves.

*   *   *

Once the children had decided that staying in damp country cottages was not their idea of a holiday, they started to go off for their own overseas adventures, leaving Ann and me to holiday without them. Working within these new parameters, we arranged a number of foursomes with old friends—taking package holidays to more or less identical tourist hotels in German, Croatian, Italian, French, Turkish and Greek resorts. In time, and assured by friends that it was not too bad, we even went on packages organised by Saga. We salved our consciences over this particular humiliation by taking on each holiday one or two of their day excursions to view historic sites, although we despaired of this eventually because of the guides' chronic inability to separate fact from fiction. After that we spent our time just relaxing, reminiscing and eating before drinking more than the estimated average consumption at the Saga free bar. By these means foreign destinations became homes from home. Only once did we raise the possibility of moving outside these safe confines when Ann and I caused two chums to pass several sleepless nights by suggesting, deep in our cups, that next year we should give package holidays a miss. It would be a really grand idea, would it not?, for we four to drive across Europe and China in a camper van and then walk along the length of the Great Wall . . . . No, it would *not*! It would have served us right if they had agreed.

Left to our own devices Ann and I tried to plug some of the gaps in our knowledge of the nearby world. Ann took me several times to Ireland, which I came to love almost as much as she did—perhaps because on such visits she carefully kept me and her relatives apart. Ruth Bereson arranged for us to spend time in the flat of her friend in Paris during which we were able to enjoy the galleries uninhibited by the need (still strong even when one was visiting with friends) to pass smart and insightful judgements on the exhibits. We enjoyed the same kind of relaxed gallery crawl in Amsterdam, where we were able to content ourselves with simply saying to each other 'I like this,' without the need to go further unless the other said, 'Oh do you? Why?' Then one was challenged by having to explain in ordinary language, without employing the meaningless clichés of the exhibition catalogues, which would have reduced the other to incredulous laughter.

* * *

Ann and I laughed a lot together. I can never remember us falling silent in each other's company for more than half an hour. But on one holiday, in the Italian lakes, we had one of those brief but intense conversations, in which a relationship is momentarily pulled apart and examined before being reassembled in a slightly different form. For many years we had managed to be more or less honest with each other about the occasional squalls which briefly threatened to blow our relationship on to the rocks. We had both confessed when we felt attracted to someone else, and chuckled together over others' absurdities—such as the lady who, briefly enamoured of me, said that she thought my wife was surely the luckiest woman in the world (Ann thought that hilarious). A male friend, in an attempt to seduce Ann, told her that I regularly slept with my female colleagues, to which she replied she knew I didn't, as I would have told her. Denis at one time asked me whether Ann and I were 'going to go our separate ways', having (as Ann told me) told her *in vino* that he would like to roll her up and take her home in his luggage (we had baulked slightly at that one, as his luggage consisted of one small, dog-eared canvas bag).

But back to the Italian lakes. One night after dinner we were sitting on the balcony of our hotel room. We were unwontedly silent until Ann observed that she had noticed that back in England I had been seeing a great deal of one of my woman friends, and that now on holiday I had become pensive and withdrawn. Was that relationship now becoming serious? So, she said half-smilingly, did I want us to separate and for us each to go our separate ways? I can recall taking a few seconds to reply, caught amongst other things by the uncharacteristic phrase she had used. For a moment I looked into the abyss—the pain and sense of waste such a parting would give rise to, in particular the turbulence it would bring to our children's lives, me perhaps living in a bedsit with a new partner (but who? I had never even thought of such a thing, still less discussed it with anyone else), and Ann going her own way with, whom? *Denis!!?* You cannot be serious! I had been on the verge of dodging the question and asking playfully, 'Well, do *you* want to go your own way?', before suddenly seeing the danger. Ann might just possibly—jokingly even—say yes and we both knew that however light-heartedly the question may have been put, the wrong answer could take us into uncharted realms of doubt, suspicion and darkness. 'No, of course not,' I said quickly, 'I certainly don't want us to separate.' Softly, 'Nor do I.' The silence hung in the air Momentarily stirred by all that had been left unsaid, we sat for a while gazing out on to the calm waters of Lake Garda, before pouring ourselves another glass of wine. And then talking about something else entirely.

Networking at City: Lady Hall, Sir Peter Hall, JP, Tony Field

❧12❧

Failure

To RETURN to my life in London. As she was coming to the end of her first parliament, the Prime Minister, Mrs Thatcher, on whom we later pinned too much of the blame, was being lauded for having brought a new sense of 'reality' into national life. In my neck of the academic woods she was credited by some with bringing a 'new realism' into the affairs of the Arts Council. Quite what that 'new realism' consisted of, save for the adoption of a new commercial vocabulary to describe activities formerly described in more nuanced terms, was never clear. In truth the world she was said to represent seemed to some of us to be profoundly unreal, *surreal* even, a verbal lunge towards a Narnia comprising nothing but 'efficient' production lines with clunking 'outcomes'.

The language of her government was certainly belligerent and—to use a word still in use as a smokescreen to cover noisy political vacuity—'robust'. But then the political language of each age is on one level merely a record of the phobias and superstitions of the time. Sometimes it may be no more than a jungle growl, even though it may at the time convince people of the reality of forces and powers that in fact have no existence at all. At that time of extreme political hysteria it did not seem to occur to Mrs Thatcher's more fervent followers that this 'new reality' might finally be composed of nothing but cold air—no more revolutionary and no more meaningful than many other political slogans, of right or left.

A brief illustration. After the Lady's election victory it happened that I was to lead an international conference for the British Council on Administering the Arts. One of their Bertie Woosterish officers insisted that the programme should include a plug for this exciting 'new realism', and offered to lead a discussion on 'Value For Money' in the arts. The session, when it came, was deeply embarrassing. The students, more intelligent than the session leader, quickly realised that he had, quite literally, no idea what he was talking about. He appeared not to know of Wilde's famous aphorism on the subject and thus to have given no thought at all to the various possible meanings of the term 'value'. So they peppered the poor man with loaded questions: 'Was a Picasso painting *worth* the money paid for it?', 'Had the poetry of the impoverished John Clare no value?', 'Could poor people not enjoy great music?', 'Did pricing art take precedence over determining its value?'

Nevertheless Mrs Thatcher's dogmas were seized upon as banners beneath which all kinds of robust action—whether sensible, heartless or just plain vile—could be justified. And her government had caught, and helped to create, a popular mood. The post-war consensus around the Welfare State was imploding, and it was now described by the sneering right-wing term, Nanny State. The middle classes seemed to have grown bored with its too-well-advertised concern for the oppressed and downtrodden. It was time to bring a new mercantile focus on such namby-pamby concerns. Whether it was selling off state utilities or sinking the *Belgrano*, many welcomed this new and unsentimental, even brutish, government approach. And the 'new realism' seeped into the innermost salons of the establishment. Working in the City of London, albeit as a lowly academic, gave me something of an inside view of this apparent change in the public Zeitgeist. The new mood was most memorably illustrated for me by the eminent City Father who, in my hearing, reacted to news of the rampaging AIDS epidemic by squawking concernedly, 'Just *think* what it'll do to the actuarial rates!'

Everything—religion, the law, public health, the arts, education—was now spoken of as an 'industry', with its parts named by a new breed of word-juggling bureaucrats. These new 'industries' were judged, not by the service they offered to their workers or their clients, but by their statistical 'outcomes', starkly arranged in the sort of league tables which old fashioned liberals so abhorred. Thus literary success was measured by the number of publications sold rather than by what was being meaningfully read, musical success measured by record sales and educational success by the numbers of young people being bribed to enter the new 'universities'—which, fortuitously, were springing up in every town in the land.

Universities of all vintages—whether Edge Hill, Cambridge, Wolverhampton, Bournemouth or Hull—tumbled over themselves to capitulate before this baleful new orthodoxy. From them the old humanities subjects all but disappeared, and were replaced by a job lot of takeaway, 'vocational' degree courses in 'subjects' attuned to modern students' needs with titles such as Game Design, Journalism, Surfing or Media Studies. But omnipresent, and on special offer everywhere, was the exciting new all-purpose subject, 'Management'—presumed to be a transferable set of skills which could equally well be applied to the 'efficiency' and 'outcomes' of an Accident and Emergency Department as to those of an abbatoir.

Within the universities the remaining academics found themselves enmeshed in the coils of this sinister new 'education industry'. Their departments were split up and reorganised according to a new 'industrial' designation ruled over by ever-multiplying layers of resource managers, planners, strategists, organisational experts and public relations spokespersons, whose aim was not the furtherance of scholarship, but rather to encourage the right kind of mindset among the toiling hands. Vice Chancellors were now (non-ironically) termed Chief Executives. Deans of Faculty, though expert in climbing league tables, now made no secret of the fact that they had little interest or expertise in the subjects they were supposedly leading but were solely interested in the Faculty's *interface* with funders and the media. When Deans met together (which was a more frequent occurrence than their occasional meetings with their own staffs) it was to determine or redefine the *brand image* of their university. What was the institution's Unique Selling Proposition? Its well-tended lawns? The high proportion of starred firsts it awarded to overseas students? The *relevance* of its consumer-friendly courses—in Circus Skills perhaps, or Clairvoyance or Surfing? Its on-campus leisure and recreational facilities? The opportunities it offered to meet new sexual partners?

New PR Companies, dedicated to designing each university's TV marketing, advertising campaigns and glossy appeals for funds, were founded and duly prospered. New Model Agencies supplied groups of healthy-looking, happily gurning 'graduate' lookalikes to be photographed for the prospectus, with the obligatory black student wearing the university's scarf and the bespectacled oriental girl looking demurely on from the back row. Meanwhile the newly realistic fees, for which crippling bank loans were readily available, were discreetly relegated to the final pages. By these means each university prospectus shyly welcomed new UK students in to its grinning jaws, promising each little fish three years of green lawns, customised courses and a raunchy night life—in preparation for a life spent in debt.

Meanwhile the remaining staff found that they too had been caught in the same seductive trap. Freed of any old-fashioned responsibility to be academic—preparing papers for peer-reviewed journals, for example—they now found themselves assessed by different means. As scholastic ability increasingly yielded to the cult of academic celebrity, promotion now depended upon how 'visible' the staff member was deemed to be. In essence that 'visibility' was measured by the frequency of the don's appearances on radio and the telly. To assist with this process media moguls were issued with lists of university 'experts' who could be relied upon to offer instant opinions on anything from climate change to expenditure on defence weaponry. Soon those same academics looked to develop and 'front' their own television programmes. Upon these candyfloss creations, whether ostensibly concerned with history, anthropology or social analysis, university bureaucrats looked with even greater favour. For they knew that such televised concoctions would not only bear the name of their presenter, but also the name of his or her university—thus burnishing its *brand image*!

For those chosen ones, the rigours of script conferences and shooting schedules took up so much of their time, and drained so much of their energy, that they simply could not find a moment to look in upon their own departments, or even visit the university whose name they bore. Until, that is, Graduation Day dawned, and the press and television were in evidence. Then one heard of students who had been attracted to enter a department linked to a highly visible one's name, but who had not seen hair nor hide of him until that final ceremony. However, on that day, smiling seraphically and condescending to all, the Great Panjandrum would appear, his golden radiance shining out from the graduation photographs framed on humble mantelpieces and bedside tables throughout the fee-paying world.

★   ★   ★

So how did this double whammy—the twin attacks on the universities and the arts—affect us in the City University Department of Arts Policy and Management? It dealt us a fatal blow is the short answer. But first I must beg the reader's indulgence as I reiterate the particular problems attendant upon trying to create a new department in a wholly new subject.

Arts Administration was, for a start, not yet a subject. It had no literature of its own, no substantial research to draw upon and no agreed methodology by which it might have proceeded. But any new university subject—and in the febrile atmosphere of the 1980s there were many such—ought by rights to be gradually and thoughtfully nurtured, with the ever-present possibility that it might turn out not to be a subject worthy of serious study. However, at that time, in a heady atmosphere of over-rapid expansion, such was the pressure for immediate

results that a new subject had to spring fully formed from
the womb, as it were. It had to make its own immediate
contribution to the university's *brand image,* had to be
ready to grub for instant funding and above all, ready to
compete in the market place.

I have already explained that I held what was soon
revealed as an absurd ambition. In my arrogance I
chose to believe that I could single-handedly create the
literature, undertake the necessary research, lay down
the methodology, develop the new degree structure and
teach what I chose to believe could one day stand as a
university subject. Lord, what fools these mortals be! I
know now that I was not capable of doing any of these
things, certainly not quickly, and most certainly not on
my own. In any case the ends were almost certainly not
achievable, at any rate within the realms of the 'new
realism'. But I closed my eyes to the truth, and decided
that it could *probably* be done. Then I convinced myself
that it *definitely* could—if I only had good colleagues
working with me . . . .

Aye, there's the rub! From where does one recruit
good colleagues to teach a subject which does not exist?
There are no bright young researchers coming through,
no authors of ground-breaking textbooks, no thoughtful
analyses of the value-laden language adopted by our Arts
Council. So, too rapidly, and blithely shutting my eyes
to the probable pitfalls, I appointed people who were
practitioners in the field, but who seemed intelligent
and independent-minded. But I do not blame any one
of them for what subsequently occurred. Some were
unfitted to the task, but more importantly I grossly over-
estimated my own abilities.

Although, in retrospect, it is possible to see that some
of these appointments brought lustre to the university.
There was for example Dr Michael Hammet, who had
been Drama Officer for Eastern Arts, but who proved
himself capable of trenchant and insightful observations
about the world in general and the arts world in
particular. 'The British Arts Council,' he once smilingly
observed to a wondering group of overseas students,
'does not *administer* the arts, it is parasitic upon them.
It could not exist without them, but they could easily

exist without *it*.' There was also Dr Caroline Gardiner, who for many years led the Department's (qualitative as well as quantitative) surveys of West End audiences, and later went on to become Professor of Arts Management Studies at South Bank University. A little later came Dr John Elsom, sometime the regular theatre critic for *The Listener,* who inaugurated the MA in Arts Criticism, and whose expository devices in his subject included working with his students to forecast the annual winner of the Man Booker Prize for Literature (usually successfully) solely by means of reading the promotional material on each book's cover and calibrating it against previous winners' nationalities and subject matter.

Around the ten or so full-time staff were ranged another group of part-time teachers, who supplemented our knowledge by their specialisms. One of these was Tony Field, whose many years of experience as Finance Director of the Arts Council meant that he was able, when asked any question on any financial or admin-istrative subject, to answer with a pithy and memorable anecdote. Tony was a man of honour, who probably threw away his deserved knighthood by delivering a brave public lecture exposing the crude machinations of the Thatcher government in the field of public subsidy.

A second was the truly extraordinary Charles Arnold-Baker, the Department's Professor of Law. I did not recruit Charles; he recruited me. One day, when I was still new to my job, my office door opened to reveal a distinguished-looking, black-gowned figure who smiled warmly and said, 'I think I may be able to help you. I understand you're having some difficulty with the legal side of your subject, is that not so?' I agreed it was certainly so. Within a month he had rewritten the law syllabus entirely, drafted the outlines of a good textbook on the subject and agreed to teach it. As the department grew he became a pivotal figure, famous as much as any-thing for his riotously funny examination papers. These usually consisted of several bizarrely-imagined offstage scenarios—involving such characters as drunken tim-panists, randy ventriloquists and paint-spraying cannibals —followed by some such question as 'Who can sue whom, and with what chance of success?' I have seen candidates in the examination room, upon reading one of Charles' papers, fall to the floor helpless with laughter. In marking them Charles did not ask for precise case histories, but rather for the right approach to the problem. 'All the legal details are wrong of course,' he would say of some script to which he had awarded a high mark, 'but the *spirit* is exactly right.'

Out of a certain tact I have not mentioned those staff members who did not, in my opinion, reach these same sublime standards, or those who fundamentally disagreed with my view of the subject. It is well-known, at least amongst the small group retaining any interest in the matter, that the Department fell apart, riven by ideological divisions as fierce, and as insular, as those which sometimes rent English or Fine Art Departments. I had neither the academic focus, nor the mental or physical strength, to hold it all together. The students were only too well aware of the schisms within the Department. The outside world was made aware of them by the paragraph which later appeared beneath the editorial in the department's *Journal of Arts Policy and Management* which offered the pusillanimous disclaimer that the journal did not represent the views of all the members of the DAPM staff.

You bet it didn't! Some of the staff had come to believe fervently in the 'new realism', and hoped only to gain the approval of the Arts Council. Others were interested only in one preferred art form. Still others turned out to believe only in the subject as a practical guide to working in the contemporary UK, and faced with the increasing numbers of overseas students which the department attracted, just wanted to teach them how the British system of state arts subsidy operated—with the clear implication that one day they too could aspire to the same level of political sophistication. None of these positions was inherently wicked, though all fell short of developing arts administration as a proper university subject. It might all have had a happier outcome if we had been able to discuss things rationally, but even that seemed an aspiration too far. Charles Arnold-Baker's suggestion that we collectively write and perform a staff pantomime so we would be brought together in a common creative purpose was perhaps the most enlightened suggestion for our salvation, but that too was beyond us.

As my colleagues subdivided into warring factions, some clustered around one malevolent conspirator—a Thatcherite wannabe recently come to us as a visiting lecturer—who took on the mantle of academic broker and led a devious backstairs campaign against me and those colleagues who shared my views. In his opinion the Department needed to return to the 'real world' and accept that it must drop all that speculative inquiry and conform to the prevailing political orthodoxy of the 'new realism'. After two bitter years of plotting and counter-plotting, too tedious and too painful to recount in detail, the 'new realists' prevailed. It is true that the university grandees urged me to stay on, but they too were caught up in the commercial mood of the times, and did not understand that the battle was about principles rather than resources and numbers. I failed to make my case, even to those well-meaning people. Defeated and depressed, I got myself included in one of the Thatcher government's lists of those dangerous elements that must be rooted out from the universities, and took early retirement. My more enlightened colleagues either followed suit, or moved on to pastures new.

The remnants of the department were, I later learned, gathered together and retitled 'Department of *Cultural* Management' (which title, as a puzzled observer wryly remarked, did not exclude the study of *any* kind of activity, at any time or in any place) and in turn was lost within the cloying fug of a 'Faculty of Creative *Industries*', no less! A Department of Cultural Management set within a Faculty of Creative Industries! Phoebus! Sad and meaningless titles of course, yet in their very blankness as sinister than anything Orwell or Huxley might have created. The outward-looking subject had now descended into servile grocery, with its staff grubbing for government grants so they could either count the beans or make recommendations about the packaging. Of the heart of the arts manager's business, the forging of that unique relationship between art and its audience, that which I termed the 'aesthetic contract', the modern bean counters cannot speak. Because, as it cannot be reduced to a formula, or weighed in their grocer's scales, they do not even know of its existence.

* * *

Following my early retirement, when my appearances in the university were confined to occasional guest lectures, I began to see other ways in which the box tickers were taking over. A Chinese student, overseas fees duly paid, whom I had noticed was completely lost within the unfamiliar sounds and sights of the English language, was allowed to take examination papers in his rooms and suddenly found an unheralded fluency of expression and gained, I heard, a sound Master's Degree. An Iranian student, overseas fees duly paid, of whose ability to express herself or even to think in causal terms I had long despaired, was suddenly awarded the doctorate she had long sought but which had hitherto been cruelly denied to her. I was sent a copy of her final thesis and decided that she must have shone so brightly in her viva examination that the examiners had decided to dispense with the bother of actually reading it, as it was full of errors of spelling, expression, attribution and fact. Meanwhile throughout the university system the proportion of firsts and upper seconds grew ever greater. In the corridors of South Bank University I came across a student, whom I knew to be an affable soul but incapable of writing a declarative sentence, taking down details from a law firm's poster promising in bold type that if the student did not get the degree class they thought they deserved, they would take action to put it right. She told me that she intended to instruct the lawyers if she did not get 'at least' an upper second.

* * *

The shifting foundations of the university world also contributed in small part to my final and irrevocable split from my American friend Denis. Though the fault was largely his. As I neared early retirement, he told me that it had long been his intention, as a visiting member of staff, to submit a dissertation for a doctorate in arts administration (he already had one, appropriately, in psychology). I suggested he now offered his thesis, as was proper, to my successor. My successor duly received it and, properly, arranged for it to be examined in New York. Dr Caroline Gardiner was assigned as the City University examiner. She read the dissertation carefully and on the appointed day she and her fellow US examiner met Denis in New York. They were of a mind. It was a clear failure.

When I heard the news I had two immediate thoughts. First was a comradely feeling of sympathy for Denis, who had been used to success throughout his academic career, and would now have to cope with this unfamiliar failure. Second, and paramount in my mind, was a sense of pride that Caroline should retain such a proper sense of academic probity that she did not take any account of my well-known friendship with Denis, or of the fact that at the time Denis enjoyed higher academic status than she did. I did not budge from either view, even though it all had a bitter outcome. A few weeks later Denis wrote me a sorrowful, angry letter, full of recriminations that I had allowed it all to happen, reminding me of what we had shared, and telling me that though he would see me when I was in New York, he did not intend to come again to London, or to work with me again. I did not reply (nor did he expect me to). My family and some of our mutual friends were disturbed by this apparently inexplicable rupture in our relationship, though for a time I kept my counsel as to the cause. When I finally read some of what he had written I was if anything embarrassed. Denis's mind, once so formidable, was now, for whatever reason, shot to pieces. The sad upshot was that we neither met nor corresponded again.

★ ★ ★

Our children had by now not exactly fled but had partially detached themselves from the family nest and so we decided the time was ripe to leave the smoke and settle in greener pastures. This time we were not confined by the demands of my job, while Ann's managerial and social skills were in such demand that she could, she said, pick up a post almost anywhere. Now we looked at the convenience and attractiveness of the location. As

usual we shared brief fantasy lives in various unsuitable
locations—Matlock Bath, Cork, Robin Hood's Bay—
before yielding to more practical considerations. Bearing
in mind the increasing age of my parents, and the fact
that the Great Northern line into King's Cross was still
just about the quickest and most reliable service into
London, we elected to look for a dwelling somewhere
near Newark on Trent, not far distant from my grandmother's old cottage. We were not altogether surprised to
find that the new realism had spread to the East
Midlands and we were offered a pricey succession of
adapted gamekeepers' lodges, restored school houses and
desirable barn conversions, with fitted kitchens and
double garages, behind whose slatted blinds we could if
we chose convince ourselves that we were still living in
West Hampstead.

Eventually we settled for a pleasant but unremarkable
detached house set in a pleasant but unremarkable village
called Winthorpe. This was situated next to a derelict
wartime aerodrome, and within a short car ride of
Newark's main line station. At one end of the village,
next to the pub, lived a rich American TV performer
called Mickey Dolenz, who was romantically cast by the
awestruck locals in the traditional role of Squire, but who
made no concessions to convention by appearing at local
events in jeans, sweatshirt and baseball cap. I used to
silence party conversations by boasting that I lived in a
village with a Monkee. Sometimes Mickey's media
chums came to stay and then village tongues would be
heard salaciously wagging over what Peter Noone or
Ringo Starr had supposedly got up to at the weekend.

The disused aerodrome was, in a roundabout way,
rather more of a nuisance. It was (still is) the site of the
Newark Antiques Fair. This brought unexpected problems. The Antiques Fair brought in its wake a cohort of
skilled thieves, who would nick such pieces of porcelain,
antique pottery or decorative wall hangings that could be
seen through the downstairs windows of local dwellings.
The stolen pieces turned up sooner or later, usually at
one of the other antique fairs. We had nothing old that
was worth pinching but some of our fellow villagers had.
They knew the routine. At the time of the Fair, when

we called on them, we found that they had scooped up and hidden their precious antiques under their beds or in various dark cupboards. Even so, during the thieving season, we knew two or three families that in spite of all precautions still had their valuables pinched.

Then a number of events conspired to make us restless once more. My links with my former Department were gradually being severed. Ann had taken a post with Lincolnshire Social Services, so one way and another there was no longer a need to live close to a commuter station. My own parents, still living in the same Retford house, were by their own standards becoming increasingly frail, and too dependent on the telly and their neighbours to bring colour to their lives

It was suggested we might consider buying the home of a recently deceased relative of mine, whose home was set within four acres of dark and shadowy woodland, but Ann put a shuddering stop to that. Finally we opted for Willow Cottage, a newly-renovated building in the heart of Sutton on Trent, an interesting old village just off the A1, about twenty-five minutes from my parents in Retford.

Martyn at the Hotel Akademos,
Athens

Cath on the hearhtrug
at Minster Road

❊13❊
Sutton on Trent

NOW OUR ROLES were reversed. After our early morning tea Ann would get up, dress in her business suit, and set out on the twenty-five mile trip to her new headquarters in Lincoln. It was a challenging journey, largely on busy motorways with the rising sun in her eyes most of the way. On arrival, watched from a first floor window by her easily-amused colleagues, she would have two or three attempts at reversing into her allotted parking space, earning a little round of applause when she finally made it. She would then plunge into her working day, which involved offering assistance to the rural elderly in need. The problems which presented themselves to Lincolnshire's social workers were, she soon discovered, deeper and less tractable than those of central London. Attending to them involved a great deal of car travel to lonely cottages followed by lengthy periods assessing what assistance was needed and negotiating the means by which it might be delivered—the Lincolnshire folk being jealous of their privacy, unwilling to accept help from neighbours and also deeply suspicious of all forms of official aid. After an exhausting day attending to these intricate dilemmas, Ann would climb wearily back into her little Fiat and set off on the return leg with the sun now dropping down the Western sky—and once more shining in her eyes.

Meanwhile, what was I doing? Well, occasionally I caught the train down to London to teach in the Department, but generally I stayed home, did the housework and—a secret pleasure—tended the garden and pottered around in the greenhouse. I shopped in Sutton's three main shops; the butcher, the post office and the Co-op supermarket (avoiding the newspaper kiosk run by the village burglar who was said to prick up his ears when his customers cancelled their orders because they were 'going away'....). I would sometimes, though not regularly, have a lunchtime drink in one of Sutton's two extant pubs—either in the tarted-up one which ran a sort of restaurant and had framed memorabilia tastefully adorning its walls, or the dowdy one which had neither of these things but which I preferred. I took pleasant country walks. And in the course of these bucolic pleasures, I would sometimes stop and pass the time of day with my fellow villagers.

At those words the reader, lulled into clichéd thinking by the rhythms of my slumberous prose, may be summoning to mind images of straw-chewing, flat-capped yokels whose only conversation was of last year's gales and this year's harvests. Nothing could be further from the truth. My fellow villagers were a varied crowd with an eclectic range of interests. And their homes were equally diverse. For example, near Willow Cottage was what looked for all the world like a film-set version of an old Elizabethan inn. It was in fact a twentieth-century private hotel. The key to the *Old England*'s unexpectedly olde worlde appearance was the fact that the family which owned the site had been friends with one Henry Spencer, the local auctioneer. It had been assembled from left-over bits and pieces from abandoned Dukeries mansions whose contents had been put up for auction prior to their demolition. Film stars such as David Niven and more modern notables such as the Beatles had once stayed there, but it was now in decline and run only as a venue for lah-di-dah wedding receptions.

Directly over from us lived the surviving daughters of Sutton's last Master Basket Maker*, with a boarded-up

---

* This sounds like a tongue-twister, but it recalls an important part of local history. In Sutton, which lay at the limit of the tidal Trent, willow trees grew profusely, their roots churning up the local paths like the tentacles of rampaging Triffids. The twenty or so basket makers who had once plied their trade there had chosen Sutton because of its willows, rather than because of the special qualities of the inhabitants' urine.

outhouse on the roadside in which, the daughters told us, the baskets had once been made. Apparently, in order to make the willow fronds suitably supple, their father would dunk them in vats of human wee—for which precious liquid the locals used to be paid half a crown per bucketful, which sounded like a generous rate. By way of variation, down by the Trent there lived a gregarious security adviser who as a precaution against being robbed (which would have been professionally embarrassing) kept an eclectic menagerie of barking dogs, quacking ducks, bouncing wallabies and screeching monkeys wandering through his extensive grounds. And for good measure, round the corner in an ivy-covered mansion there lived a retired captain of industry who invited guests to his house, not just to enjoy his generous hospitality but to play with the extensive model railway system which he had laid out in a room above his garage.

Next door to us lived another surprising couple, Mike and Ann Gardiner. Mike owned a Formula Ford stable of racing cars, and each weekend he, together with his son John, would drive these snarling beasts around European motor racing circuits. My dear wife—capable of exhibiting motherly anxiety even when her grown-up children were undertaking a short journey on public transport—marvelled at the fact that Mike's wife could remain so calm while her husband and son were hurtling round a race track. That was until our neighbour explained that the reason why she didn't worry was that both of them were expert mechanics and personally prepared the cars they drove. So it was a terrible shock when one day Mike was fatally injured—not in a racing crash, but attending to a neighbour's broken-down Mini. Out of pure kindness, as was his wont, Mike had gone over to repair the lady's car. But he had left the engine running while bent under the bonnet making adjustments. The clutch had slipped and the car had lurched forward, injuring him horribly. He died a few days later in hospital.

While we are walking on the dark side, I should add that Sutton even had its own serial killer, an ex-railwayman who, in addition to committing murder,

sometimes kidnapped young girls and held them to
ransom. He lived in a white-painted cottage up the hill
in Sutton. Once, rather horribly, he had kept one of his
victims in a wheelie bin in a yard in nearby Newark.
After his arrest the red top newspapers descended on the
village and one published a blurred photograph of Willow
Cottage (which was also painted white) as the 'Home of
the Wheelie Bin Killer'. It was then discovered that the
killer had helped out at the previous year's village fête—
the Sutton Threshing Festival—and had made a brief
appearance on the video recording the event. One of the
red tops offered the organising committee £5,000 for it—
an offer I thought we should take up as we rarely made
that much on the festival and it would save us expending
energy on organising the whole shebang yet again. Which
shows how little I understood the underlying purposes
of a country festival. The newspaper's offer was curtly
rejected and the Sutton residents set to work instead
painting signs, carving wood, baking cakes, forcing root
vegetables, fashioning candles, making jars of chutney
and all the rest of the expensive and time-consuming
activities which are essential precursors to rural fund-
raising.

The Threshing Festival was of course a major local
event. It largely took place on land belonging to the
village's best-known farmer, John Marshall, whose
family had farmed in those parts for centuries. The
Festival celebrated the old method of bringing in the
harvest. A week or two in advance, on a chosen day,
an old-fashioned cutter and binder went to work in a
local cornfield. The assembled villagers gathered up
the sheaves and arranged them in stooks. When the
sheaves had dried out they would be pitchforked on
to horse-drawn wagons and stacked in John's yard. At
the Festival itself, the sheaves would be fed through a
dusty old threshing engine, whose antiquated workings
would always draw a fascinated crowd. Some of the other
Festival attractions—the old steam organs, the craft
stalls, the flower and vegetable show, the beer tent selling
Springhead Bitter (the local brew)—were arranged
about an arena in which the more spectacular open-air
attractions took place.

There was each year a 'flyover' by an RAF Spitfire, which led to one of the two notable contretemps which occurred while I was helping to organise the arena attractions. I had arranged for a Falconry Display to be given in the middle of the afternoon. In the arena the hawks and eagles were doing their stuff and all was going well until—at least fifty minutes ahead of schedule— the Spitfire arrived and swooped down upon us, with its unmistakeable click-clacking engine going full pelt. Terrified of this monstrous contraption the winged performers abandoned their performance and took to the nearby trees, from which not even whole lumps of dead sheep could (for a while, anyway) tempt them back into the arena. Their owner was not best pleased, though the spectators seemed to enjoy his attempts to lure down the birds as much as the formal display.

The second crisis was not directly attributable to me, but I record it nevertheless because at the time it threatened to become one of those absurd legal situations which Charles Arnold-Baker delighted to put in his examination papers. The organisers had booked a historical re-enactment society to re-stage some long-forgotten but no doubt highly significant piece of local history. The re-enactment involved a specially-manufactured property cannon firing—presumably blank balls?—at the climax of the performance. However, before the costumed combatants could take to the arena, we had been instructed by the insurers to issue a warning over the public address system that the cannon was going to fire and stress that it would be very *loud*. This warning was given twice, at a volume which meant it was plainly audible to the revellers in the beer tent, and those who, having been temporarily taken short, were apprehensively crouching in the distant Jakes. Following which the re-enactors variously marched and gambolled into the public arena, and after a few moments of incomprehensible shouting, proceeded to lay about each other with swords and staves. This continued for several minutes, with the lady members of the troupe expressing concern from the sidelines. It seemed to be a stalemate until, quite suddenly, with a clod-scattering thump, the cannon fired, purple smoke billowing from its muzzle. Following which, as its reverberation died away, a number of the performers fell cautiously over. A victorious standard was raised, three hearty cheers were given by those still standing and a good time was had by all.

So the organisers were surprised when, a few weeks later, they received a solicitor's letter telling them that a female client had been harmed by the cannon's boom. Her resulting deafness had required expensive treatment, and therefore she sought damages as she held the organisers to be guilty of criminal negligence. At first the organisers were scornful. If her hearing had been sound beforehand why hadn't she heard the warnings? But was she also—sudden thought—also blind, and unable to read the notice boards? Did she enter the site after the warnings had been given and, being blind, had leant on the cannon for support while awaiting her carer? Doubts began to grow in the organisers' minds. But fortunately their worried silence was taken as a refusal to treat. It was then revealed that the lady was a rich local eccentric who had for several years been as deaf as a post, but amused herself by sending solicitors' letters to organisers of local events, in the hope of having a bit of court action.

The villagers took it as further evidence that you should have nowt to do with the law. And indeed it was only when they were directly in the public eye that they bothered at all with elf n' safety regulations. Left to themselves they instinctively obeyed a darker, more primaeval law. I once attended a closed meeting of local residents which was addressed by an official from the County Council. His cause was not a popular one, his manner patronising and his delivery monotonous. A few minutes after the meeting had begun, I noticed that a group of the local lads had slipped out—because, I surmised, they had found that neither the speaker's platform style nor his sentiments were to their liking. And in a way I was right because, when the speaker had concluded his oration and left the hall, he found that his car had been gently levered by unknown hands into the shallows of the nearby River Trent.

★   ★   ★

I celebrated the Millennium in Sutton on Trent, and a very curious celebration it was. At the time of the first Millennium, as regular readers of the *Anglo-Saxon Chronicle* will need no reminding, the population was in superstitious dread of the wrath of the Gods being visited upon them. There were flying dragons seen in the sky, and all peoples of the earth must expiate their sins by self-abasement and fasting. We might smile indulgently at such primitive fancies, were it not for the fact that such views also seemed to be held by the New Labour government and by its worried little Home Secretary, Jack Straw. In the weeks preceding the second Millennium, there had been dire prognostications that all the computers on earth would crash on the stroke of midnight, causing airliners to crash all over the globe. That rumour died away as the fateful day approached, only to be replaced by another and greater fear— that on this fateful New Year's Eve all men would run wild, uttering strange cries and tearing each other to bloodstained shreds. In preparation for this orgy of wild destruction, all police leave was cancelled, some elements of the Army Reserve were called into action, and hospital wards cleared in readiness for the expected casualties.

New Year's Eve revellers found themselves under curfew. On the night the pubs either charged for admission (refusing to serve or even admit non-ticket holders) or closed early. Ann, Tish and I spent the evening in the less salubrious of the Sutton pubs, which advertised the fact that in compliance with government instructions it would close at 11 o' clock. And indeed it did. It was one of the most miserable evenings I have ever spent. The usual barflies were sunk in gloom. Frank, always good for a tale or two about the bodies he had fished out the Trent, fell silent. The village policeman, normally the one to set the snug in a roar, was on duty in nearby Newark, helping to control the blood-maddened crowds. At closing time we all slunk soberly off to our silent homes. The next morning we were awakened by the news that my mother's long-term neighbour had died in hospital, having been forced to leave her comfortable ward, which was required for the casualties, and instead take her final rest on a stretcher in a cold and draughty corridor.

Now I was living in what my London friends called the far North (though to my Northumbrian mates it was the soft South) I did far less performing and public speaking. I did though, often by courtesy of the aforementioned loaf-faced comedian Eamonn Jones, do a few scattered music hall gigs. One, at Boston in Lincolnshire, yielded a story. It is sometimes the case (as it was on this occasion) that the Chairman, in swirling cape and polished top hat, mixed with the punters beforehand, ostensibly to drink with them, but in fact in order to prise out of them the names of local bigwigs that could be used on stage to get a cheap laugh. For this show a local name was needed to insert in a number during which Eamonn burst into the auditorium as a 'Salvation Army Lass'. In the bar on opening night I learned that a gentleman in holy orders, extremely popular in the area and able to take a joke, would be attending. He sounded ideal. He was a Canon Fluck, who happened to be the brother of Diana Dors but who unlike his sister had retained the family name. Before curtain up I relayed the information to Eamonn, who was backstage enjoying a pint of guinness. 'Fluck you say? Fluck? Are you shore now?' 'I'm sure, yes. No, I'm not having yez on.' 'Fluck?' A meditative sip. 'Fluck, eh? Well, I'll have to practice dat.'

I know that I could cap the story in five different ways, all equally droll, but I'm afraid that would be tampering with history. The prosaic truth was that when the moment came, Eamonn pronounced the Canon's name perfectly ('So Canon Fluck thaves fallen women. I hope he'll thave one for the chairman!') and we got an affectionate round of applause. But when I returned to the dressing room and saw the Canon's name written in eyebrow pencil on the mirror and saw the empty guinness bottles I knew it had been a demn'd close-run ting.

I still attended occasional conferences, and gave a few public sermons on the subject of the iniquities of the riven Tory government. Which is an appropriate time to confess that I actually *voted for* Tony Blair and his 'New Labour' project—a brief infatuation that lasted less than a month, by which time Blair had already been persuaded, allegedly by Bernie Ecclestone, to cancel the party's proposed legislation on tobacco advertising. And I still did some work for *Associated Speakers* but it was borne in upon me that if you wanted to live off that sort of work (which I didn't) you really had to be mixing with the right sort of media crowd, and that meant working from London. Unless you worked at burnishing your reputation (which I most certainly didn't) living in the countryside buried you well away from the media world. When one of my country neighbours recognised a comment attributed to me in the *Daily Telegraph*, she excitedly showed me the cutting and, not considering the possibility of a more straightforward explanation, exclaimed, 'Look, he's got the same name as you.'

*   *   *

But Sutton proved a blessing in other ways, not least because it united me once more with three of my oldest friends. The first reunion occurred through an improbable combination of unlikely circumstances. My daughter Cath was at the time on the production team for a TV serial which was telling the riches-to-rags story of a Northern dynasty, and on this particular Thursday she had to be at the TV studios in Leeds. She didn't drive and there was also a national rail strike in progress. She could take a coach up to Nottingham but no further, so she rang and asked could I possibly drive over to Nottingham and collect her, and after she'd stayed overnight at Willow Cottage, could she please have a lift up to Leeds? Next morning, with that accomplished, and Cath safely in the BBC studios, I thought that as this was the first time I had been in Leeds since far-off student days, I would take a walk around. Some of the city centre—such as the Harvey Nicols emporium in one of the restored arcades—looked very different, but there were bits that were more familiar. I nosed around the streets I knew until suddenly, walking towards me, was my friend of student days, Ben Roberts, whom I had not clapped eyes on for nigh on thirty-five years, and looking much the same as he ever did.

We recognised each other almost simultaneously, and though I had changed more than he had, he politely didn't draw attention to the ravages of time. Eschewing showy physical contact we smiled our manly greetings. (After all, we were British!) I drew attention to the demn'd stroke of luck that had brought us back together. Ben (picking up the tone perfectly) added drily that yes, fate could be a bit of a bastard sometimes. I told him that I had two children, and he capped that effortlessly by saying that he had four. Borrowing a pen from a nearby kiosk lady—who was probably wondering why the fates had ordained that two raddled old variety comedians should choose her pitch for their rehearsal—we exchanged addresses and telephone numbers. I pressed him to visit us at Willow Cottage. A week or two later he and his wife Jane (whom I had not previously met) did just that, and so began a series of delightful weekends, alternately in Leeds and Sutton, in which we continued and expanded our former friendship—and, in Ben's wry phrase, ate and drank for Britain.

Jane was a delight. She ran their vast Roundhay mansion (which had a library, grand pianos in the sitting room, and a wonderfully stocked dining kitchen) with a downbeat nonchalance ('I'm such a slut') which could not mask her considerable organisational and culinary powers. She was, quite simply, the best cook I have ever known. This, coupled with Ben's generous way with the bottles, made a meal in their home a truly memorable experience, though it made us slightly ashamed of the hospitality that we offered in return. On one occasion, when they had arrived on a Friday lunchtime I suggested, as Ann was at work, that we three might stroll down for a drink and a snack at the dowdier of the two local pubs. The drinks were fine, but then Jane thought she might like a ham sandwich. Now in the Roberts' home this delicacy involved two slices of newly-baked crusty bread, spread with good salted butter and packed with chunky wedges of glistening home-cured ham all slathered with English mustard. In the Sutton pub by contrast it consisted of two listless pieces of factory-sliced bread, a scrape of some sort of ersatz butter and a film of tasteless pink mystery meat, sliced so thinly that it was to all intents and purposes transparent. Jane, normally the politest of ladies, lifted up this flabby concoction and broke into slow giggles, which mounted bit by bit until

Ben and I began to join in. Soon we were all hooting with hysterical laughter, all reason flown before the sight of that limp testament to bad pub catering which dangled lifelessly from Jane's shaking hand.

Such experiences did not however lead us to shun either the Nottinghamshire or the Yorkshire pubs. And on our way back from them, perhaps in a forlorn attempt to relive the recklessness of earlier days, we revived the practice of bawling out crude limericks, dredged up from our time in Leeds forty years before. Ben had if anything enlarged his repertoire:

> When Titian was mixing his madder,
> His model went off up the ladder.
>> Her position to Titian
>> Suggested coition,
> So he went up the ladder and 'ad her.

Others conjured up orgiastic pictures reminiscent of the wilder prints of Hieronymus Bosch:

> A randy young actress called Gloria
> Was screwed by Sir Gerald du Maurier,
>> Jack Hulbert, Jack Payne,
>> Jack Hulbert *again*,
> And the band of the Waldorf Astoria.

I had forgotten most of them but Ben and his family had apparently sung them for years on their car trips. Apropos of which he proudly told the story of one of his daughters, a professional folk singer, who throughout her career had been able to control even the rowdiest of audiences by means of knowing more bawdy choruses than they did. 'Ah yes,' murmured Jane from the back of the car, 'In the end it's all down to upbringing.'

My second reunion was less dramatic but every bit as important. I resumed close contact with the only friend of whom I am in awe. I had known Ian Robinson since my school-days and we had never really lost touch. He and his wife Hilary had occasionally stayed with us in London, and we visited them often in their Gringley home. But my contact with Ian had been maintained on another level because I read his many books and subscribed to *The Human World* and *Gadfly*, the two critical quarterlies he had edited (or conducted, as he sometimes preferred). Ian's was always a distinctive voice, in which he melded the critical sharpness of his mentor F. R. Leavis with a traditional Church of England theology. He has made scholarly and witty contributions to literary studies, theology, linguistic theory, politics and the sociology of the media, all demanding close and informed scrutiny. Which may explain why, when slick marketing and manufactured celebrity are prized more than scholarship, that save for loyal followers and the church grandees whom he sometimes goads, he is not widely read. His dedication to his causes has however never wavered.

Some years ago he stepped aside from his full-time academic post in order to concentrate on running his publishing imprint, The Brynmill Press. In addition to publishing the quarterlies and collections of Ian's essays, the press has published a variety of critical studies, and was at that time engaged in reissuing the collected works of T. F. Powys, the bucolic novelist that F.R.Leavis had championed.

Soon after I had moved to Sutton, I had resolved to write a summary of all my hostile attitudes to the Arts Council in one short polemic, provisionally titled *Vile Jelly* (though its title may be new, my critics tartly opined, it was still the same book I always wrote). I offered it to Ian and as part of our ensuing negotiations he suggested that I might join Duke Maskell and Barrie Mencher on the Board of the Brynmill Press. It was a generous offer but I had private reservations. They were all, one way and another, Leavisites and perfectly capable of collectively loosing off those canonical judgements which you may find bizarre or inexplicable, but concerning which you are curtly told that unless you can *see* that (for example) Iris Murdoch is the greatest living author writing in English, there is no point in arguing with you. So I accepted with some apprehension. I need not have worried. My nervous judgements were not dismissed out of hand, but carefully considered and *then* dismissed, which is as it should be. My fellow board members were wiser and more knowledgeable than I. However we enjoyed many convivial Board meetings, though I think my input (consisting of various over-optimistic schemes for marketing the books) was ultimately of little value.

For in truth the whole enterprise continued to depend upon Ian, who in the early days had typeset many of the Brynmill publications on his own hot metal press, in addition to designing, marketing and posting the books to purchasers. But it was rare for his efforts to be adequately rewarded, even when his press was offering works of real merit. At a lower level, both *Vile Jelly* and *Managing Britannia* (a later book I wrote in conjunction with our friend and former English master, Robert Protherough) were well reviewed, and sold well enough to the Brynmill regulars, but neither achieved the kind of general sales figures we all thought even they deserved.

The third, and totally unexpected, reunion was with my one-time Cambridge Vice Principal, John Irwin. He had seen something of mine on a remaindered shelf somewhere and had written to reintroduce himself. Of course we invited him down, and when he emerged from his rusty white caravette (he hadn't realised we intended him to stay *in* our house) the years rather fell away. He was as slim and lantern-jawed as ever, and with the same shy grin. The only essential difference was the fact, not immediately obvious in the glow of the afternoon sunlight, that he had dyed his springy mane of hair a rich purple. As we talked it also emerged that, since the time in Cambridge (where at my suggestion he had sent a script to Tony Britten) he had by slow degrees managed to leave well-paid academia and turn himself into an unsuccessful and impoverished writer. He was not actually living in a lonely garret, but in another dwelling equally appropriate to his calling—a small, rat-infested cottage in the wilds of Cumberland. His daughter was paying his mortgage.

He had brought numerous typescripts—poems, plays, essays and novels, many of them rejected by some of the best publishers in the land. I looked forward, genuinely, to reading them. But he wanted me to do more than that—to edit the scripts, to act as his agent, and hardest of all to find backers and producers for his plays. Like so many people who are trying to get their plays staged, or their books published, John was convinced that all he had to do was to attract one powerful supporter from inside the establishment and all would be well. I told him that, although I should try to help, I was certainly not inside the establishment, and had no influence with anybody important.

In any case the theatre had undergone several revolutions since the days when Binkie Beaumont pulled all the strings in the West End. Actors no longer worked primarily in playhouses. There was only one repertory company still working in Britain, and every other kind of show was patched together in touring circuits and new receiving houses. In the world of literature the change had been even greater. The insistent march of information technology had in many ways rendered what used to be known as the literary world obsolete. 'The reading public' was now becoming a network of kindle users. 'Publishers' were being replaced by online dissemination, and 'literary criticism' submerged within a kind of electronic populism, in which the ultimate accolade was going viral and accumulating 'likes'. I explained to John that I was too old to learn these new technological tricks. It remains true to this day. I have no mobile phone, nor a page on Facebook, nor have I ever tweeted or skyped. Nor do I want to. I choose to believe that overall information technology has harmed civilisation more than it has benefited it. I am quite happy to be the world's last remaining Luddite.

There is of course an irony in the fact that, holding the views I do, both of my children have spent much of their working lives in the world of film and television. During our time in Sutton they visited us regularly, bringing news of their latest enterprises—Cath doing four seasons on the *Eleven o' Clock Show,* which launched the careers of Ricky Gervaise, Sacha Baron Cohen, McKenzie Crook and many others, Martyn directing his first live-action film, *Green,* for Channel 4. They still came for the family Christmas, for which Willow Cottage, with its low beams and open fires, proved a Dickensy setting.

And it was at Sutton that we first met the partners with whom both were to settle down. Martyn, following his divorce, introduced us to the lovely Sharon, a fellow

artist, with whom he now lives in Notting Hill. Cath
brought Simon, an information technology man but also
an artist who, like Sharon, is possessed of a wry sense
of humour—though in other ways they do not resemble
each other. In due course we also met and stayed with
both Sharon and Simon's parents. Family gatherings
thus became ever more populous, so by the time Simon
and Cath had brought Bonnie Mia, their first-born
and our first grandchild, up to see us, the joys of the
expanding family had driven from our heads all thoughts
of technology's evils.

★   ★   ★

But as the family tree grew new roots, as is the way
of things, some of its tallest branches withered and died.
I must record the last years, and the passing, of our
parents.

Ann's father was considerably older than her mother
and, in his ninetieth year, and after only a brief illness,
he died in Eastbourne. His widow lived on for some
years in their flat, regularly visited by Ann and her sister,
and very happy to welcome all her grandchildren to the
sunshine coast. However, by the time we were preparing
to move North she had begun to exhibit distressing
signs of that senile dementia which is always, though
not always accurately, termed Alzheimer's Disease. This
condition is nowadays so common that its symptoms
do not need detailed description, but it will always hurt
and bewilder those who observe its ravages from without
much more than it hurts the sufferer. Ann's mother
became disturbingly forgetful of recent events, and her
erratic behaviour began to alarm her neighbours. Pat and
Ann saw that she could no longer be left without regular
and sympathetic companionship, so it was decided that
she should move into a comfortable and well-run care
home on the edge of Newark. We all visited her regularly,
including Pat who at weekends drove doggedly through
the Dartford Tunnel and up the crowded A1 to join
us. She and Ann would have lunch and walk with their
mother in the home's beautiful gardens. Sometimes
we brought her over to spend the day with us. She was
always a pleasant guest though on one occasion, upon

returning to her care home and being asked whether she had enjoyed herself, smilingly said she was glad to be back because in our house there had been far too much fighting.

In her later years she reverted often to her tempestuous Irish childhood but even at the height of her dementia she remained always the same sunny lady, thanking me 'and the other Derry boys' for bringing her food and drink, before (to use one of a well-known Irish comedian's flights of fancy) she picked up her Fenian needles and knitted another tank. One sunny day we used our camper van to transport her and my parents to a picnic in nearby Clumber Park. All seemed to be hunky dory until, looking out from the camper van's low-slung windows, I saw the retreating figure of my father, attempting to catch up with the much smaller figure of Ann's mother who was legging it purposefully off into the Clumber rhododendrons. We watched and waited—until at length the two of them reappeared, arm in arm. When they sat down and my father had caught his breath he explained that Ann's mother had been on her way home to Dublin. Quite oblivious of any incongruity involved in setting off to walk from Sherwood Forest across the Irish Sea, she smilingly explained that she was walking there because she hadn't wanted to put me to the trouble of driving her back. Not giving trouble was always her way. When she finally died, peacefully in her sleep, the staff of the care home joined the family virtually *en bloc* as we celebrated her life: 'She was a lovely lady.'

My father had rarely been ill, though in his eighties he began to slow down a bit, no longer meeting his friends two or three times a week for golf, but channelling his formidable competitive instincts into long games of Scrabble with my mother, whose vocabulary may have been larger but whose spelling was probably worse. So they were well-matched. For arbitration in these keenly-fought contests they had a well-thumbed Shorter Oxford Dictionary to hand. My father meticulously kept the scores on a notepad specially ruled out for the purpose and, if he happened to be on a good run of results, would leave it open on his chair-side table so visitors could chance upon it and congratulate him. But towards the end he became too exhausted even for Scrabble. He even stopped going out to potter in his little greenhouse. Finally, having achieved the same age as Ann's father, he took to his bed and quietly died.

Which brings us to my mother, who had surely been a candidate for an early grave. Throughout her life she had deliberately chosen to eat unhealthily (salads were 'rabbit food'; lacking a thick crust of congealed carbohydrates a shepherd's pie was 'not a proper pie'; unbuttered potatoes cooked in their skins were 'pig potatoes'), had most certainly enjoyed her sherry and until her ninetieth year had been a determined chain-smoker. Yet in the event she lived the longest of all. When my father died, she lived on in the same small ill-equipped house, tended thrice-daily by home carers, and visited by me two or three times a week. Then one day she suddenly collapsed and the carers rang to say she had been admitted to the local hospital. After a week or two there was an improvement in her condition and (though not without a few hard words —'You can't wait to be shot of me, can you?') she agreed to go into a new purpose-built care home in the village next to Sutton.

She was now well over ninety, but had not lost any of her gloomy truculence. 'Hello Mother,' I would gaily trill, walking into her sun-drenched room with its modern en suite facilities, 'Isn't it a lovely day? Ann sends her love. I've brought you some of that mint cake you like.' 'Why didn't you come yesterday?' 'Well I came the day before, and I told you that yesterday I was working in London. Now—did you enjoy your lunch?' 'No, I didn't.' 'Oh, why?' 'That Honker (a quietly spoken girl called Veronica, against whom my maternal parent had inexplicably taken) was there, watching me.' 'It's her job, Mother.' 'Well, I've got my eye on her.'

I wish I could say that she died peacefully, but I cannot. To the last she was convinced that not only was I shamefully neglecting her but also that I had the carers—whom she thought of as prison warders—in my pay. 'Tell them I'm watching them—*and* I'm taking notice,' she would instruct me in her best schoolmarm voice. The day before she died she had been brought down to the lounge to sit amongst the other residents. I walked in after lunch with a piece of news for her. She had taken a lifelong interest in the Queen Mother, claiming (after the manner of royalty fans) to know what the Queen Mum thought about things as disparate as fox hunting and Fergie's love life. However, though she was pleased that her favourite had lived to a great age, my mother still wanted to outlive her. So I had come to tell her that the day before the Queen Mother had indeed died. In order not to alarm the rest of the room's occupants, I conveyed my sad news in a low and suitably sombre voice. 'What?' she said, flapping her hands to draw me towards her, 'What d'you say?' I tried again, a little more loudly. 'For Gawd's sake! Speak up!' So I filled my lungs and bellowed at the top of my voice, 'The Queen Mother is dead!!' 'Good!!' my dear old Mother shouted back, momentarily pleased that at last events were unfolding in the right order. The startled residents looked on, appalled.

It was the last conversation we ever had. At ten o' clock that evening the home's matron rang me to say my mother had died, and did I want to see her before she was taken away? I had been asked the same question at my father's death, and was asked again when, much later, Ann died. In each case I gave the answer 'no'. I was grievously saddened in each case but to pay homage to lifeless flesh has always seemed to me to be a superstitious ritual that answers no longing and expiates no guilt. However the matron seemed to imply that it was expected of me and so I offered an excuse—something that sounded plausible but did not, on this occasion, happen to be true: 'I'm afraid I've been drinking. I couldn't drive over tonight'. Even as I uttered the lie I seemed to hear my mother's bitter comment—'You can't even be bothered to see me when I'm dead!' Her manner was always gruff and stern, but she was nevertheless capable of considerable sympathy and, for certain sorts and conditions of men, compassion. At her funeral I was pleased, though not altogether surprised, to receive several unsolicited letters from her former pupils, telling me what a difference she had made to their lives.

★   ★   ★

That same autumn, our remaining ties with the area having been finally severed, we left Nottinghamshire for the last time. We had considered many possibilities for what would probably prove to be our final destination, including a Yorkshire mill town, a return to London or even (very briefly) a croft in a Highland glen. Eventually we decided, after paying it two or three scouting visits, that we would, like so many others before us, retire to Eastbourne. The town did not set the heart racing but it did tick most of the boxes. It was the sunniest place in Britain, and set by the sea (two things which pleased Ann). It was moreover easy to get out of, whether one chose to walk on the Sussex Downs, take the train up to the London theatre, or fly out from nearby Gatwick. Chichester, Glyndebourne, Brighton and Lewes were comparatively near. We also learned that houses in the town centre were comparatively cheap, because most of those retiring to the sunshine coast preferred to hunker down in a well-guarded service flat. At that time we could not for the lives of us think why.

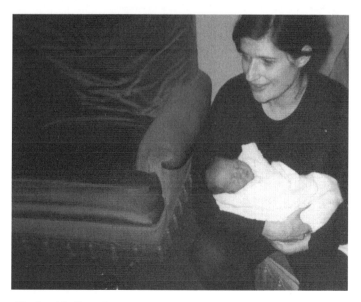

Cath with Bonnie

early retirement: Ann, JP

❧14❧

Eastbourne

EASTBOURNE EXISTS within a curious time warp. Its long, defiantly old-fashioned promenade is studded with pre-war ice cream booths, browning palm trees kneeling before the wind and blue-painted benches staring vacantly out over the English Channel. Its Victorian pier, like all of its kind, has long outlived its original purposes and is now dotted with a silent gaggle of kiosks, with a raucous cacophony of slot machines chattering to themselves inside the old music pavilion.* To the West of the pier squats the pre-war bandstand, where military bands no longer play, but whose concrete base still juts pugnaciously out on to the steeply sloping foreshore. Eastbourne's beach is virtually devoid of sand and instead consists almost entirely of cobblestones, making the building of sandcastles or the playing of games impossible unless the tide is completely out. In bad weather, there being no undercover attractions on the front, luckless visitors are reduced to trudging round the Arndale shopping entre, or to watching it rain from one of the town's innumerable coffee shops.

In a word, Eastbourne exists almost entirely for the convenience of its elderly residents and visitors, so it suited us just fine. Without difficulty we bought and

---

* No longer! In 2014 the Musical Pavilion was burned out. The pier itself had to be partly rebuilt, but the opportunity to rethink its purpose cut no ice with the preservationists, who wanted it restored *just as it was*.

moved in to a narrow, five-storey dwelling in the heart of
the town, with shops, pubs, bus stops and railway station
all just around the corner. From an upstairs window we
could see the sea, just a couple of streets away, and when
the weather was good it was a simple matter to take
our books and our canvas chairs down to the Western
lawns and join the other wrinklies in staring myopically
at the horizon. When we both felt more active, we walked
out to Holywell or along to Sovereign Harbour. Ann,
mindful of the days she used to accompany her father
to have his daily dip, sometimes braved the waves and
swam. Cowardly by nature, I would guard her clothes
and towels, ready at her signal to pick my way down to
the water's edge with the rubber slip-ons which allowed
her to walk up the cobbles without risking injury.

Friends, perhaps surprised to find that Eastbourne
was a real place and not just an invention of cartoonists
and comedy writers, found excuses to visit us. Ian
Robinson discovered an acquaintance from the English
Prayer Book Society who lived in the area. David
Norman, another old school friend, stayed with his wife
when he sang with his choir over at Rye. Kate and Ian,
together with a number of their emigrating cats, found
it a convenient stopover when they were driving over
to their French home. Ben and Jane used the alibi that
they wanted to revisit the Devonshire Hotel where Ben's
brother had annually taken a suite as he audited the hotel
chain's accounts. Robert, down from Hull with Judith
and Margaret, said that he was most interested to see
Eastbourne because when his father was driving his
family along the South Coast he had always 'missed it
out'. They were all of them prepared to overlook our
embarrassing choice of retirement venue, kindly affecting
not to notice the flaws in our characters which had led us
to sink so low.

Of course some visitors came just to see us, rather
than just to take a fascinated peek at God's Waiting
Room. Ruth, for example, spent three weeks in Eastbourne writing a book and celebrating a significant
birthday with a visit to nearby Glyndebourne. Ann's
friends (whom I called by the nicknames we gave them)
visited in rotation; 'Yappy' brought news of the current

thinking of the left, 'Himmler' of the right, and 'Mad Margaret' brought us news of her latest affairs, while treating her wheezing bulldog to a dump on the prom. Mary, whom Ann had known since her undergraduate days, had an annual 'birthday tea' with Ann at the Grand and was one of a regular group attending the local Film Society. Another memorable visit was from Ann's 'Revision Group', a posse of LSE postgraduates alongside whom she had worked for her M. Sc. and who met annually to compare notes on their subsequent careers. On that occasion I cooked their anniversary lunch for them, and was rewarded by a little spatter of applause as I passed through the dining hall on my way out to my own lunch at Wetherspoons.

Few of these visitors expressed any interest in moving to Eastbourne although for a short time Ann's sister Tish did just that. She first moved into one of the tightly-constructed faux Georgian terraced homes that seem to spring up on every brownfield site in Eastbourne. But the ticky-tackyness of the house, and Eastbourne's asphyxiating gentility combined to unsettle her. She soon sold up and moved to an altogether more bosky dwelling in nearby Hailsham, which led on to fields and good walking country. There she was, I think, much happier. On our frequent visits to her we would all eat at the Hailsham Wetherspoons, a stylish establishment set in an old inn, and conveniently just by the stop for the Eastbourne bus.

Ann put her energies into charitable work, and soon made herself useful working in the local Oxfam Shop, while I (probably against my better judgement) sought to put my long experience as a cultural planner at the service of the local Council. In pursuance of this noble end I chaired a number of the Council's various regeneration committees, was elected Chairman of the civic pressure group, the Eastbourne Society, spent much time in writing discussion papers, and expended much energy in persuading influential people to advise us. However, my efforts to persuade the powers-that-be of the benefits of holistic cultural planning proved unavailing. There was, among the populace as well as in the ranks of the wary Council officials, a deeply-rooted hostility to change, particularly if it threatened the officers' personal interests. So, after a few months, I detached myself from the morass and, with no great pleasure, watched the town's planning efforts congeal into vacuity.

From a selfish point of view however, my involvement with the town's progressive element led to a number of friendships with unusual and interesting people who, I couldn't help noticing, were generally not Eastbourne natives. The most extraordinary of them all was probably Hugh Riddick, a lawyer who had spent much of his life in private practice in the town, and who had been a distinguished rugby player. Years before, Hugh had been instrumental in helping to set up the town's Citizens' Advice Bureau and the local branch of the Samaritans (an important service, given the town's proximity to Beachy Head). He was also one of the original Trustees of the local Hospice, and indeed a mover and shaker in many of the local societies. Not the least surprising thing about him was that he had been to school in Gloucestershire with my friend and English Master Robert Protherough. Dapper in appearance, and quietly spoken, Hugh remained to the end a master of the unexpected. Wandering together through a deserted Eastbourne hotel —which we had our eyes on as a possible home for a town museum—Hugh looked at the raised stage in the ballroom and murmured to me, 'Ah yes, that's where I put a firecracker under the Mayor's chair'. On another occasion two beautiful young girls came up to him in a pub restaurant, shouted 'Hugh', threw their arms around him and kissed him warmly. It was obvious that through one of his charitable endeavours he had helped them in some way. When they had done with embracing him, and after they had bidden him an emotional goodbye, I asked Hugh admiringly who they were. Wiping his glistening cheeks he shook his head, professional to the last. 'I've no idea,' he said.

One always respected Hugh's opinion, even if it was not always flattering to oneself. After the death of Muriel, Hugh's third wife, Ann and I regularly met with him in the slightly posher of the two Eastbourne Wetherspoons. Ann would come over when she had finished her morning stint at Oxfam, and we talked as we tucked into our all-day breakfasts. Usually these conversations meandered through familiar territory—the narcissism of our local MP for example—but on this particular day Hugh had taken to asking Ann in some detail about her charity work. After a while I realised that what he was doing was cunningly suggesting to her that she might consider working with the Samaritans. I confronted Hugh with this, adding tartly, 'Why don't you ask *me* to be a Samaritan?' The little smile and shrug Hugh gave me not only answered the question but indicated the kind of character analysis I would be given were I to persist in posing as a caring citizen.

Then of course there was Jane Montague, the enigmatic and talented daughter of the celebrated theatre architect Henry Montague. Jane is an architect, a teacher of Yoga, an artist (one of her paintings forms the cover of this book) and, if I may say so, a delightfully wacky conversationalist. I count myself lucky to have known her during what would be, I was sure, a short stay in Eastbourne. The same applies to two other members of the Eastbourne enlightenment—Tony Crooks, an outstanding IT man who seemingly had the power to hack into the local Council's grubbiest secrets, and the sometime editor of the local papers, the alarmingly fit Peter Austin. Both men became great lunchtime friends. The three of us rather favoured eating in the Eastbourne *Bibendum,* the restaurant opposite the Town Hall. We took great pleasure in watching the Council staff take lunch there because—after spending a busy morning screwing the pensioners, watering the workers' beer and so forth— it was a delight to watch the smiles drain from their pasty faces as soon as they clocked this triumvirate of smilingly inebriated cynics.

There was the indefatigable Pam Kuhn, who led two music hall performances at the Hippodrome, which I came out of retirement to chair. The Musical Director for the first was the multi-talented Mark Jones, who co-wrote with me the history of that venue, *Mr Phipps' Theatre: The Sensational Story of Eastbourne's Royal Hippodrome.* Mark was the first of us to decamp from the town, going off with his wife and son to live in Malta. Before that the book's launch had been successfully engineered by the Royal Hippodrome's highly successful manager, John Pleydell, who, with his lovely wife Pat, later turned his home into the nearest thing Eastbourne had to a *salon des artistes*. It helped that he was, in addition to everything else, a wonderful cook.

Finally there was—the Quiet Man. Whereas most of my new acquaintances would announce themselves from the opposite side of the street with a whooping and a hollering, anxious to fill me in on the latest probably untrue but still riveting piece of local gossip, Len Smith went about the town stealthily, with a quiet smile playing about his lips to indicate that he knew of things the rest of us didn't. For he had really achieved something of significance in Eastbourne. When his family first moved to the town after the war young Len, together with a gang of his like-minded cronies, had started a Youth Club football team. Gradually, and of course with different players, the club had progressed through local and then county leagues, the old Southern League and were now playing, in a well-equipped stadium, in the National League. If you get to know Len well he may tell you the whole astonishing story, may even show you photographs of himself, first as a youthful left half, then digging ditches and humping soil to set up their Priory Lane ground, and finally as the proud Chairman of Eastbourne Borough F.C.

What he may not tell you, because he is also a political animal, is that the Borough Council, which one way and another loses up to two million pounds a year running its three theatres, has not only refused to assist its best football club, but has also on occasion stood in the way of its expansion. The Council officers would explain that they could not offer help to Borough without offering the same assistance to the town's other two semi-professional sides. 'If only the three clubs would combine,' one of the dafter officers once wailed in my presence, conveniently forgetting that the Council throws shedloads of cash at its three separate semi-professional theatres, which *could* well benefit from combining into one. But Len knows the real reason for the Council's hostility. It is nothing to do with the scale or manner of the club's activities, which are exemplary. For in addition to hosting the football teams, Priory Lane has a crèche, bowling club, all-day restaurant, beautifully-run bars and is a community centre for the nearby estates—it is indeed Eastbourne's most-used cultural facility. But, against this, and trumping all other arguments, the sad truth is that Eastbourne Borough FC operates at *the wrong end of town.* And, unlike the frequently deserted Devonshire Park, Priory Lane *cannot be seen from the windows of the Town Hall.*

★ ★ ★

In spite of Ann and I being old retirees, there remained a creative buzz around our family gatherings. Cath and Martyn were regular visitors. They had a residual affection for Eastbourne, remembering the summers they had spent with their grandparents. But their lives had spun off in all sorts of directions. We briefly invaded the media world when we went up to see the recording of a TV sit-com for which Cath was on the production staff. We were ridiculously proud to see our daughter waving her magic clipboard over this frothy confection (observing one at work, I had a late-life fantasy that I could perhaps repackage myself as a warm-up man). We all went over to Brighton to see the première of *The Age of Stupid,* for which Martyn had animated the scenes of global desolation which gave the film its impact. A year or two later Martyn brilliantly directed his first feature film, *Ultramarines,* with John Hurt, Terence Stamp and Sean Pertwee. He gave us a handsome DVD set of the film, which we proudly showed to everybody who stayed with us, whether they were *Warhammer* fanatics or not. Meanwhile I was pleased to be asked to work with Sharon's father on his life story, *The Strong and Silent Man,* which recounted his rise from an East End childhood to acting as show business accountant to the Beatles, Cilla Black, George Raft and many others. Sharon herself published a beautifully-illustrated, hugely successful book, *Drawing With Impact,* which was not only an immediate best-seller, but found itself translated into several languages.

Meanwhile Cath and Simon, chary of bringing up Bonnie and her brother Mackenzie in the wilder reaches of North London, had decided they would move to the boskier environs of Lewes, not very far from us in East-bourne. Of course we were privately delighted. They found a centrally-located four-bedroomed house and managed the complexities of moving, finding schools, changing jobs and so forth with great success. Soon Simon had successfully qualified as a schoolmaster and was teaching IT in a local Academy, in his spare time coaching a youth soccer team for which Mackenzie (already showing signs of being a remarkable midfielder) regularly played. Cath continued to build her career as a resource producer for television programmes, sometimes undertaking the arduous daily commute from Lewes to Victoria, and then returning home to help with her young children. We tried to help when we could, going over to collect the grandchildren from their First School, and watching both Bonnie and Mac playing matches after school on the school's attractive but freezing cold playing fields.

Watching our grandchildren grow up was a great, and unexpected, pleasure to us both. Seeing Bonnie become a talented and beautiful young lady, and Mackenzie develop not only as an outstanding sportsman but also as a café wit, gave us both great pleasure, and in view of what happened shortly thereafter, it is comforting to remember how Ann delighted in them—as indeed she did in all of her family.

★　★　★

Quite early in our time in Eastbourne Ann, who was meticulous about having regular check-ups, was diagnosed with breast cancer and, having been success-fully operated on in Eastbourne DGH, undertook a course of immersive therapy involving six weekly treatments of about ten minutes each in Brighton. Ann always took a companion, usually me, with her on these journeys to act as 'carer'. Some of her other companions however were much less fit than either of us were. They found the cramped bus journey, uphill walk to the hospital, and long wait with her on hard benches for the invariably-delayed treatment, extremely trying. The result was that on those occasions the patient, Ann, ended up comforting and attending to the needs of the carer. However, it all passed and soon she was declared free of cancer. In typical fashion she immediately joined an area committee dedicated to educating medical personnel in the best ways of breaking bad news to patients and families. (A dreadful indication of the compartmentalisation of the NHS was that the chairman of that committee, a cancer specialist under whose general care Ann had been, was to write to her some six weeks after her death from cancer to send her the agenda for the next meeting.)

After her recovery from breast cancer, Ann renewed her voluntary role with Oxfam, and aside from frolicking in our strange corkscrew house, we occupied our time in visiting old friends and new places. In those years we tested the adage that Eastbourne was an easy place to get away from to near destruction. We went by (someone else's) car to stay with John Offord in his Normandy château, where his spacious grounds offered a splendid opportunity to relax into *la vie Françoise,* while John continued, as always, to work on his computer. We went, part of the way at least, by ferry to visit Eddie and Di in the Isle of Wight. We rumbled up by train to visit Ben and Jane for yet more limericks interleaving their generous hospitality. Most unexpected of all, we visited Robert, Margaret and Judith in their new Oxford home, by train *and* coach. Easy peasy! We took the train up to Victoria, stepped outside the station and caught the 'Oxford Tube' which deposited us as close to their door in Headington as Eastbourne Station was close to ours.

The term 'Tube', so suggestive of speed and economy, was no doubt bestowed upon it by some donnish prankster with an overdeveloped sense of irony, as in reality the 'Oxford Tube' consisted of a bog-standard coach, which juddered its way slowly through London's suburbs in a wholly conventional manner, staying well above the ground. We supposed that it was not acceptable among the dreaming spires to call the conveyance by vulgar titles such as 'bus' or 'coach'. To this end we noticed that Robert, while being perfectly happy to adopt modish Oxford terminology in the right context—for example, describing an Oxford piss-up as a 'gaudy'— shrank fastidiously from calling a jolting bus journey by a name which suggested rapid subterranean transit.

We also went by coach on a number of those mini-
breaks that are such a feature of Eastbourne retirees'
lives. At various times we explored new regions of
France, German vineyards and the glorious Scottish
Highlands. We also enjoyed several visits to Ireland—
watching with horrified fascination the irresistible rise,
followed by the unstoppable collapse, of that falsely-
engineered economic boom that went by the unfortunate
name of 'The Celtic Tiger'. These trips usually lasted
for less than a week but were almost always impeccably
organised with programmes tailored to the needs of their
clientèle, who were usually well stricken in years. One
company was so well-organised, so caring for the needs
of its elderly travellers, that a taxi picked up and returned
each of their customers to his or her very own doorstep.

It is therefore salutary that an alteration to the
programme of one of these coach holidays which
cemented a pleasant acquaintanceship into a new and
deeper friendship, and may have been one of those
'turning points' which some say lurk undetected beneath
the surface of our lives. I had, more out of inertia than
anything else, carried on giving occasional talks in the
area. When booking this particular holiday I had carefully
noted that we returned to Eastbourne on the morning of
a day when I was due to give an evening talk to a local
society on 'Eastbourne's Theatres'. I thought that would
give me plenty of time. But a few days before departure
we unexpectedly received an amended programme. We
were now to be returned to base at some unspecified
time during the afternoon! It still might have been all
right but I couldn't take the risk of letting down the
bookers. Nor did I want to cancel the holiday. What was
to be done?

A few months before, Ann and I had made the
acquaintance of a new neighbour, Brian Freeland, whose
love of opera (together with his extensive DVD collection
of memorable productions) delighted Ann. In turn I was
mesmerised by Brian's long experience of theatre, and
by his stories of the extraordinarily diverse figures with
whom, and for whom, he had worked—Laurence Olivier,
Noël Coward and Joan Littlewood among them. He
would come round once a week for coffee, and we would,

amongst much else, discuss the way the local Council was dealing with its three once-vibrant but now slowly disintegrating theatres. So Brian would be a wonderful replacement. He not only had far better theatrical stories than I did, but knew at least as much about Eastbourne's crumbling theatrical edifices. So, knowing that he also had considerable experience of public speaking, I took my courage in both hands and asked him if he would give the talk. He agreed and, needless to say, was a resounding success. The group never asked me again, though Brian returns to them regularly (as he does to most of his gigs). Indeed his kindness in taking my booking may have helped to nudge him towards resuming and greatly enlarging his role as a professional speaker.

Meanwhile Ann and I continued our sequence of short breaks. One of the most memorable was a visit to the rolling green landscapes of the Ribble Valley, where the ancestors of Ann's father had once lived and worked. The climax of that holiday was a three hour boat trip down the Manchester Ship Canal. We embarked from the Salford Quays, with the lights of the new BBC Centre shining expensively out into the misty Summer morning. 'Money to burn, them buggers,' commented our fellow passengers with Lancastrian finality. We glided through the huge locks, past the swinging canal bridge and the unexpected bird sanctuaries, before finally cutting across the sunlit Mersey and mooring in the august shadow of Liverpool's Liver Building. We disembarked hand in hand. There was, for us both, a deep significance in this symbolic 'return' to the city of Ann's childhood, from which she had set out with her gauche young husband some fifty years earlier.

A few weeks later Ann went on a short walking holiday with her sister. On her return she said that when away she had felt more tired than usual, and had developed a slight cough. As she got off the train she called in to the medical 'Drop In Centre' in Eastbourne Station, to get their advice. They had said that there was probably nothing to worry about, but she should see her doctor as soon as she could. The next morning she did. The doctor made arrangements for her to have an immediate X Ray at the nearby Esperance Hospital. She then went back to the surgery to hear the result, uncharacteristically refusing to let me accompany her. When she returned she stood uncertainly in the hallway, looking grey and drained. As we clung to each other she whispered to me, 'It's not good news, love.' Then, barely audibly, 'I've got lung cancer.'

❧15❧
Death

DURING THE FOLLOWING DAYS there were brief moments of sunshine, as when our concerned neighbours brought round bunches of flowers and treats to tempt Ann to eat. But there were also long periods of dark foreboding. A worried Tish came over, slept and sat for many silent hours with her sister. One day Ann sat up and tried to be bright for her grandchildren who had brought over their tributes—Bonnie a videoed play performed by her and her friends, and Mackenzie a personally animated film, which began as a Western but finished, inevitably, with the mounted cowboy scoring a cracking goal, right in the corner of the net. Ann loved them both. Dr Stewart, whose care for all of us was exemplary, tried on his many visits to convey that the end was inevitable and that he would do everything he could to ease Ann's passing.

To say I was not ready for Ann's death is platitudinous of course. One is never totally ready for a loved one's death, any more than one is prepared for one's own. And the awkward truth was that Ann and I had prepared ourselves for a quite different outcome. We had operated on the assumption that, with my heavy drinking, overeating and refusal to take unnecessary exercise, I should (deservedly) be the first to go. All our financial affairs—bonds, insurances, pension schemes and so on—were predicated on the reasonable expectation that, after making decent arrangements for my cremation and after paying my outstanding bar bills, Ann would be able to enjoy a long and busy retirement. We had regularly joked about this all-too-likely prospect. But now there was no laughter, and indeed no time for anything else, for the only redeeming feature of Ann's untimely death was the brevity of her last illness. Only three weeks elapsed between that moment when she told me that she was suffering from lung cancer to the terrible empty afternoon when, deadened by morphine, she finally slipped out of consciousness, and I phoned Martyn and Cath to break the dreadful news.

There followed a purposeful, purposeless fortnight, filled with arrangements for Ann's cremation, and the opening of a seemingly endless stream of letters and cards commiserating with us on our loss, and making a brave attempt at saying all that Ann had meant to them. David Norman wrote with a memory of him and his engineering mates passing Ann and me when we were walking along a Leeds pavement and wolf-whistling loudly (he says at Ann, though at the time I thought it was aimed, ironically, at me). Harry Pinsker, who had lost his own dear wife Ana, wrote touchingly. Others rang and, condolences having been given and received, the line would fall silent save for the sound of two people politely breathing, each waiting for the other to terminate the exchange. When I bumped into friends in the street they would, I noticed, cradle my elbow as they expressed their sorrow. One theatrical friend who hailed me in Grove Road less than a week after Ann's death, hugged me wordlessly to his bosom, cradled my elbow, looked deeply into my eyes, and sighed, 'Oh poor *John!*', adding in a brisker tone, 'So—will you marry again?' Typically, Jane Montague got it exactly right. A day or two before the 'Celebration of Ann's Life'—the civil ceremony which nowadays seems to have replaced both Funerals and Services of Remembrance—Jane came round to South Street with a special bottle of brandy, smiled, said, 'Don't drink it all at once' and disappeared.

It had been our custom to make light of every family event—'except for Weddings, of course' my crusty old father would add—but now we touched in each other unexpected depths of emotion. My children and their families were wonderfully supportive, of me and of each other, busying themselves about the town when I wanted to be alone while I, forcing myself to remember that it was equally their loss, tried as best I could to respond to their feelings. The lady who was to lead the atheist service of remembrance came and gently interrogated Tish and me on the details of Ann's life, and Martyn and Cath helped to choose the sound tracks which were to be seamlessly inserted into her eulogy (which, irreverently, reminded me of *Desert Island Discs*). Then Sharon arrived and calmly and wonderfully, and with the help on the day of her kind sister Barbara, made all the arrangements for the post-remembrance reception at South Street.

I have, like everybody else, been to many funerals, and indeed arranged those of my own parents, but I think that until that day I had always regarded them with half a theatre-director's eye, looking for example at which mourning couples were studiously avoiding each other's eyes, as they tend to do in the opening scenes of a macabre whodunnit or, in comic mode, speculating inwardly at the slapstick scenes that would surely ensue were the dead one to throw open the coffin lid, and spring out with a cheery cry of 'Surprise, Sur-prihise!' It had no doubt been a childish defence mechanism, but however much I may have wept in private, at public ceremonies I had always found it impossible to remain appropriately mournful. For example, at Ken Rowat's service of remembrance, there were at the back of the church two or three rows of elderly ladies in what looked like widow's weeds, some wearing veils. They were probably innocent relatives, but I had them down as a parade of past mistresses of Ken, who would at a signal stand up, strike attitudes and wail in unison like a demented Greek chorus. At the chapel ceremony for one of my more militaristic aunts, I became convinced that her grieving husband would shortly call for a parade-ground inspection of the dress of the mourners, after the manner of General Montgomery, whom she slightly resembled. At the funeral of my cousin Jill I had a different kind of fantasy. In the funeral oration I was startled to hear that she had been a devoted fan of Cliff Richard. She had never mentioned this particular shortcoming to me, and the information made me glance nervously around the church, fearful that I had wandered into the wrong funeral (which, together with being in the wrong costume on the wrong stage in the wrong play, is another one of my recurrent nightmares).

I had no such fantasies on the day of Ann's cremation. Sharon, arranging this with the same meticulous care that she had everything else, had ordered a car to take me to the Crematorium. Once there, I remember greeting Ann's friend Susan, Malcolm Webster, Ian Robinson, who had driven over from Hereford, and Pat Moulder who had driven from Cambridge, then running up the drive to greet Ben and Jane who took the laurel wreath for long-distance mourning by having driven down from their home in North Yorkshire. Then I remember ducking away to hide as I couldn't bear to watch the arrival of the funeral cortège and Ann's coffin being carried in to the chapel. Then we passed inside. This time no untoward flights of fancy. Only memories of the many years Ann and I had spent together, interspersed with bafflement at the unfeeling fate which had determined that we should die in the wrong order.

Then, ferried by Mary's daughter Jess, I was back at the house, made unexpectedly fragrant by bowls of lilies, drinking from wine glasses charmed out of the neighbourhood restaurateur by Sharon, and eating the delicious canapés she and Martyn had conjured up from somewhere, all served to us with much gravitas by our handsomely-dressed waiters, Bonnie and Mackenzie. It was a sunny afternoon and I wound my way out to the garden bench in our tiny, rather overgrown, back yard. I remember drinking too much wine, chatting with Ian Robinson, Tony Crooks, Edward Thomas and some of Ann's LSE friends, and then gravitating indoors to talk to Ben and Jane and drinking a lot more wine before Ben, with the air of a master strategist proposing new and revolutionary tactics to break an impossible stalemate, suggested that it was about time, surely, that we had a drink and something to eat. I remember walking with him and Jane the fifty yards or so to Morgans bistro, and crying a little, but nothing at all after that.

It was the following days which were the most difficult to fill. Just as you are always told that following a car accident the best thing you can do is to get right back in the car and drive, so you are supposed, following the death of a loved one, to try as far as possible to resume normal life. But almost every aspect of my normal life had so far involved Ann, as aspects of hers had involved me. For some reason an old pop single kept running through my mind:

> First the tide rushes in,
> Plants a kiss on the shore . . . .

Then it lazily rocks to its haunting climax, the banality of the lyrics transmuted into something more meaningful by the infinite richness of Sinatra's voice:

> In the rain, in the dark, in the sun,
> Like the tide at its ebb,
> I'm at peace in the web
> Of your arms.

But in spite of snatching at such consolations I felt empty and drained. Of course there were some warm family moments—Cath and Simon coming over with their family and Simon cooking us all a sumptuous Sunday lunch of Scottish salmon, Martyn and Sharon spending an extended farewell evening with me in Wetherspoons, Tish chatting consolingly to the neighbours—but the most important person was always somehow missing from these events. I still reached for her as I woke up each morning, still out of habit put her cup out on the tea tray and still found myself memorising little comic incidents in order to recount them to her when we were alone.

Friends rallied round of course. Brian, happily for me, resumed his Monday morning visits, for which we both prepared piles of paper—programmes, old newspaper articles and the like—about which we would happily reminisce while discovering, to our growing incredulity, how often our paths seemed to have crossed in the past without either of us ever having previously met the other. John Pleydell invited me to delicious meals at his home. Tony and Peter resumed the occasional Bibendum lunches, I suspect largely for my benefit, and we three also met up occasionally at Eastbourne Borough games —on one occasion even being invited by Len into the holy of holies, the *Directors' Box!* I went up a couple of times to the National Theatre, once with Ruth to see an absurdly overegged pudding made of Goldsmith's *She Stoops to Conquer* and then with Brian to see a much more restrained production of G.B. Shaw's *The Doctor's Dilemma*. The fashion for cinema presentations of live opera performances having finally reached Eastbourne Brian and I were able to enjoy an excellent Royal Opera House *Eugene Onegin* for a tenner without leaving town. I found I now enjoyed such delights distantly, without getting emotionally involved, as once I had.

Hugh Riddick, whose third wife had died not long before, drove me out to lunch in Alfreston and (with his attractive daughter Fiona, over from her work scanning the Spanish skies) on another occasion to eat at a splendid pub in the Cuckmere Valley. And one special autumn day he took me to Sheffield Park, where we quietly talked of the passing of the seasons as we walked by the lakes. In the garden shop Hugh bought spring-flowering bulbs to be planted in loving memory of Ann. I was pleased when, the following spring, I was able to show them to him shyly flowering by the side of my front path.

Ann was more prosaically recalled by the slow untangling of her 'estate'. This was both larger and more labyrinthine than any of us had realised. Our next door family solicitor, Sheila Cramp, proved to be not only highly efficient but a sympathetic friend, explaining legal and financial intricacies to Martyn, Cath and me (Ann had no fewer than sixteen accounts—including one in Switzerland, for heaven's sake!) and answering our questions patiently. Before it was all wound up, it more than once occurred to me that for those fortunate enough to have a little money, unravelling such fiscal intricacies was becoming, in our mercantile age, a replacement for the traditional funeral service. Instead of pulpit eulogies for the goodness of the departed, together with hopes for their eternal life, the priests of modern finance now complimented the deceased on the cash they had squirrelled away, and on their skill at hiding it from the Inland Revenue.

And so, uncertainly at first but with increasing inevitability, I fell into the daily routines of the aged widower. Going out first thing for a daily paper and a few provisions, then preparing my breakfast of toast, mandarin oranges and a glass of tomato juice, before attempting the *Guardian* crossword. Then morning coffee, opening the post (if any) and an hour or two on the computer. Although I attempted a little housework from time to time, I knew that if I were left to my own devices, my home would soon resemble the set for a well-known play by John Arden, and so I determined to employ a part-time housekeeper. Here I had an extraordinary piece of luck. Through the good offices of John and Pat Pleydell, I met the wonderful Sue McPherson, who not only sorted out my strange five-storey home, but advised me cheerfully on which household appliances were wearing out and whether they should or could be replaced, what new bed linen I needed and which long-term provisions I should buy and freeze. Thus, on two or three mornings a week, Sue became a most welcome agent of normality and good order.

Lunchtime was the critical period. It could, occasionally, go the righteous and healthy way with a bracing walk along the front and a frugal salad. But it could more easily go wrong. If I knew I was going to spend the day alone too often I would around two o'clock take a book, settle down and read it in a local bar—Eastbourne has many such—having a snack meal and a couple of glasses of wine. Then home for a brief rest and then, like as not, pick up another book, have supper and drink yet more wine in Morgans bistro, just along the road. On such days I would stumble back home about nine o'clock and (sign of your lonely widower) fall asleep in front of the television, waking up to strange late-night programmes designed, I presumed, for drunken deadbeats, into which category I was rapidly falling. Lacking at this late stage any capacity for self-analysis, I adopted instead the persona of the literary outsider, fastidiously observing the foibles of others while remaining blissfully unaware of my own. I noticed for instance that the same group of shabby, moist-eyed old men was often to be seen sitting about in the pub at around the same time as I was. Looking at their loneliness and quiet desperation, and their apparent over-reliance on alcohol, I rather pitied them.

I still travelled to see friends, but with a caution that bordered on the neurotic I would now allow at least an hour to effect a change of vehicle, even if it only involved moving from one side of a station platform to the other. I began to rehearse what I was going to say to someone I didn't know, even if I was conveying the simplest of requests. Then, at the point of delivery, I would somehow contrive to mangle the words. Thus to an unfamiliar assistant at the delicatessen, 'Can I pask what the rice is of those tame guys?' Faced with baffled incomprehension, I would attempt to row back the other's sympathy by affecting a stammer, and make it much, much worse. But perhaps the surest sign of my rapidly approaching senility was the thoroughness with which I now reconnoitred my comfort stops. No would-be escaper from a prison camp has ever plotted the guards' lookout posts with more thoroughness than I mapped those lavatories. I recorded the entry points, opening times and admission prices of every public toilet in every habitation I ever visited—however cunningly the authorities may have sought to camouflage them. Soon I was grading possible destinations entirely by the number and availability of the jakes which abutted them—though without taking any concern for their fragrance or interior decoration, reasoning to myself, at any rate in the case of Gentlemen's *pissoirs*, that once you've seen one, you've seen 'em all*.

As must have been obvious to my loved ones, I was sliding gently downhill. Yet I would not want to paint myself, or my circumstances, in too doleful a light. In so many ways I was still highly privileged. My family kept a wary eye upon me and we had regular family gatherings. There were delightful Hudsons lunches with Pam, with Mary and with John Pleydell and also with eighty-something-year-old Jo with whom I had long discussions about

---

* This is not strictly true. In Hull there is near the Museum District a nest of public lavatories looking across the Humber, with hanging baskets and brilliantly polished brass, on whose immaculately tiled walls the custodian regularly displays his poetry free of charge. It is more interesting than many so-called 'arts centres'.

whether she should or should not go on the stage. Distant friends came over and I arranged little celebrations at Bibendum, Morgans and the short-lived but highly exotic Persian establishment down the road where they once advertised an evening feast with a *belly dancer,* of all unexpected Eastbourne delights! Just as memorable for me were the stylish lunches I enjoyed with Jane during which we heart-to-hearted over glasses of wine, and she offered compelling, slightly mystical insights into my widower's life. It was at one of these that she made the suggestion that was the Genesis of this book.

* * *

Meanwhile change and decay were all about me. Tony Crooks became the second of my friends to leave Eastbourne, as he and his wife departed to take up residence in the South West, near his wife Chris's family. One of Eastbourne's unjustly neglected characters, George Musgrave—the living advertisement for *The George Musgrave Museum*—suddenly died or, as he would probably have put it, went to Glory. Hugh Riddick had a stroke but, even partly recovered, was still a gracious host to his friends in the care homes where he took up temporary residence. My old university friend, David Fontana, in his time a great champion of spiritualism and ESP, died or, as he might have phrased it, passed over to the other side. As did Charles Arnold-Baker, upon which event I put a short note in *The Times* recalling his legendary examination papers. Nearer home, Margaret Protherough's increasing dementia meant she could no longer live at home in safety, and so she moved into a special care home near Oxford, with a distraught Robert visiting her every day. And dear Eddie Wainwright died, railing to the end against the fates which had dealt him so cruel a hand that he had been forced to live in great comfort, lovingly tended by Di and publishing his furious poetry without let or hindrance, until his late eighties.

* * *

In starting to write these memoirs I had of course been vouchsafed a good way of filling my long days. It was an unexpected comfort for, in common with many of my friends, I had always sworn I would never descend to such self-advertisement. I had kept no diaries, and had precious few mementos of my childhood or my teenage years, so I was forced to depend upon the notoriously fallible source of personal memory. To arrange my life in plausible sequence I first relied upon known national or international events on which to peg events. This proved easy enough until the early sixties. The dates for the opening and closing of the Second World War, the Suez Crisis and the shooting of President Kennedy were readily recalled. But thereafter dates became more blurred in my mind, and I found it easier to mark out my life by Prime Ministerial reigns rather than by the dates of such things as the signing of various European treaties, the Balkan wars or the intermittent invasion of Middle Eastern countries by the Western powers. I presumed my readers, like me, would more readily recall the triumphant entries to and inglorious departures from Downing Street by the Iron Lady or the oleaginous Mr Blair than the year of the Prague Spring, or the date of the Tehran Hostage Crisis.

I had not got very far with this book when I began, for the first time in my life, to feel my age. It was not a straightforward physical deterioration. My eyesight did not suddenly blur—I had lost the sight of one eye some time before, but the other was fine—nor did I lose my ability to walk, though I was becoming increasingly afraid of stumbling and falling on Eastbourne's uneven pavements. I started to use a metal walking stick as a sort of prop, tucking it briskly under my arm if I saw a female acquaintance approaching along the street. I began to make elaborate mental and physical arrangements before I crossed over the road, and when I was out in the town, found myself calculating the distances to the next bench on which I could rest. I stopped going to the station to greet my family and visiting friends. Instead of visiting good but distant shops, I started to buy inferior produce at the Asian store over the road. Keenly aware that I was his best customer Ahmed kept my preferred purchases under his counter so that he was able, when I entered his emporium each morning, triumphantly to pull out a heap of delights comprising that day's *Guardian*, and various other treats he thought I might like—such as blue Turkish curries, microwaveable fish or tinned and luridly dyed vegetables. Though Ahmed was as honest as the day, his manner of revealing my bundle made the daily transaction feel not only furtive but faintly illegal.

In spite of these signs of increasing decrepitude, I continued to believe deep down that I was immortal, and that just slowing down a bit and making a few changes to my routine would keep me on an even keel, without any outside medical assistance. But when shuffling over to the shop one day I realised that even after a few steps I was getting out of breath. I took it easy at home for the rest of the day but by the following morning I saw that in addition my ankles had swollen—a symptom I remember noticing years before when visiting one of my relatively immobile, deeply asthmatic aunts. So, for the first time in my life, I rang for the doctor. I nonchalantly described my symptoms over the phone, expecting he would prescribe a pill and advise a few days' rest. However, he arrived very quickly, briefly examined me, and succinctly explained that two parts of my heart were not synchronising as they should. Fifteen minutes later I was lying in an ambulance and on my way to Accident and Emergency.

❧16❧

Resurrection

I DIED on August 23rd 2013 at Haywards Heath Hospital, surrounded by friends and loved ones. By my bedside were Cath (destined to play a pivotal role in my dreams), Martyn (wondering whether Max Miller's songs would be quite suitable for my funeral), Sharon and Tish together with the blessed Brian, who had twice been roused from his bed and driven through the night so the close family could be with me at my passing. And Jane, who sprinkled flower petals upon me and offered a brief incantation. But there was not, I'm told, over much weeping and wailing. That was how I would have wanted it. I had enjoyed a good innings and if now, in my seventy-seventh year, Jesus wanted me for a sunbeam, nobody could reasonably complain.

My time on the other side was comparatively brief and unmemorable. I may have exhibited all the outward signs of having passed over to the Happy Hunting Ground, but inwardly this 'I' was feeling and seeing nothing at all. But then the various pieces of hospital machinery that were attached to me started to kick in and (aided, my family were certain, by Jane's petals) this 'I' began to breathe again. Not that 'I' was conscious of it but, as the philosophers might have said, there was some breathing going on.

I had first gone into hospital because my heart was not functioning properly, but shortly after I had been discharged from the Cardiac Unit something worse had taken hold of me. A few hours after coming home I had found myself glued to my chair, paralysed to the extent that I could no longer hold a pen in my fingers or lift a cup to my mouth. Back into hospital I went, and after three weeks of waiting was finally diagnosed with a comparatively rare condition known as Guillain-Barré Syndrome. I was then sent to Haywards Heath Hospital, where there was a specialist G-BS unit, and there began to suffer the dreadful hallucinations which afflict about a third of those with this condition. After some weeks of treatment I had a rip-snorting heart attack, followed in short order by an intestinal collapse which led to my losing a great deal of blood and being rushed through the night, sirens blaring, to the Brighton Hospital. There I was operated upon and placed for five weeks in Intensive Care. Just about the only thing I clearly remember from that period of sedated languor was asking one of the kindly nurses in ICU whether I was going to die. Well-versed in the niceties of patient-centred care, he said exactly the right thing; 'Only if *you* want to.'

I apologise for imposing this catalogue of medical detail upon my reader, as I apologise retrospectively for my bored demeanour in past years when people recited their medical histories to me. My excuse is that to me illness was a new experience. For seventy-seven years I had never been really ill. It is true that when I was very young neighbours and relatives would regularly remark upon my unpleasant and sickly appearance, and throughout the ensuing decades people had frequently warned me that, because I was drinking too much alcohol/not eating enough salad/not jogging regularly/ eating too much meat/not eating enough oily fish/not going on enough long walks/consuming too much sugar and/or salt, I was going to make myself ill. But in spite of this I had remained defiantly fit. I had never consulted a doctor, had never (except when I was deliberately playing hookey) had a day off work, and had never had reason to use the NHS—though I had like everybody else paid in to it.

Now I was getting my money's worth in spades. And I played the role of invalid to the manner born. For the first time in my life I became a keen listener to other people's medical problems. I enjoyed those cosy huddles around my bed when my visitors would recite their latest symptoms to me and I could proudly take my turn re-telling, and slightly embroidering, stories of the latest scans, X-rays and probings to which I had been subjected. However, I also learned that when recounting one's medical history one is only as good as one's last procedure. So, when the consultants told me that I would be having a further operation to mend a hernia (from which apparently I had been suffering for some years) I was strangely pleased. The recounting of my recent infirmities was already becoming too familiar to my little circle, and this would give me something new to boast about.

During these months observers frequently remarked that I had surprised them by my stoicism and good humour in the face of such adversity. I smiled bravely and said that it was only through my extraordinary acting talent (think Noël Coward's *In Which We Serve*) that I was offering this stiff upper lip to the world—beneath it all I was in *agonies,* darling. Yet the truth was that, once on the road to recovery, I was finding my hospital stay rather more congenial than I had found those months after Ann's death, when I had been too much alone with my thoughts. In hospital cheerful people would distract me, talk to me and feed me. Friends brought me news of the outside world together with welcome gifts of fruit and flowers and solved crosswords with me, letting me think that I had found the solutions by myself. Though looking forward to being on my feet again, I was for the time being happy enough to be a bed blocker.

In almost a year in hospital I grew familiar with hospital talk—the coded messages in the nurses' bedside phrases —'Just give me a minute' (meaning 'I'm going on a long break'), 'I'm going to look for someone to help me' ('I'm off to another ward') 'I'm afraid I'm not allowed to touch that' ('Tune your own radio, you idle old sod')—as I became, for short periods, intimate with those temporarily embedded alongside me. There was the Christmas Island survivor who had been through so much hospital treatment that he was able to correct the spelling and pronunciation of the drugs he was prescribed. Other old hands were able, like travel correspondents, to compare the food and quality of care in hospitals all over the world. (Don't ever get taken ill in Korea, was their message.) One delightful old lad was smilingly tolerant of one and all by day, but in his sleep would roar out the words of what sounded like Masonic curses threatening bodily mutilation to the faithless—the content of which he had, presumably, once sworn to keep secret.

Sufferers from Guillain-Barré Syndrome almost always recover, but the process, in the elderly, can take some time. Neither the Brighton nor the Eastbourne hospitals had expert knowledge of the condition so, beset with the need to reach externally imposed targets, their hospital staffs decided that I was recovering far too slowly for their prescribed timetables. Some darkly suggested that I was *deliberately* extending my post-operative stay. So they made determined attempts to speed my recovery up, giving me regular bouts of vigorous physiotherapy while trying to ignore my screams as I imagined, in the course of another hallucinogenic delirium, that they were casually throwing me over Beachy Head. This led one of the lady physios to ask brusquely, 'Were you always such a wuss?'

During my many sleeping hours, however, I dreamed serial dreams which were far more pleasant. In those I acted out a long fantasy sequence in which Ann and I were waited upon by a silent corps of black-garbed women. The action took place in a variety of settings, including a canal-side hotel in Wales and the inside of a circus tent which, for no apparent reason, had been pitched on a hill near to my grandfather's house in Ranby. None of the settings corresponded directly to reality, nor did any of the characters behave as they did in real life. A recurrent plot theme was the contemporary circus performance, with killer clowns, designed and produced by my Aunt Sarah—a particularly improbable plot line as during her life the lady had, as I recall, set her face sternly against entertainment in any form. However, a welcome aspect of these lurid imaginings was that if the action in them did not please me I could, as in the making of a film, rewrite and shoot them again. In one such scene a group of arrogant American doctors had taken over my house and were using it as a hospital. I wanted them out, so in the re-shoot Cath (playing a brilliant lawyer) gave a coruscating courtroom performance and got rid of them. In another Martyn, at the controls of a motor launch full of bearded clerics, scattered my floridly kilted enemies. (No, I don't know either.) The plots of these fantasies were all repetitious in the extreme, but for all their absurdity they were more real to me than reality itself. I remember waking from such a dream and asking Cath, seated by my bedside, why it was that Ann never came to see me? 'Mum's dead, Dad,' she said, wonderingly.

A surreal existence, but one that had to end. So it happened that, of all the good days of all the good old year, on Christmas Eve I was without warning pitched over to the Irvine Rehabilitation Unit at Bexhill on Sea, where all was jingle bells and carols and rectangular chunks of processed turkey. For a couple of weeks I received no treatment at all, while staff and patients made merry, but then normal Irvine service was resumed. Now able to use the top half of my body without difficulty, and relatively *compos mentis*, I was much more aware of what was going on. It soon became clear to me that there was no common view amongst the physios about how, or indeed whether, I should be rehabilitated. This was first apparent when I was told by one of them that I was going to have hydrotherapy (being suspended in water so I could exercise my joints by swimming). I was pleased to hear this. On the chosen day an assistant came over from the pool but the in-house staff could not, or would not, accompany me and it all fell through. A few weeks after that I was told by a pleasant physio lady that I would spend the weekend in a 'patient's flat' kitted out with a mock-up kitchen to see if I could boil a kettle, use a toaster and spread butter and so forth. I excitedly told my family, but the weekend came and went and nothing happened. I never saw the lady physio again, so I never had chance to ask her the reason (though I think I could guess).

There was also simmering dissatisfaction amongst the nursing staff, some of whom seemed rather too ready to denigrate the skills and experience of their colleagues. And their angst was sometimes turned against the patients. One of the ghoulish night staff woke me in the

early morning to hiss in my face, 'You don't fool me—
you're wasting our time!' Others were more kindly
disposed. But it was clear the way the prevailing wind was
blowing when one of the senior consultants, a Dickens-
ian character with flowing grey locks, a music-hall
chairman's waistcoat and a red flower in his buttonhole,
glared down at me suspiciously and said, 'I hear you're
not co-operating with the staff!' The charge surprised me.
I at once suspected that the truth, although I was some
way from being ready for rehabilitation, was that they
wanted my bed.

On reading the consultant's words, and bearing in
mind the night nurse's analysis, the reader will of course
suspect that I have glossed over aspects of my hospital
behaviour and that I had, in fact, been proving a bit of
a pillock. And swinging the lead into the bargain. But I
swear that the extent of my 'non-cooperation' was my
inability to get on with my recovery at their prescribed
box-ticking rate. Upon further racking my brains to discover reasons for the consultant's judgement, however,
I recalled that I had publicly sympathised with the
grumbles of some of the nursing staff, who'd had
to accept a minuscule pay rise while, they said, their
managerial bosses were lining their pockets*. I suppose
I might therefore have reasonably been charged with a
refusal to take the side of senior management, rather
than the fanciful allegation that I, still half-paralysed, was
some sort of bedridden Wat Tyler.

However, as is often the way, once the accusation had
been made, the charge of non-cooperation stuck. Fairly soon
afterwards all physiotherapy was cut off. An urgently-
convened meeting was then held with my family, during
which a doctor, whom I had never met, surreptitiously
read up my medical notes while the chief physiotherapist
promised that when I had returned home I should have
daily visits from the community physios (now that
would have been something!). A condescending and
uninterested social worker was assigned to ask me
questions and to fill in forms relating to my now
imminent departure. And, my allotted span of rehab

---

* Within a year of my 'rehabilitation' the East Sussex Trust was put in
'special measures' and the Chief Executive 'resigned'.

having terminated, in April 2014, with my demobilisation bag hugged close to my chest, I was decanted back into a hospital bed that had been set up in the dining hallway of my Eastbourne home and I resumed abnormal life.

★   ★   ★

The deployment of all the apparatus required to ease my daily existence at home in South Street had been overseen by Cath and Brian. That good man had also, with great kindness, offered to 'sleep in' for a few weeks, help with shopping and so forth. In fact he stayed with me for more than a year—in addition to fulfilling his ever-expanding programme of speaking engagements all over the UK. I was further tended (at mind-boggling cost) by a kindly team of home carers, who helped me wash and dress and levered me daily into my wheelchair, from which I took lunch and tea. There were some memorable characters among them; Eileen, who had spent many years in hospitals in the Middle East and who had a fund of hair-raising stories, the smiling Lesley, a cheerful transvestite called Simon, a lugubrious Irishman called Larry who coined for my daily record book the menacing line, 'He was all right when we left him....' I intend one day to write a play about them—them and the Community Nurses. The overstretched community physios did come a few times (though certainly not daily) but then discontinued their efforts saying that I now needed an operation to loosen my tendons.

Negotiations over that operation soon descended into farce, as any visit to the hospital, according to elf'n'safety, needed no fewer than four ambulance men to carry a stretcher down my front steps. The first appointment for the op. was cancelled because only two ambulance men turned up. On a subsequent occasion, four chaps *did* turn up, but with the wrong sort of stretcher, so that a further ambulance team was called to bring the right equipment—meaning that for a time there were no fewer than three ambulances standing, lights flashing, outside my home, and, thinking it was the scene of some major disaster, a small crowd of rubberneckers gathered at the gate. The farcical climax was reached when, having finally got four ambulance men arriving on the right day with the right equipment, the pre-op unit called it off because they had no facilities to receive a stretcher.

A great joy of my current cloistered existence has been the ability, through phone and email, to get back in touch with my distant friends—with Robert, Margaret and Judith, together with Susan, Allanah, Keith and Heather and of course Ben and Jane Roberts. Other email correspondents—Ian Robinson, Adrian and Helen, Ruth, Caroline and Jane—have also travelled (sometimes a considerable distance) to see me. And then there is my regular rota of callers, my neighbour Hilary, John and Pat Pleydell, Brian and Louise Jones, Mary Britten, Peter Austin, Tom Hollobone, Edward Thomas, Malcolm Webster and of course the much-travelled Brian Freeland (who, thank heaven, still calls in for our cake-fuelled chats). And so much of my life now revolves around the wonderful Sue McPherson, who is both a general factotum and close friend.... These names may mean little to a general reader but to me they mean a companionship which I feel I have done nothing to deserve but which lights up my declining years.

A further joy is that my partial recovery has lifted some, at least, of the emotional burden placed upon my family. Whereas at one time they were ringing the hospital every day, and visiting two or three times a week, they are at present able to get on with their own lives. Tish, a regular visitor to the hospitals, shows no outward sign of advancing years and recently celebrated her eightieth birthday in fine style, assisted by, amongst many others, Sally and Dee, Martyn, Cath, Simon, Bonnie and Mac. At Christmas, with Sharon doing noble duty as chef, the family gathered around me for the traditional fare. And they have been able to take holidays, even returning to Greece. Martyn and Sharon followed an idyllic visit to Santorini with a stay in Athens, and in the same year Cath and Simon and the grandchildren took a family holiday in the beautiful coastal resort of Tolo.

Another pleasure has been that I've been able to continue, and almost bring to a close, these un-called-for memoirs. Originally begun at Jane Montague's suggestion as a therapeutic measure to help me recover from the shock of Ann's death, the effort of trying to recall events from years past has proved to be (as must surely be the case with most autobiographies) an aid in trying to uncover, to myself, what sort of person I really am. With the alleged benefit of hindsight, is it possible for me to see what threads have bound my shallow personality together?

Even before considering that weighty question, I have had to ask myself just how much of the story told in these pages is actually true. When recounting things that probably did more or less happen I know that not only am I being selective in what I describe but am too apt to fall prey to the temptation to round things off too neatly. Apparently I will, as one of my critics once remarked, do anything for a laugh. This is particularly true of those well-worn anecdotes which I have told and retold to friends or family over the years. The details have mutated through repetition, to the extent that, although some of the details are certainly invented, I now actually *remember* it all happening exactly as I say. Did I really fly all the way to Buenos Aires in order to have a meal in 'the best steak restaurant in the world'? Did I sit giggling with Tony Field in a Turkish restaurant while we watched various members of the Arts Council keep their shady lunchtime assignations in Shepherd's Market? Did I really once cross swords with Donald Sinden about his Polonius? Did I once skid off an icy surface in my VW, fall twenty feet down an embankment, and not only finish the right way up but then drive cautiously across a frozen field and resume the road? I *believe* these things happened, as I believe everything in this book happened, but I am only too well aware of False Memory Syndrome and of the fact that, in common with so much of human kind, I cannot bear over much reality.

And if the facts themselves are selectively chosen, incomplete or distorted, what are we to say of those passages when I confidently assert what my *mood* was at the time? My mind, like everyone else's I hope, is at any one moment a jumbled kaleidoscope of speculation, amusement, terror, self-righteousness and wonder, all jumbled up with sexual fantasies, geometrical problems and biscuits. Plus (and I hope this reaction is not confined to me) even as things are actually happening I am thinking how I will describe the event and aggrandise or lessen the part I played in it. So even as I hear my wickets tumble and before I have trudged back to the pavilion I will have already fashioned my unconvincing excuse: 'You'll never believe it, but a couple of foxes ran right across my line of sight!'

Furthermore, if I am so confused about my own character and memories, by what right do I describe the thoughts and actions of others? I can only say how, at a chosen moment, one aspect of their being may have struck me. And even that fleeting moment is distorted in the retelling. In these pages I have separated out particular incidents and particular memories of people whose personalities are by themselves big enough to fill a much larger volume than this. I know there was a lot more to Frank than his morose tales of dragging drowned bodies out of the River Trent, just as I know that there are so many more aspects of David Norman than are touched on here, and that there is much more to be said about Caroline Gardiner, John Coultas and twenty others. My excuse has to be that while I was trying to make my own life sound at any rate mildly interesting, I left too little space to do justice to others'. I have drawn out a few threads from the tangled fabric of my many relationships, nothing more.

And finally, like everybody else, I have lived my life in compartments. There are people who know me only as a poor club golfer, an indiscriminating jazz fan, an amateur magician, a keen Ripperologist or a dedicated cricket watcher but, to nobody's particular surprise, none of these activities—or the people associated with them—has been described here. Nor have I imposed upon the reader my tastes in music or painting, my involvement with CAMRA or my years as a cinema buff—now extended into old age by courtesy of Martyn, who selects remastered classics and watches them with me every time he visits.

And of course I have thus far kept hidden (don't we all?) my most secret self—my sordid personal habits, my facile escapism, and my shameful private rituals. I sometimes think it might be fun, in a spirit of full disclosure, to explain that in old age I still, like a scurvy orang utan, scratch behind my ears, or that I sometimes still daydream of sexual congress being achieved in an unlikely setting such as inside a washing machine, or that my escape from night time demons is invariably foiled by two dray horses obstinately dragging a gypsy caravan across my path. But on reflection I think not.

Yet it may be that my memories may reveal more than I thought. I have after all lived through a huge social change. The beliefs by which we lived when I was very young—the Christian ethic, respect for the past, loyalty to one's family and friends, living within one's means, the nobility of charitable giving—have all been swept aside, together with any respect for the institutions that once embodied them. George Orwell's dystopian vision —a society driven by base materialism, wherein there is no privacy or personal honour, where citizens are electronically spied upon, their minds forcefully emptied and refilled with nothing but empty slogans—has rooted itself in Britain. In almost every respect we now live in a one-party state, ruled by a brutish 'middle-of-the-road' consensus, from which any kind of dissension seems not just foolish but positively dangerous. Thus we are, like Winston Smith, lost in a waste land of terror.

Yet there are, of course, crucial differences between Orwell's world and ours. In *1984* citizens lived in poverty and with the dread of physical torture by the Big Brother state. By comparison most of us now live in luxury—but are made to fear that unless we conform to the centrist rules our Big-Society state imposes we shall lose it all and descend once more into the toils of anarchy. We are told that it is only our rulers' financial skill that is preventing us from being overrun by refugees, or from military take-over by left or right, and that unless we conform to their way of thinking, the whole financial edifice on which the Western world sits will fall apart, the stock market will collapse, banks and pension funds will dissolve into thin air and life as we know it—except for those prudent enough to own offshore islands or stash their fortunes in places of refuge—will come to a painful and murky end. Thus money, once touted as the root of all evil, has now become our one true salvation and the foundation of all goodness.

I have now been told I shall spend the rest of my life in a wheelchair. The thought does not alarm or depress me, although it means rethinking and overhauling my living quarters, so I can operate on wheels rather than legs. In some ways it has even helped me to grapple with the problems that have for long interested me. Is this 'I' merely the sum of my parts—recollections of all my attitudes, my interventions and dreams, together with those long-forgotten memories which presumably, as no-one else now remembers them either, exist no longer and to all intents and purposes never existed? Or is there a 'me' which binds them all together, and which—so some wise ones tell us—might even survive my physical death? So many of my fellows seem to be striving for an electronic immortality—blogging, going on face book, texting, twittering, skyping, counting followers and their 'likes', every part of their existence stored away in a 'Cloud', which itself has no tangible existence. If that is the modern immortality, and if the immortal soul is now vouchsafed merely by having the right password or tweeting on Facebook, then I can have no part in it, for I do not even understand, let alone partake in, these strange practices. So, dear reader, I can only stake my poor claim to immortality, as so many nobler and infinitely wiser beings have done through the ages, by means of that which you are now holding in your hands—a printed book.

JP
2015

INDEX